The Art of Nick Cave

The Art of Nick Cave
New Critical Essays

Edited by John H. Baker

intellect Bristol, UK / Chicago, USA

First published in the UK in 2013 by
Intellect, The Mill, Parnall Road, Fishponds, Bristol, BS16 3JG, UK

First published in the USA in 2013 by
Intellect, The University of Chicago Press, 1427 E. 60th Street,
Chicago, IL 60637, USA

A catalogue record for this book is available from the
British Library.

Cover designer: Holly Rose
Copy-editor: MPS Technologies
Production manager: Tim Mitchell
Typesetting: Planman Technologies

ISBN 978-1-84150-627-2

Printed and bound by Hobbs, UK

Table of Contents

Introduction

Nick Cave, Twenty-First Century Man

John H. Baker

Few who were lucky enough to witness a gig by The Birthday Party would have imagined that the snarling madman on vocals would live much beyond his mid-twenties, let alone be acclaimed as one of the most significant artists currently operating within the field of 'popular music' in the early twenty-first century. Until the late 1990s Nick Cave was most certainly a cult artist, adored by a small but committed fan base and known, if at all, beyond this circle as a drug-crazed, possibly misogynistic, chronicler of murder and mayhem. He was also associated, however unfairly, with the Goth movement, mainly because of The Birthday Party's 1981 song 'Release the Bats' – an association that misses the song's strongly parodic element.

Flick forward to 2012. Cave is now 54 years old, married and a father. Many fans of The Birthday Party would have been startled to find him still alive at this age, but their jaws would certainly drop if they were told that the middle-aged Cave is not merely still with us, but more famous and successful than ever. The contemporary Cave, while not exactly a 'mainstream' artist, has produced nine top 40 albums in the United Kingdom with the Bad Seeds and two with his new band Grinderman. Two of these albums – *Murder Ballads* and *Dig, Lazarus, Dig!!!* – charted in the UK top ten. His most recent album with the Bad Seeds, *Dig, Lazarus, Dig!!!*, was his most successful yet, charting at number four in the United Kingdom, and was met with almost universal critical acclaim – 'this is how rock stars are supposed to age', wrote Stephen M. Deusner for Pitchfork, while the *NME* put aside their usual adulation of youth to offer some patronizing praise for 'Cave and his wizened cronies' (Deusner 2008; *NME* 2008). His albums have also sold well outside the United Kingdom, particularly in his native Australia, Scandinavia and Germany. He has been less successful in the United Kingdom as a singles artist, with three top 40 singles, but his 1995 duet with Kylie Minogue, 'Where the Wild Roses Grow', narrowly missed the top ten and earned him an appearance on 'Top of the Pops'. He continues to tour, playing to packed houses with the Bad Seeds and Grinderman, his onstage vitality putting performers half his age to shame.

The Cave of 2011 is rightly regarded as a songwriter and performer of tremendous range, talent and charisma, ably supported by a range of superb and sympathetic musicians in the Bad Seeds and Grinderman – most of whom he has worked with for many years. No longer can he be characterized as a lunatic shrieking demented imprecations at his cowering audience (indeed, a man in his fifties doing so would be an undignified spectacle). Although he is not primarily a musician himself, his abilities as pianist and guitarist have grown steadily over his career, as has the range and versatility of his singing voice – he can still scream and howl like his younger self if he wishes, but, as albums like *The Boatman's Call* demonstrate, he can also sing softly with considerable beauty and emotional power. The range of his songwriting is extremely wide, although he regards himself as primarily a writer of love songs – he can craft a gripping narrative like 'John Finn's Wife' as readily as a haunting lament like 'Lucy' or an ironic commentary on fading sexual prowess like Grinderman's 'No Pussy Blues' (Cave 2007: 13). His abilities as a lyricist are extensive and his command of language often masterly – he has few rivals in the field of 'popular music' in this respect, perhaps only Morrissey and Jarvis Cocker being artists of his generation worthy of comparison. The publication of his *Complete Lyrics 1978–2007* in 2007 – all 460 pages of them, from The Birthday Party to Grinderman – allows readers to judge for themselves. Musically, his work with the Bad Seeds ranges from the hymnal 'Foi Na Cruz' to the demented 'Jangling Jack', from the hilarious epic 'Babe, I'm on Fire' to the melancholy fragment 'Watching Alice'. His more recent work with Grinderman, in particular, is testament to his often-neglected sense of humour. It should also be pointed out that although he has claimed to care little for the medium in his commentary on his collected videos, his promotional videos form an impressive and imaginative body of work in the field (Cave 1998). If his talents lay solely in songwriting and performance, his work in these fields for over 30 years would be enough to earn him comparisons with his heroes Bob Dylan and Johnny Cash.

What would surely startle a Cave fan from the early 1980s, though, is the sheer breadth of Cave's artistic achievement. Not content with his success as a songwriter and performer, the Cave of latter days has produced startling and acclaimed work in a number of other genres. *And the Ass Saw the Angel*, published in 1989, though widely admired, was long seen as a one-off venture into prose fiction on Cave's part until his second novel, *The Death of Bunny Munro*, appeared 20 years later and won praise from broadsheet newspapers like *The Times* and *The Observer* (Litt 2009; Thomson 2009). In addition to the musical and literary worlds, Cave has also enjoyed considerable success in the world of film. He has made occasional appearances as an actor, most notably in John Hillcoat's *Ghosts … of the Civil Dead* (1989) (see Johinke's chapter in this volume), but has enjoyed more success in recent years as a screenwriter and composer of film scores. He wrote the script for John Hillcoat's powerful *The Proposition* (2005) and composed the film's soundtrack with his bandmate Warren Ellis; more recently he and Ellis have scored *The Assassination of Jesse James by the Coward Robert Ford* (2007) and Hillcoat's cinematic adaption of Cormac McCarthy's *The Road* (2009), and a selection of their soundtrack work has been released as the album *White Lunar* (2009). His most recent cinematic venture, the Hillcoat-directed *Lawless*, for which he wrote the script and composed the soundtrack with Ellis, opened in August 2012. He has also branched out into composition for the theatrical stage, with three collaborations to date with the Icelandic theatre company Vesturport.

The Cave of 2012, then, is widely admired as an artist of startling versatility and range. He gives the appearance of a man whose personal and professional lives dovetail exceptionally well, balancing his roles as husband and father with the professional demands of songwriting, touring, writing and composing. The often-mocked order and discipline of his working life, as well as his recovery from drug addiction, have allowed this most professional of artists (he always wears a suit to the office, 'as a worker', and works six days a week) to forge an impressive career that shows no sign of slowing down – it is to be hoped that there are many more albums, novels, scripts and soundtracks to come (Snow 2011: 186, 214). It is undoubtedly a cliché to call Cave a contemporary Renaissance man, but the term seems apposite.

This collection has its origin in a one-day conference on Cave organized at the University of Westminster in July 2008. The call for speakers emphasized that the purpose of the conference was to consider Cave's art as a whole, and that papers on his work outside songwriting would be particularly welcome. The range of papers given at the conference reflected this, with topics including Cave and the Presley myth, the use of his lyrics in the college classroom, Cave as a Gothic artist and *Ghosts ... of the Civil Dead*. Five of the presenters at the conference feature in this collection, but their chapters are accompanied by ten others that, together, cover the entire range of Cave's achievement and clearly demonstrate that his art is worthy of serious consideration from a wide variety of critical approaches.

The collection is divided into five parts, each of which focuses on a different aspect of Cave's art. The first part contains four chapters that each discuss the most familiar aspect of Cave's work – his songwriting.

Peter Billingham's chapter focuses on one of Cave's most important albums, *The Boatman's Call* (1997). This album, a sombre and often beautiful meditation upon lost love, came as a shock after the blood-soaked *Murder Ballads*, and Billingham offers a song-by-song reading of the work that focuses upon the way Cave intertwines themes of desire and spirituality across the album. He uses Wim Wenders' 1987 film *Wings of Desire* to anchor his reading, viewing the songwriter as a sort of fallen angel like those in Wenders' film, making a spiritual journey across the album from the cautious hope of 'Into My Arms' to the lonely despair of 'Green Eyes'.

Carl Lavery's chapter analyses a single song, 'When I First Came to Town' from *Henry's Dream* (1992), in order to explore how Cave uses his voice – his performance – as much as his lyrics to place the listener in the same position as the paranoid wanderer of the song. He is particularly interested in the way the song stages a religious theme, a 'dialectic of abandonment' that runs throughout much of his work (see also my own chapter in this volume for more on Cave and religion).

Paul Lumsden examines Cave's lyrics from a very different perspective – that of a college professor of English literature using them in the classroom while teaching first-year students. The chapter demonstrates that the richness of language and imagery we see in Cave's lyrics makes them ripe for close analysis; it also examines the way Cave uses intertextuality, not only through references to literary figures like John Donne, Shakespeare and Andrew Marvell but also to more contemporary figures as disparate as Philip Larkin and Johnny Thunders.

David Pattie, by contrast, is less interested in Cave's work as a lyricist than he is in his often ignored work as a musician, and collaboration with the Bad Seeds. It is all too easy to elevate Cave's gifts as a lyricist to the extent that his very real talents as a musician are neglected, and this chapter pays particular attention to Cave's musical collaboration with two of his most gifted fellow-travellers, Blixa Bargeld and Warren Ellis. Pattie argues that much of the power of the Bad Seeds' music lies in its simultaneous espousal and subversion of existing musical forms and structures like blues, gospel and confessional songwriting.

Although Cave is a versatile songwriter, he is particularly well known for his ability to craft violent narratives of murder – murder ballads. The second part of the collection focuses on this grim aspect of Cave's work, paying particular attention to his most gruesome album, the Bad Seeds' album *Murder Ballads* (1996).

Nick Groom places Cave's album in the murder ballad tradition, presenting a history of this grisly subgenre before arguing that the songs on *Murder Ballads*, like their eighteenth- and nineteenth-century predecessors, express and interrogate contemporary social anxieties. *Murder Ballads*, for all its horror, proved to be Cave's best-selling album to date upon its release, and Groom argues that Cave had successfully tapped into the contemporary Zeitgeist with these brutal but often darkly humorous narratives.

Dan Rose examines perhaps the most shocking song on *Murder Ballads*, 'Stagger Lee', Cave's adaption of a 'toast' (a sort of proto-rap) given by the 'black huster' Big Stick in 1967 (Wepman, Newman and Binderman 1986). 'Stagger Lee' is the horrific tale of one of the titular character's murderous escapades, which features the gunning down of a bartender and a man being forced to perform fellatio before being shot. Rose places the song in the context of the history of the Hustler archetype and its significance in black culture before examining its perverse attractions in the light of psychoanalytical theory.

The next part of the collection considers Cave's work in the fields of film and theatre. Karoline Gritzner explores the range of his theatrical work, from his early and largely unperformed one-act plays to his three collaborations with the Icelandic theatre company Vesturport in their productions of *Woyzeck*, *Metamorphosis* and *Faust*. Gritzner examines the essential contribution Cave's music and personae as a cult musician makes to Vesturport's innovative and imaginative theatrical productions.

Rebecca Johinke focuses on Cave's most memorable role as an actor, as the maniacal Maynard in John Hillcoat's Australian prison film *Ghosts ... of the Civil Dead* (1989), but also examines the film itself more widely in the context of the genres of Australian Gothic and prison films. She studies the film's origin in the writings of the prisoner Jack Henry Abbott and Cave's considerable role in its creation (in addition to acting in the film, he collaborated on the script and composed the score with Blixa Bargeld and Mick Harvey). In particular, she investigates Cave's performance as Maynard in terms of the abject and self-mutilation.

William Verrone explores possibly Cave's greatest achievement so far in the film genre – John Hillcoat's *The Proposition* (2005), for which he wrote the script and composed the soundtrack with Warren Ellis. Verrone examines the ways in which the film simultaneously adheres to and subverts the genre tropes of the western through its Australian setting and its engagements with issues usually elided by the traditional western – femininity, class and race – as well as the way in which Cave's script reflects many of Cave's central preoccupations, including spirituality, violence and the nature of love.

The fourth part of the collection contains three chapters that examine different ways Cave's art is influenced by outside factors. Cave is often thought of as a 'Gothic' artist, and Isabella van Elferen's chapter moves beyond 'Release the Bats' to explore Cave's Gothic modalities. Van Elferen argues that Cave can be seen as a pivotal figure in modern Gothic, not merely through his obvious interest in 'dark' subject matter and the often sinister nature of his music but specifically through the way his work evaluates the relationship between the past and the present – simultaneously nostalgic, transgressive and haunted.

Nathan Wiseman-Trowse considers an often-neglected aspect of Cave's art – his frequent habit of recording cover versions of songs by other writers as disparate as Johnny Cash, Lou Reed and Alex Harvey. Cave's first single with the Bad Seeds was a cover of Elvis Presley's 'In the Ghetto' and he has recorded an entire album of cover versions, *Kicking Against the Pricks* (1986). Wiseman-Trowse explores the significance of Cave's choice of cover versions and argues that they are never wholly simple reproductions, but more complex attempts by Cave to position himself within (or against) a particular tradition as part of a continual process of reinvention on his part.

Sarah Wishart's chapter focuses upon the way Cave has used the Spanish concept of the *duende* in his work, making particular reference to Federico Garcia Lorca's depiction of the *duende* as an inexplicable power capable of sending waves of emotion through those watching or listening to a performance of 'deep song'. Cave uses Lorca's essay 'Play and Theory of the Duende' as a framework upon which to build his important lecture 'The Secret Life of the Love Song' (1999) in an attempt to explain the pain at the heart of any true love song. Wishart interrogates Cave's argument and the way the spirit of the *duende* can be seen to inhabit his work.

The final part of the collection examines one of the most important aspects of Cave's work – his engagement with spiritual and religious themes, and the numerous ways his work enmeshes the sacred and the profane. My own chapter asks whether we can see Cave as a Christian artist, and argues that a profound change can be identified in his work around the time of the release of *The Boatman's Call* in 1997 – a change that involved a new focus on the figure of Christ on Cave's part and an abandonment of many of the 'Old Testament' trappings of his earlier work. I argue that it would be inaccurate to argue that Cave had somehow 'found God' or become a Christian at this period; instead, his new focus on Christ allowed him to resolve an artistic impasse and reach new conclusions about the artist's role that have had profound aesthetic and spiritual effects on his more recent work.

Steven Barfield's chapter pays particular attention to Cave's exploration of sacred and profane love. Like Cave himself, Barfield sees Cave as primarily a writer of love songs that endeavour to explore love in all its dark complexity. He compares Cave's work to that of the surreal poets and uses psychoanalytical theory to explore what Cave called the 'secret life' of Cave's own love songs, particularly 'Where Do We Go Now But Nowhere' and 'Straight to You'.

Finally, Fred Botting boldly tackles perhaps the most controversial way in which Cave interweaves the sacred and profane – his uncompromising approach to themes of sexuality. Like Barfield, Botting uses a psychoanalytical approach – not to psychoanalyse Cave himself, but to illuminate the work. Cave has often been accused of misogyny and Botting makes use of the writings of Georges Bataille to explore his disturbing representations of women and female sexuality. Botting demonstrates that Cave's work is not misogynistic, but marked by a profound engagement with themes of male inadequacy, transgression, abandonment and sovereignty.

Ultimately, then, this collection endeavours to take Cave's work as a whole and engage with him as an artist who has produced, and continues to produce, stimulating and provocative work in several genres. He is far from being a simple singer-songwriter; indeed, as the range of topics and approaches in this collection demonstrates, he is one of the most diverse and uncompromising artists of our time.

References

Cave, Nick (2007), *The Complete Lyrics 1978–2007*, London: Penguin.

Cave, Nick and the Bad Seeds (1998), *The Videos*, DVD, London: Mute.

Deusner, Stephen M. (2008), 'Review of *Dig, Lazarus, Dig!!!*', http://pitchfork.com/reviews/albums/11375-dig-lazarus-dig/. Accessed 26 August 2011.

Litt, Toby (2009), 'From Bad Seeds Grow Fruitful Trees', http://entertainment.timesonline.co.uk/tol/arts_and_entertainment/books/book_reviews/article6820321.ece. Accessed 26 August 2011.

NME (2008), 'Review of *Dig, Lazarus, Dig!!!*', 21 February 2008, http://www.nme.com/reviews/nick-cave-and-the-bad-seeds/9484. Accessed 26 August 2011.

Snow, Mat (2011), *Nick Cave Sinner Saint: The True Confessions*, London: Plexus.

Thomson, Graeme (2009), 'The Death of Bunny Munro by Nick Cave', http://www.guardian.co.uk/music/2009/sep/06/death-bunny-munro-nick-cave. Accessed 26 August 2011.

Wepman, Dennis, Ronald Newman and Murray Binderman (1986), *The Life: Lore and Folk Poetry of the Black Hustler*, Los Angeles, CA: Holloway House.

PART I

Cave, the Songwriter

Chapter 1

'Into My Arms': Themes of Desire and Spirituality in *The Boatman's Call*

Peter Billingham

I n his 1999 lecture 'The Secret Life of the Love Song', Nick Cave observed that

[w]e all experience within us what the Portuguese call '*saudade*', which translates as an inexplicable longing, an unnamed and enigmatic yearning of the soul, and it is this feeling that lives in the realms of the imagination and inspiration and is the breeding ground for the sad song, for the Love Song [...] The Love Song is the light of God, deep down, blasting up through our wounds.

(2007: 7)

In this chapter I shall explore the ways in which this profound sense of 'inexplicable longing' informs Cave's love songs. I shall frame my discussion and analysis initially in terms of Wim Wenders' 1987 film *Der Himmel über Berlin/Wings of Desire* (hereafter *Wings of Desire*) in which Cave featured in a cameo role (Wenders 1987). The principal themes in that film offer an interesting, comparative commentary upon some of the central concerns of Cave's album *The Boatman's Call* (1997) that this chapter focuses on. The album's opening track, 'Into My Arms', has become an evocative signifier of Cave's wider back catalogue of love songs. They are characterized by a deep, poetic, melancholic introspection. Secondly, I will be discussing the extent to which *The Boatman's Call* explores and conveys Cave's search for a radical Christian theology that might offer the possibility of an existential, spiritual redemption.

Wings of Desire

I first encountered Nick Cave's music through his cameo appearance with his band the Bad Seeds in Wim Wenders' award-winning film *Wings of Desire*. Wenders won 'Best Director' for this film at the 1987 Cannes Film Festival. The film is haunted by an almost overwhelming sense of loss and alienation. In it, Wenders explores flight, both as desire and as a metaphor for transcending the limitations of our human existence. In *Wings of Desire* strange angel-figures watch over the lives of the citizens of a pre-1989, Cold War Berlin. The angels are seen standing behind readers in libraries and on Berlin's rooftops watching the crowds passing below. The citizens' lives and their relationships are enmeshed in the complex and poetic web of a fractured city. This evokes themes of mortality, loss and rebirth throughout the film. Cave's appearance as a post-punk, anarchic prophet burns with brief, savage intensity into the film's narrative like a cigarette stubbed out on its celluloid. Cave was living in Berlin at this time.

There is an interesting synchronicity in the decade or so that separates *Wings of Desire* from *The Boatman's Call*, reflected in Cave's own musical and spiritual journey in this period and its resonance for the many admirers of his music. This journey is expressed in his ongoing struggle to discover a non-reductive, radically redemptive spirituality. In the 1980s Cave continued to battle with fracturing life-events from much earlier in his life. For Cave, the earliest and most formative of these traumatic experiences was the premature death of his father in a road accident when Cave was still a teenager. This tragedy occurred when Cave was embroiled in a rebellious adolescence. The traumatic experience of loss remained a dark star that hovered over much of the rest of his life. Simultaneously the album revisits another crippling metaphorical bereavement in Cave's life immediately prior to the writing and release of *The Boatman's Call*, the traumatic ending of his tortured love affair with the singer-songwriter PJ Harvey. Lines from the song 'Brompton Oratory' convey with razor-sharp poetics Cave's devastation at the unsought ending of this relationship: '[n]o god up in the sky/No devil beneath the sea/Could do the job that you did/Of bringing me to my knees' (2007: 278). This dichotomy of desire and its emotional, psychological and existential cost in human existence is central to the characters in *Wings of Desire*, in which Kantian, trench-coated angels silently witness the existential angst of the troubled human lives they watch over. As well as watching Berlin's citizens the angels are able to listen to the internal thoughts of those they observe. The film is shot in such a way that the angels' perspective on human existence is presented monochromatically; by contrast, the human beings' viewing perspective is filmed in colour. However, these angels, whilst possessing the power to hear the inner desires and anxieties of humans, cannot becalm them or, more crucially, 'be-come' them. They cannot intervene in the human condition, forced as they are to be mere witnesses of history. This unique role bestows upon them a metaphorical otherness or transcendence of the limitations of human mortality. One of the central characters of the film, an angel called Damiel (played by Bruno Ganz), experiences an overwhelming attraction towards Maria, a young female trapeze artist in a travelling circus (played by Solveig Donmartin). Damiel simultaneously experiences a transformative, disruptive and overpowering phenomenon: human desire. He recognizes that the only way in which this desire can be fulfilled is through a kind of radical reincarnation: his transformation from angel into human. In that sense he risks, like Lucifer, a form of fall from the spiritual into the material world.

The songwriter as fallen angel

In *The Boatman's Call* I propose that Cave uses his narrator voice as a kind of quasi-'Damiel', which enables Cave to observe and explore his own and our human experience in an equivalent way to that of the angel in Wenders' film. Therein lies the potential for empathy and catharsis for Cave, through that character's emotional, psychological and spiritual journey. There is simultaneously an equivalent and therapeutic function for the listener. In that sense, both songwriter and listener(s) are afforded insight and release through an observational role similar to Wenders' fictional angel. As with Damiel, our sense of detached, dispassionate witnessing is challenged by the power of desire explored in the album. Is this the 'secret life' of the love song to which Cave refers, one that can activate a powerful and destabilizing empathy? This metaphor of emotional and spiritual falling has, of course, powerful resonances in the mythic narrative of Lucifer's descent from the sublime otherness of heaven: a fallen angel. There is also, of course, the myth of Icarus: an embodiment of transgressive desire being punished by death. It becomes even more thematically layered and enriched if Cave's traveller-narrator is viewed as a form of radicalized Christ overwhelmed by transformative suffering. His journey takes him across the 12 tracks that make up the album. It is hauntingly resonant that 'tracks' is also the colloquialism used by heroin addicts for the marks made by a syringe on their body. Like some doomed Romantic, Gothic journeyers of Schubert and Schumann *lieder*, Cave's imagined soul searcher seeks a kind of salvation: one that can only be realized through a provocative and dangerous entry into his particular kind of Gethsemane. It is only through a courageous embracing of a cross of emotional and spiritual brokenness that the fallen angel might ultimately find a radically alternative salvation. The singer-songwriter invites his listener(s) to make a profound choice to 'fall' and be embraced by desire: into its arms. This coming together of songwriter and listener through the medium of the fictionalized alter ego resonates with the act and function of the Mass, as Cave stated in his radio talk 'The Flesh Made Word', originally broadcast in 1996: '[t]here is a communion, there is language, there is imagination. There is God. God is a product of the creative imagination and God is that imagination taken flight' (1997: 137).

For those like this author who recognize Cave as a fellow traveller, these love songs serve as signifiers of the sublime. Cave's fallen angel faces some final existential reckoning in the bleakly humoured title of the penultimate track 'Idiot Prayer'. In it he is able to challenge the binary moral certainties of conventional Christian theology:

Is Heaven just for victims, dear?
Where only those in pain go?
Well, it takes two to tango
[...]
If you're in Heaven then you'll forgive me, dear
Because that's what they do up there
But if you're in Hell, then what can I say
You probably deserved it anyway
For we will meet again
And there'll be Hell to pay

(2007: 285)

Songs for Charon

Charon was the ancient boatman who, for a fee, ferried the souls of the dead across the rivers Styx and Acheron to Hades in Greek mythology. Employing this as a framing device for this section of the chapter I want to propose that the songs on *The Boatman's Call* might be viewed as landing stages on a river journey to a destination of the death of desire. Whilst there is seemingly no alternative destination possible, Cave's traveller is on a redemptive journey. This journey of love and loss carries its own possibility of an inherent transformative power. It is also one of immeasurable cost, far beyond the coin traditionally paid to Charon.

'Into My Arms'

This song is characterized by a dialectics of faith and doubt and certainty and unknowing. Its synthesis is the centrality of love. This is a love that is located primarily and experientially in the one that is loved: the object of desire. The primacy of the beloved allows the possibility of a faith in the power of love to endure and also offer emotional liberation. With subtly melancholic harmonies on a nuanced dying fall, the gentle rhythm and tempo of the song communicates a subtext and subcurrents of desire. For Cave, faith is not predicated on a belief in an externalized other, but, much more powerfully, in the experiential reality of the lover. It is her presence in his world that reinforces and validates his spirituality. This is a 'God' embodied in female form and presence, and a love whose divine dimension is incarnated in and as mutual, reciprocal desire. This enables the narrative speaker to affirm that he 'believe[s] in Love' and in 'some kind of path/That we can walk down, me and you' (2007: 273). This path is travelled upon with its direction and destination perfected in the lovers' destination: a shared embrace, which in Cave's terms embodies a communion. Thus, whilst the beloved believes in an 'interventionist God', who is simultaneously external to perceived reality and able to enter it to affect change in human existence, her lover-narrator experiences the divine in and through her presence (2007: 273).

'Lime-Tree Arbour'

Track two opens with the line that gives its name to the album: '[t]he boatman calls from the lake/A lone loon dives upon the water/I put my hand over hers/Down in the lime-tree arbour' (2007: 275). The 'loon' is both a diving sea bird and also a common (if insensitive) colloquialism for someone who hovers perilously on the edge of sanity. This 'lone' loon is a solitary bird swooping in and out of the water. It also serves as a metaphor for the narrator's lonely immersion within the desire he feels for the woman. It suggests that desire itself may be a form of madness. These thoughts hover over the lovers in the secluded shade of the lime-tree arbour. Tactile experience reaffirms itself again, as in the opening track's potent image of being held in the beloved's arms. This time it is in the repeated image of the hand that is protectively 'over' that of the beloved as if it affords protection to the fragile nature of their mutual desire. 'There will always be suffering/It flows through life like water': this sense of water as a kind of transmutable phenomenon through which the speaker travels, and also as a metaphor for his existential *angst,* is powerful (2007: 275). As the narrator plunges desperately, loon-like, in and out of 'life like water', it is as if he too might drown in his own desire (2007: 275).

'People Ain't No Good'

By track three the quiet (if problematic) optimism and sense of a love known experientially begins to be questioned. This is conveyed and interrogated by a song whose title expresses its moral perspective. It also subliminally suggests the early-hours anguish of a Hank Williams or Johnny Cash lament: '[p]eople just ain't no good/I think that's well understood/You can see it everywhere you look/People just ain't no good' (2007: 276). The song opens with plaintive discordance and pain communicated through the sharply amplified strings of the piano, embodying a sense of emotional exhaustion. The intrinsic, irredeemable failure of people is mournfully rearticulated throughout the song. Cave places it into a beautifully haunting context of almost predestined doomed love affairs and marriage: '[w]e were married under cherry trees/Under blossom we made our vows/All the blossoms come sailing down/Through the streets and through the playgrounds' (2007: 276). This is suggested by an image of lustrous poetic economy and searing emotional pain: '[t]he windows rattling in the gales/To which she drew the curtains/Made out of her wedding veils' (2007: 276). This is a world in which people's destructive incapacity for love is signalled with razor-sharp specificity in images of 'jilted lovers', 'pink-eyed pigeons' and 'coffins of wood' (2007: 277). The hope of a transforming love that was immanent in embrace ('Into My Arms') and protective hands ('Lime-Tree Arbour') has now become an emotional disaster area, hauntingly evoked by an agonized violin and single, discordant chimes from the vibes. The attempt at a conditional consolation – '[i]t ain't that in their hearts they're bad' – is ultimately and bitterly condemned: '[t]hey'd stick by you if they could/But that's just bullshit, baby/People just ain't no good' (2007: 277).

If the two opening songs provided the possibility of a heaven on earth embodied experientially as God-as-desire, this third track summons up a desolate vision of the impossibility of love and desire being sustained. In its absence is an unremitting purgatory of lost love and future anguish: '[t]o our love send back all the letters/To our love a valentine of blood/To our love let all the jilted lovers cry/That people they just ain't no good' (2007: 277).

'Brompton Oratory'

The mood changes again in the following track, whose title refers to a famous London Roman Catholic church. Something of the solidity of architectural materiality seems to inform a sense of recovered perspective on behalf of the narrator. The word 'Oratory' comes from medieval Latin and means 'place of prayer'; Brompton Oratory was founded by John Henry (later

Cardinal) Newman. It is in this song that there is, apart from 'Into my Arms', the only formal, explicit reference to Christ and the Bible on this album. This is when the narrator tells us that the Bible reading for the day is from Luke, Chapter 24, '[w]here Christ returns to his loved ones' (2007: 278). In this final chapter of the Gospel according to Luke, Christ reappears after his death in a resurrected form, one that is material and somatic: '[b]ehold my hands and feet, that it is I myself: handle me, and see; for a spirit hath not flesh and bones, as ye see me have' (Luke 24: 39). Once again, and central to my analysis and discussion, we have a God who is located in the human. This is also a God who, in showing his disciples and friends his 'hands and feet', embodies a love that may be encountered and sensuously embraced. There is also a subtly evocative reference to a major event in the Christian calendar, Pentecost: '[u]p those stone steps I climb/Hail this joyful day's return/Into its great shadowed vault I go/Hail the Pentecostal morn' (2007: 278). Within Christian teaching and its calendar of major events and festivals, Pentecost describes the time after the ascension of Christ when the Holy Spirit appeared as 'cloven tongues as of fire' and anointed his followers (Acts 2: 3). Central to this narrative is the way in which, as the fire fell upon them, the believers were able both to understand languages not their own and also to speak 'in tongues': a spiritual language of prophecy and spiritual vision.

Even as the architectural and spiritual dynamics of the church's interior offer some small comfort and reassurance, they are located within a cruel paradox. This is that the very certainty that the church and the Pentecostal service seem to convey is viewed by the narrator from his condition of alienation and doubt: '[a] beauty impossible to define/A beauty impossible to believe' (2007: 278). Whilst a fragile sense of hope faintly glows, the death of the relationship extinguishes that light. This is perfectly expressed in the image of '[t]he blood imparted in little sips/The smell of you still on my hands/As I bring the cup up to my lips' (2007: 278). The lyrics place the lost love affair in the context of suffering and sacrifice (the crucifixion of Christ re-visited through the Communion wine) with the fragrance of the departed lover. The song has a sacramental and redemptive function. If there is no 'interventionist God', then the cultural accoutrements of religion are no more than crumbs of bitter bread in a time of emotional famine: '[a]nd I wish that I was made of stone/So that I would not have to see/A beauty impossible to define/A beauty impossible to believe' (2007: 278).

'There is a Kingdom'

This song seems to serve as a kind of bridge between the resigned stoicism of the previous track and the ultimately misplaced hope of the song that will follow it, '(Are You) the One that I've Been Waiting For?'. The song opens with an evocative image of a bird that begins to sing in celebration of the day and light even whilst in the darkness prior to dawn:

Just like a bird that sings up the sun
In a dawn so very dark

Such is my faith for you
[…]
And all the world's darkness can't swallow up
A single spark
Such is my love for you
Such is my love

(2007: 279)

This opening reference to a light that darkness cannot overcome carries a clear association to an iconic image from the opening chapter of the Gospel of St John, in which Christ is referred to as the 'Logos' or 'Word' that originates all creation (and creativity) (John 1). Christ is also described as the 'Light' that enlightens all human beings born into the world (John 1: 4). In the Authorized Version, it is expressed poetically as the darkness being unable to 'comprehend' the light (John 1: 5). The love and the faith that Cave seeks to affirm are in a 'Light' that not only cannot be overcome by the darkness of despair and life's sufferings but also cannot be 'comprehended' through rationality alone. However, that understanding is *a priori* experiential and empirical in the transcendent sense. Rational deduction cannot, in its own framework of knowledge, 'comprehend' or 'know' that ontological reality.

This is confirmed and developed when the voice, in a Kantian manner, identifies and affirms '[t]he starry heavens above me/The moral law within/So the world appears/So the world appears' (2007: 279). It is as if, for Cave, the 'starry heavens' above carry with them a clear association of a transcendent reality. In their breath-taking scale and presence they evoke, however imperfectly, a hope that '[t]here is a kingdom/There is a king/And He lives without/And He lives within/And He is everything' (2007: 279). This is no empty triumphalism or shallow, uncritical certainty on Cave's part. Cave can only sense the anticipated experience and consequent knowledge of light because of his own intimate acquaintance with darkness.

'(Are You) the One that I've Been Waiting For?'

The placing of this song immediately prior to the emotional and spiritual desolation of 'Where Do We Go Now But Nowhere?' signifies the last dying breath of hope in terms of a love affair that is destined to failure. The song opens with its poet-narrator articulating once again what might be known and anticipated experientially: 'I've felt you coming, girl, as you drew near/I knew you'd find me, 'cause I longed you here/Are you my destiny? Is this how/you'll appear? […] Are you the one that I've been waiting for?' (2007: 280). The song exists musically within a deliberately restrained melodic range and has a gentle rhythmic intensity, like a small boat ebbing through the pessimistic countercurrents of experience. His beloved is 'longed' into presence, almost as an occult act of will. With this summoning up of a lover, who might yet prove to be a form of psycho-emotional salvation, the lover-narrator allows himself a moment of ultimately misconceived certainty:

As you've been moving surely toward me
My soul has comforted and assured me
That in time my heart it will reward me
And that all will be revealed
So I've sat and I've watched an ice-age thaw
Are you the one that I've been waiting for?

(2007: 280)

However, even as he dares to anticipate the possibility of a restorative and transformative desire and relationship, the image of Kant's 'starry skies' is re-invoked. This is not as evidence of a deeper, spiritual reality but as a harbinger of destiny and death: '[o] we will know, won't we?/The stars will explode in the sky/O but they don't, do they?/Stars have their moment and then they die' (2007: 280). The reassurance of knowing – and, with it, the possibility of some kind of fragile emotional certainty – is ransacked by the knowledge that many of the stars visible to us on earth have, in fact, died, even as we witness the 'proof' of their existence through their seemingly 'eternal' light.

'Where Do We Go Now But Nowhere?'

The title of this song powerfully evokes its emotional territory: a desert of unbearable loss that crackles in a heat of bitter despair. The opening lines of the song delineate the signifiers of this purgatory: 'I remember a girl so very well/The carnival drums all mad in the air/Grim reapers and skeletons and a missionary bell/O where do we go now but nowhere' (2007: 281). The woman he loved is now perpetually remembered as 'a girl' – anonymous and barely recollected. She is now no more than a ghost: a 'ravaged avenger' (2007: 281). 'I remember a girl so bold and so bright/Loose-limbed and laughing and brazen and bare/Sits gnawing her knuckles in the chemical light/O where do we go now but nowhere' (2007: 281). A funereal tempo requires the listener to meditate upon a litany of images of death, destruction and bitter retribution. A desire that had liberated is now reduced to a mechanical, penetrative sexual act: '[i]n a colonial hotel we fucked up the sun/And then we fucked it down again' (2007: 281). The possibility of offering or receiving a transformative forgiveness is rendered impotent: 'I turn the other cheek and you lay into that' (2007: 281). A haunting one-line refrain punctuates the journey both of the song and of the album overall: '[o] wake up, my love, my lover, wake up' (2007: 281). What possible meaning or future can be resurrected? The desolate female lover has contrived to create a perverse cake to 'celebrate' the spiritual death that now threatens to yoke them to a hellish infinity: '[y]ou come for me now with a cake that you've made/Ravaged avenger with a clip in your hair/Full of glass and bleach and my old razor blades/O where do we go now but nowhere' (2007: 281). For the poet-narrator there can be no consolation, no imagined future. Like Coleridge's mariner, whose transgressive act results in his eternal suffering, Cave's anti-hero carries around his neck a memento mori of endless regret and guilt:

> If I could relive one day of my life
> If I could relive just a single one
> You on the balcony, my future wife
> O who could have known, but no one
>
> O wake up, my love, my lover, wake up
> O wake up, my love, my lover, wake up

(Cave 2007: 282)

'West Country Girl' and 'Black Hair'

I am grouping these two songs together as their placement in the album's narrative has a shared significance and is principally one of a kind of remembered invocation of the female lover. With 'West Country Girl' Cave offers not only a geographical context and past for the woman, but also a geography of desire and its encounter. With its imagery of 'black cats' and a 'widow's peak' there are traditional associations with witches, witchcraft and the occult power of desire (2007: 283). Significantly, this is a desire that has filled him

> [w]ith love, up to the brim, and killed me
> And rebuilt me back anew
> With something to look forward to
> Well, who could ask much more than that?

(2007: 283)

This sense of a sensual and dangerously disruptive desire is echoed in the title and content of 'Black Hair', in which we discover that

> [h]er hair was midnight black
> And all her mystery dwelled within her black hair
> [...]
> All my tears cried against her milk-white throat
> Hidden behind the curtain of her beautiful black hair
> As deep as ink and black, black as the deepest sea

(2007: 284)

The powerful sensual imagery of the blackness of hair and the depths of the sea serve as potent reminders of the power implicit within both the female beloved and the desire she has invoked in him. This is a desire that threatens to 'smother' and drown our love-wrecked mariner.

In some ways these two songs, though clearly linked as a pair that speak to each other, are strangely and awkwardly positioned within the overall narrative of *The Boatman's Call*. They have the function, perhaps, of the lover needing and taking one last, lingering look at the former object of his desire before consigning her and their relationship to the one-way journey of a 'train to the West', from which she (and they) can never return (2007: 284).

'Idiot Prayer'

In this powerful song of utter alienation, Cave adopts another parallel persona for his journeying narrator. The opening verse of this song is characterized musically by the disruptive rhythm of a nightmarish fairground. A discordant violin wheezes malice and invites us into a world where the narrator faces imminent execution:

> They're taking me down, my friend
> And as they usher me off to my end
> Will I bid you adieu?
> Or will I be seeing you soon?
> If what they say around here is true
> Then we'll meet again
> Me and you
>
> My time is at hand, my dove
> They're gunna pass me to that house above
> Is Heaven just for victims, dear?
> Where only those in pain go?
> Well it takes two to tango
> We will meet again, my love
> I know

(2007: 285)

The savagely interrogative irony of '[i]s Heaven just for victims, dear?' communicates a conviction that it is his former lover who defines herself as the 'victim' of their doomed relationship (2007: 285). However, the speaker is equally sure that they 'will meet again' (2007: 285). This is a dark article of faith: a malevolent prophecy of their shared destiny and acknowledgement of their responsibility and guilt.

The song ends with a dedication of the song to the former beloved, albeit expressed with images of doves (traditionally associated with peace and, in Christian theology, the Holy Spirit), idiocy (madness) and damnation:

> This prayer is for you, my love
> Sent on the wings of a dove
> An idiot prayer of empty words
> Love, dear, is strictly for the birds
> We each get what we deserve
> My little snow white dove
> Rest assured

(2007: 286)

As we approach the final two songs of the album and the last stages of its emotional, psychological and spiritual journey, it is as if a song such as 'Idiot Prayer' offers the distorting mirror image from a fairground hall of mirrors. This is a world of desire translated into death. Charon has brought us to another shore in which desire seems destined to carry, within its fragrant blossoms, the cankerous seeds of its own self-destruction and self-loathing.

'Far From Me'

> For you dear I was born
> For you I was raised up
> For you I have lived and for you I will die
> For you I am dying now
> You were my mad little lover
> In a world where everybody fucks everybody else over
> You are so
> Far from me
> So far from me
> Way across some cold neurotic sea
> Far from me

(2007: 287)

These are the opening lines of the album's penultimate song. There is a violin accompaniment, which is conveyed by a desolate punctuating of anguished vibrato. In one sense the song might have made a perfect 'bookend' track to the album's opening song. From the liberating experience of the sublime expressed in the spiritual sexuality of 'Into My Arms', like some postmodern Adam and Eve, the lovers are now cast out of that paradise. The haunting chords of a Hammond organ, resonant of both Gospel music and its secular cousin soul, bring contemporary neo-Gothic darkness to 'light' their path to – where? Nowhere.

The sole, bitterly earned, knowledge of love and life that has been secured through the album's journey is a kind of anti-knowledge, that which might be encountered or experienced in a psycho-spiritual black hole:

> There is no knowledge but I know it
> There's nothing to learn from that vacant voice
> That sails to me across the line
> From the ridiculous to the sublime
> It's good to hear you're doing so well
> But really can't you find somebody else that you can ring and tell?

(2007: 287)

By the end of this song the two former lovers are as distant from each other as one horizon from another, as alienated from the album's opening embrace as it is possible to be. Heaven has become hell and the space between the two is measured in the endless waves of recrimination, regret and loss in a 'bleak and fishless sea': '[f]ar from me' (2007: 287).

A matter of faith: a postscript

In the final song of *The Boatman's Call* there is a postscript to a journey that led from the banks of a river named desire to a distant shore of alienation and despair.

The song 'Green Eyes' (a term traditionally associated with jealousy) opens with a repeated image of physical desire: '[k]iss me again, re-kiss me and kiss me', before immediately plunging into '[s]lip your frigid hands beneath my shirt' (2007: 289). This is an experiential reality that is no longer characterized by mutual sexual desire and fulfilment. This is more of a bargain-basement soft-porn sex show: '[t]his useless old fucker with his twinkling cunt/Doesn't care if he gets hurt' (2007: 289). All hope of a love sublime lies tattered and discarded. We are left with a shaman's relics of desire-as-death: '[i]f it were but a matter of faith/If it were measured in petitions and prayer/She would materialise, all fleshed out/But it is not, nor do I care' (2007: 289). Whatever occult spirit of sexual gratification has been summoned up cannot atone for the death of a purer desire. 'This morning will be wiser than this evening is': however, it is wisdom purchased at the chilling and overwhelmingly destructive price of his soul (2007: 289). He asks only to be left to his 'enemied dreams' and that this fabricated occult-marionette of his former beloved should leave quietly (2007: 289). He will be left like a lonely, impotent Prospero on an island filled with the dark magic of remorse, regret and death.

Nick Cave's album *The Boatman's Call* is, I believe, one of the major achievements of his long and distinguished career as a singer-songwriter. The emotional and psycho-spiritual depth and expanse of its journey through an inner landscape of desire and its ultimate death is moving and darkly visionary. As the shadows of a real-life love affair haunt the cityscape of a pre-1989 Berlin, Cave shares his stigmata with a reckless but breath-taking courage and, in so doing, invokes a fragment of light that might, just might, survive. Can the trapeze hold the weight of such expectation?

References

Cave, Nick (1997), *King Ink II*, London: Black Spring.
_____ (2007), *The Complete Lyrics 1978–2007*, London: Penguin.
Wenders, Wim (1987), *Der Himmel über Berlin/Wings of Desire*, Berlin: Orion Classics.

Chapter 2

The Performance of Voice: Nick Cave and the Dialectic
of Abandonment

Carl Lavery

[F]or all the serious discussion that Nick Cave's music inspires these days, what tends to get a little overlooked, I reckon, is music itself.

(Walker 2009: 32)

The set-up

By concentrating on the two meanings inherent in the *sense* of sound – the fact that songs are material artefacts that simultaneously invite (and resist) linguistic interpretation – I want to use the ideas of Roland Barthes, Simon Frith and Jean-Luc Nancy to explore the duplicitous performance of voice in Nick Cave's song 'When I First Came to Town' from the album *Henry's Dream* (1992). In specific terms, I am concerned to show how Cave's voice in that song stages a religious theme or trope that runs throughout much of his work, and which I refer to in this essay as the 'dialectic of abandonment'. My argument is that Cave's performance, and ultimately, of course, its significance, does not just remain at the level of the lyrics, but insinuates itself into the ear of the listener via the affect generated by the sounds themselves. By 'touching' our senses with his voice, Cave manages to put the listener in the same anxious and wretched position as the narrator of the song. We are 'parachuted' into the place of Other, seduced into going somewhere else, towards a place where we, too, are abandoned and lost. Importantly, this loss is not absolute; rather, it is more accurately approached as a necessary prelude to a possible experience of grace.

Through this focus on voice as a material or sensible phenomenon, I want to build on, as well as move away from, those academic studies that analyse Cave's performance in visual and lyrical terms alone (Broadhurst 1999; Jayasinghe 2009; Pattie 2010). (Two critics who listen to the music as much as the lyrics are Lynn McCredden (2009) and Tanya Dalziell (2009)). This shift from eye to ear is concurrent, too, with a reversal in how the question of authenticity is usually perceived by critics interested in popular music. Whereas many scholars in the burgeoning field of Cave studies (if I may use that term) go to great lengths not to confuse person with persona, I want to sidestep this issue, and instead listen to how authenticity plays itself out *within* Cave's songs, in those places where voice meets text. It seems important to acknowledge that my recourse to an aesthetics of listening does not, in any way, purport to be musicological. Not only do I lack the skills needed to carry out such a reading of the voice, but I doubt if musicology by itself has much to tell us about the affect of music. As Roland Barthes cautions in his influential essay 'The Grain of the Voice', any attempt to account for the performance of a voice is always bound to be a personal matter, and what he says about his methodology in that essay is a worthy epithet for my own relationship to Nick Cave's music in the chapter that follows: '[w]hat I shall attempt to say of the "grain" will, of course, be only the apparently abstract side, the impossible account of an individual thrill that I constantly experience in listening to singing' (Barthes 1977: 181). For Barthes, the grain refers to the materiality of voice: not just its timbre and pitch, but the ligature of the throat, its sonorous presence.

Two additional points before I begin. First, my use of the pronoun 'we' is a rhetorical attempt to translate my 'individual thrill' of music into the possibility of and for shared experience; second, when I refer to 'Cave', I am referring to the singer, not to the person. To use Giorgio Agamben's vocabulary, the name 'Cave', in this chapter, is posited as an authorial 'gesture', a proper noun that 'marks the point at which a life is offered up and played out in the work. Offered up and played out, not expressed or fulfilled. For this reason, the author can only remain unsatisfied and unsaid in the work' (Agamben 2007: 69).

The dialectic of abandonment

In her recent essay 'Fleshed Sacred: The Carnal Theologies of Nick Cave', the Australian scholar Lyn McCredden highlights the complexity of Nick Cave's eclectic representation of religion:

> Cave's sacred is part prophetic Jesus, part Father in the Christian tradition, part Old Testament force of retribution, part metonym for human love and sexual energy, part violent power with unknown capabilities, part absence, part extension of the Cave ego. Is there a system to Cave's sacred?

> (2009: 168)

While I have no intention here of answering McCredden's question – 'is there a system to Cave's sacred?' – I do want to draw attention to one of the idiosyncratic ways in which religious experience manifests itself in and through Cave's texts. As McCredden and the literary scholar Robert Eaglestone point out, Cave is hostile to institutionalized religion (Eaglestone 2009). The song 'God is in The House' on *No More Shall We Part* (2001) is much more than a mere satire of a stereotypical Christian congregation horrified by the spectre of abject others in its midst; it is also a refusal of the church as 'house', a sacred site or building that would act as a space where God can come into presence through the mediation of a minister or priest:

> We've laid the cables and the wires
> We've split the wood and stoked the fires
> We've lit our town so there is no
> Place for crime to hide

Our little church is painted white
And in the safety of the night
We all go quiet as a mouse
For the word is out
God is in the house.
God is in the house
God is in the house
No cause for worry now
God is in the house

(Cave 2007: 324)

For Cave, God cannot be contained architecturally or channelled through ministerial supplication. In his writings, God is typically Pauline (and, we might say, Protestant). His redemptive gift of grace can be experienced by anyone anywhere: killers on death row ('The Mercy Seat' (1986)); dumb mutes in a fortress of dogshit and mantraps (*And the Ass Saw the Angel* (1990)); and all the multiple outsiders – those broken lovers, drunks and murderers – who wander disconsolately and lost through the landscapes of Cave's writing(s). Cave spells out the essentially unmediated and non-voluntarist quality of grace in the final stanza of 'Get Ready for Love' (2004):

I searched the Seven Seas and I've looked under the carpet
And browsed through the brochures that govern the skies
Then I was just hanging around, doing nothing and looked up to see
His face burned in the retina of your eyes

(2007: 384)

Cave is equally disparaging of theological attempts to understand or equate God with a set of moral precepts. In his lecture performance, 'The Flesh Made Word', Cave proposes that

what Jesus most despised, what He really railed against time and time again, were the forces that represented the established order of things, symbolized by the scribes and Pharisees – those dull, small-minded scholars of religious law who actively dogged his every move. Christ saw them as enemies of the imagination, who actively blocked the spiritual flight of the people and kept them bogged down with theological nit-picking, intellectualism and the law. What was Christ's great bugbear, and what has sat like dung in the doorway of the Christian Church ever since, was the Pharisees' preoccupation with the law, in preference to the *logos*. Said St Paul to the Corinthians, 'The Letter killeth, but the Spirit giveth life'. So how can one be elevated spiritually if they are loaded up with chains of religious jurisprudence? How can the imagination be told how to behave? How can inspiration or for that matter God be moral?

(1997: 140)

The second part of Cave's question, 'how can God be moral?', is an important one. As well as contradicting his Kantian claim in 'There is a Kingdom' (1997) that we are ruled by 'the starry heavens above [and] the moral law within', his reflections in 'The Flesh Made Word' cause us to consider the perverse role played by abandonment in what Robert Eaglestone has correctly identified as the 'shifting complexity of Cave's relation to religion' (Cave 2007: 279; Eaglestone 2009: 15).

But what does abandonment mean for Cave? And how, in his songs, does it accomplish its theological labour? A helpful point of comparison is offered by reading Cave's songs in tandem with the ideas of the Danish philosopher and theologian Søren Kierkegaard. In his 1843 text *Fear and Trembling*, Kierkegaard deliberately distanced himself from the religious thought of the dominant German philosophers Kant and Hegel by insisting on the fundamentally 'absurd' nature of faith. Whereas Kant and Hegel, admittedly in very different ways, posited a symmetrical fit between ethics, rationality and religion, Kierkegaard maintained that religious experience transcended human understanding and had little to do with knowledge *per se*. Taking his inspiration from Genesis 22, and constructing his philosophy as a type of fictional meditation, Kierkegaard's narrator, the amusingly named Johannes de Silentio, reflects on Abraham's willingness to sacrifice his only and beloved son as a token of his faith. In de Silentio's words, Abraham's commitment, the strength of his belief, constitutes him as a 'Knight of Faith', someone whose leap into the absurd allowed him to 'transform [...] a murder into a holy act well-pleasing to God' (Kierkegaard 1954: 64).

For Kierkegaard/Silentio, Abraham's willingness to offer his son Isaac as a tender 'prey' to God discloses a schism between the realms of the ethical and divine (1954: 34). In the three problems posed in *Fear and Trembling*, Kierkegaard/Silentio equates the ethical realm with the universal, the law and the *res publica*: '[t]he ethical as such is the universal, and as the universal it applies to everyone [...]. Conceived immediately as physical and psychical, the particular individual is the individual who has his *telos* in the universal, and his ethical task is to express himself constantly in it, to abolish his particularity in order to become universal' (1954: 64–5).

According to Kierkegaard – and this is what marks his radical divergence from Kant's investment in the categorical imperative, and Hegel's all-encompassing notion of spirit or mind (*Geist*) – religious and moral experience operate in different realms. To exist in the Kierkegaardian universal, as Jacques Derrida has explained in *The Gift of Death*, is to subordinate's one's singularity to language, to follow a socially constructed set of human commandments rooted in rationality and reason: '[t]he first effect or first destination of language therefore involves depriving me of, or delivering me from, my singularity' (Derrida 1996: 60). To be ethical in Kierkegaardian terms, as Derrida points out, is to consent to mediation, to commit oneself to the human world, a world where everything, in Hegelian fashion, can be explained and known, and where one needs to obey the laws of universal reason. Consequently, to reject that world, to go against the universal as Abraham did in his willingness to sacrifice Isaac, is to suspend the ethical, to leave the human world behind and to assert that in the divine realm 'the individual as the particular is higher than the universal' (Kierkegaard 1954: 66).

> [Abraham] acts by virtue of the absurd, for it is precisely absurd that he as the particular is higher than the universal. This paradox cannot be mediated; for as soon as he begins to do this he has to admit that he was in temptation (*Anfechtung*), and if such was the case, he never gets to the point of sacrificing Isaac, or, if he has sacrificed Isaac, he must turn back repentantly to the universal.
>
> (1954: 67)

Although they are in no way identical, Kierkegaard's paradoxical notion of faith nevertheless permits a method for approaching how religious experience functions as abandonment in Cave's work. In both cases, if the subject is to move closer to God, to experience an unmediated relationship with the divine, then s/he has to be willing to sacrifice the world of the universal, the world of language and law. Or, as Cave muses in 'Hold On To Yourself' (2008) 'does Jesus only love a man who loses?' (Cave 2008). This question – and it is surely rhetorical – accounts for why Cave's narrators and anti-heroes are so often 'monsters', men who have gone too far, and who have committed violent acts that finish by distancing them from the values of the community. As in the novels of Jean Genet, the ethical world in Cave's songs is evil, the source of a temptation that must be resisted. In the song 'People Ain't No Good' (1997), Cave proposes that '[i]t ain't that in their hearts they're bad/They can comfort you, some even try/They nurse you when you're ill of health' before concluding '[b]ut that's just bullshit, baby/People just ain't no good' (Cave 2007: 277). Similarly in 'Dig, Lazarus, Dig!!!' (2008), Lazarus or Larry finishes by rejecting the human world that 'asked him to forsake his dreams' and put him 'back on the streets of New York City/In a soup queue, a dope fiend, a slave, then prison, then the madhouse, then the grave' (2008). Abandonment in Cave's work, as it is in Kierkegaard's *Fear and Trembling*, is inherently dialectical: the more one distances oneself from the world of morality, the better one's chances of experiencing grace. To borrow a phrase used by Jean-Paul Sartre that echoes the language of 'Hold On To Yourself', Cave's characters play a game of 'loser wins' (Sartre 1988: 229). To lose the human world is to attain the 'mercy seat'.

However, if Kierkegaard's argument in *Fear and Trembling* allows us to make sense of one of the themes constituting Cave's composite, and often contradictory, relationship to Christianity, a major difference separates the behaviour of Cave's narrators from that of Abraham. Whereas Abraham, the Knight of Faith, does not doubt that he will be able to return to the ethical world and to live a 'happy life' within it, Cave's characters are always inclined to renounce God for the temptations of the human. Their faith, in other words, is not as strong as Abraham's, their resignation not as infinite. In 'The Mercy Seat', the narrator protests his innocence until the final stanza, in an attempt not to lose human sympathy; and in 'Brompton Oratory' (1997), human love appears to triumph over divine love.

Up those stone steps I climb
Hail this joyful day's return
Into its great shadowed vault I go
Hail the Pentecostal morn.

The reading is from Luke 24
Where Christ returns to his loved ones
I look at the stone apostles
Think that it's alright for some.

And I wish that I was made of stone
So that I would not have to see
A beauty impossible to define
A beauty impossible to believe.

A beauty impossible to endure
The blood imparted in little sips
The smell of you still on my hands
As I bring the cup up to my lips

(2007: 278)

In this instance, what McCredden identifies as Cave's 'blasphemy' is more than romantic posturing; it expresses his failure to commit himself to the radical concept of absolute duty laid out in the Gospel of Luke (McCredden 2009: 170). In Luke 14, as Kierkegaard reminds the reader in *Fear and Trembling*, Jesus declares that no man can be 'his disciple' if he does not hate 'his own father and mother and wife and children and brethren and sisters' (Kierkegaard 1954: 82). From this perspective, the singer's reluctance to forget his lover in 'Brompton Oratory' as he listens to Luke 24 offers a privileged insight into the tension that exists in Cave's work between the human and divine, the ethical and religious, and the universal and individual. Intriguingly and ingeniously, Cave's solution to what we might call after Kierkegaard the 'temptation' of the ethical is to transgress human law: to arrive at the divine through evil. Such a strategy, of course, places the onus on negation, that is, on failure, melancholy, anger and violence. As Cave points out in his lecture 'The Secret Life of the Love Song' (1999), the love song, especially when it sings of defeat, can produce its own profound sense of abandonment; one, moreover, that leads the subject away from the human community and back 'into the arms' of the divine: '[t]hough the Love Song comes in many guises – songs of exultation and praise, songs of rage and despair, erotic songs, songs of abandonment and loss – they all address God, for it is the haunted premise of longing that the true Love Song inhabits' (2007: 7).

The theological torsions inherent in the practice of transgression in Cave's lyrics are also at play formally, in how, that is, his songs are constructed and ultimately performed. Cave's focus on form is especially crucial to grasp when it comes to the question of abandonment, since the very fact that one decides to sing one's abandonment is, in itself, inherently problematic. If the abandoned subject is a subject who refutes the universal (the human world) for the singular (his solitary relationship to God), then is not the attempt to communicate abandonment a contradiction in terms? Does not the song invariably connect the singer back to the human community that he needs to escape from if the miracle of grace is to be experienced? As I will show in a close reading of 'When I First Came to Town', abandonment can be communicated in the extent to which both singer and listener are separated from each other through their experience of the song. In this respect, and this of course complicates Cave's claim in 'The Flesh Made Word' that 'whenever two or more are gathered together [...] there is God', song-writing is the opposite of hymn-writing (1997: 137). Whereas hymns are traditionally intended to provide the congregation with a sense of communion, a sharing of the Word (*logos*), Cave's songs of abandonment are focused on transporting the listener to the most solitary of places, places where s/he is as lost and forlorn as the narrator himself. Cave's compositional practice and vocal performance also problematize the largely metaphysical view of the *logos* that he upholds in 'The Flesh Made Word'. In 'When I First Came to Town', the *logos*, by itself, is no longer, as Cave suggests in the essay above, a bridge to God; rather, language and voice play with *and* against each other to leave us naked and alone. In Cave's dialectic of abandonment – and it is, I stress, only one aspect of his religious thought – redemption is not achieved through doing good works or via the mediation of spirit in language; rather it is experienced, if it is experienced at all, by exposing oneself to God's gift, opening oneself to an irrational and absurd love that transcends the logocentric values of language and reason. In so far as he privileges song over mere speech, Cave is closer to John the Baptist than he is to Christ, since the voice (*vox clamintis in deserto*) is what predates the word. Mladen Dolar explains: '[i]n the beginning was the Word, but in order for the Word to manifest itself, there has to be a mediator, a precursor in the shape of John the Baptist, who identities himself precisely as [...] the voice crying in the desert, while Christ, in this paradigmatic opposition, is identified with the Word, verbum logos' (2006: 16).

My decision to focus on 'When I First Came to Town' is guided by the fact that the song offers what I believe to be the purest and most formally astute expression of the dialectic of abandonment in Cave's work to date. Whereas songs and novels such as 'The Mercy Seat', 'Brompton Oratory', 'Foi Na Cruz', 'Let the Bells Ring' and *And the Ass Saw the Angel* deal with various aspects of abandonment, 'When I First Came to Town' illustrates how abandonment is, quintessentially, an agonistic religious state characterized by melancholy, violence and despair. The outlaw in Cave's songs and film scripts offers an alternative figure of abandonment. In the final scene of *The Proposition*, a film written by Cave, abandonment takes on a cosmic significance (Hillcoat 2005). In this context, see also Cave and Warren Ellis' song 'The Rider Part Two' (2005) (from the film's soundtrack).

In 'When I First Came to Town', loneliness and rejection are prerequisites for unmediated religious experience. From a formal perspective, moreover, the song's architecture with its grounding in deceit and trickery illustrates the extent to which abandonment, for Cave, is a performance, something that draws us in before revealing its own empty core. In this way,

'When I First Came to Town' combines, without resolving, the two opposing tendencies that dominate so much of Cave's writing: namely, his ironic quest to undermine stylistically the semantic meaning of his own songs. (For a good discussion of Cave's irony, see Carol Hart's 2009 essay on postcolonial laughter).

Here, the distance that Cave assumes with respect to his own material becomes a vital component in the song's affective economy. Indeed, the performative qualities of the song, suggested by the narrator's inconsistent and purposefully artificial delivery, are integral to the song's content. For, as I mentioned above, abandonment is not something we simply understand semantically; it is also something we undergo through our listening.

'When I First Came to Town'

'When I First Came to Town' takes its title from the opening line of the nineteenth-century American folksong 'Katie Cruel', which is an updated version of an eighteenth-century Scottish ballad about a camp-follower or prostitute, 'Licht Bob's Lassie'. The most famous version of the song is by the American folksinger Karen Dalton on her album *In My Own Time* (1971). The lyrics tell the story of 'a fallen woman', rejected by the same townsfolk who had once welcomed her into their community, either, it seems, because of an addiction to drink: '[w]hen I first came to town/They brought me the bottles plenty/Now they've changed their tune/They bring me the bottles empty', or because she might have fallen in love with another woman:

> I know who I love, and I know who does love me
> I know where I'm going
> And I know who's going with me
> Eyes as bright as coal
> Lips as bright as cherry
> And 'tis her delight
> To make the young girls merry

(Wikipedia 2008)

Whatever the actual cause of the narrator's transgression, Katie's exile is absolute, and she stumbles through the 'bogs and mire' like a wandering pariah: '[o]h that I was where I would be/Then I would be where I am not/Here I am where I must be/Go where I would, I can not' (Wikipedia 2008).

As in the original 'Katie Cruel', the narrator of 'When I First Came to Town' has been banished for committing an unspoken (and possibly unspeakable) crime. However, while Cave retains, and indeed exploits, the 'mystery' at the heart of the folksong, his focus is ultimately very different. Not only is his version a vertiginous exercise in baroque orchestration and poetic imagery, he introduces a new religious element that sits uneasily between the opposed logics of the Old and New Testament.

In the first two stanzas, the narrator tells the story of a deception, of how he was invited into a town and treated like a guest, before an inexplicable and malevolent reversal took place:

> When I first came to town
> All the people gathered round
> They bought me drinks
> Lord, how quickly they changed their tune.
>
> When I first came to town
> People took me round from end to end
> Like someone may take around a friend
> O how quickly they changed their tune

(Cave 2007: 200)

In the third stanza, Cave's voice is joined and doubled by fellow Bad Seeds member Conway Savage singing harmony. In this haunting, quasi-schizophrenic polyphony of voices, the narrator supplies the listener with the first in a series of hallucinatory tropes. He imagines that the citizens of the town can see blood running from his hands, as if he had committed some heinous, primeval crime: '[s]uspicion and dark murmurs surround me/Everywhere I go they confound me/As though the blood on my hands/Is there for every citizen to see' (Cave 2007: 200). Following the logic of the original ballad, no explanation is given for the narrator's lament. The listener is simply invited to engage in his/her own act of interpretation; s/he is seduced by the riddle of the song, compelled to make its troubling silence speak. The next stanza appears to suggest a possible answer: the reference to 'juicers' intimates that the whole event has been imagined, a fantasy caused by the paranoid delusions of alcohol withdrawal. Again, the images proffered by the narrator are hallucinatory. But this time, the dominant trope is of fire and flames: '[a]nd from my window, across the tracks/I watch the juicers burn their fires/And in that light/Their faces leer at me/How I wish they'd just let me be' (2007: 200). However, in stanzas five and six, this reading, while never disappearing completely, is complicated by the narrator's own apparent sense of bewilderment and confusion:

> When I first came to town
> Their favours were for free
> Now even the doors of the whores of this town
> Are closed to me.
>
> I search the mirror
> And I try to see
> Why the people of this town
> Have washed their hands of me

(2007: 200–01)

Although these stanzas certainly make the listener consider the truth status of the narrative s/he is listening to (can the singer be trusted or not?), no compassion or empathy is aroused. The melodramatic quality of the singing suggests that the narrator is lying. The suspicion that the narrator is not worthy of our trust is reinforced by his claim that his experience in the town is not unique, but something that has happened again and again: '[o] Lord, every God-damn turn I take/I fear the noose, I fear the stake/For there is no bone/They did not break/In all the towns I've been before' (2007: 201). The listener's compassion is further alienated in the extended last verse of the song, when the narrator, like some Old Testament prophet, fantasizes about taking his revenge on those who have supposedly 'sinned against him':

> Well, those that sin against me are snuffed out
> I know that from every day that I live
> God-damn the day that I was born
> The night that forced me from the womb
> And God-damn this town
> For I am leaving now
> But one day I will return
> And the people of this town will surely see
> Just how quickly the tables turn

(2007: 201)

'When I First Came to Town' is a troubling and ambivalent song, the ground of which is perpetually shifting. Not only is it impossible to ascertain the cause behind the narrator's malcontent and ill-being, but the listener is unable to say with any certainty if the singer's lamentations and resentment are genuine or not. This disorientates: the listener does not know what role to adopt. Is s/he there to bear witness to the narrator's fall from grace? Or is s/he being asked to pass judgement on his actions? While both of these readings are, of course, possible, I want to suggest an alternative interpretation by arguing that the ambiguity and undecidability of the song are simultaneously structural and performative: the listener is addressed so as to allow the narrator to achieve a paradoxical state of isolation in and through the very act of trying to communicate. The narrator requires an audience so that he can stage his distance from them. In other words, the listener's function is to exist as an enemy, someone whose existence must be simultaneously affirmed and negated. In this way, the narrator manages to circumvent the paradox of his act, the sense in which to sing is to communicate with the very audience he is, by necessity, required to reject. Perversely, the key to this dialectic of abandonment is found in the choral structure of the song, that is to say, in the three appeals to God, each of which starts with the line '[o] sweet Jesus': '[o] sweet Jesus/There is no turning back/There is always one more town/A little further down the track' (2007: 201). The dialogic quality of the chorus is reminiscent of the antiphonal structures of hymns and prayers, but with the difference that there is no one here to respond back to, or indeed to sing with. Conway Savage's harmonies function as echoes; they haunt the narrator's voice and highlight his loneliness. Nowhere in the song does the singer appear so wretched and alone. Yet, this silent conversation, this one-way dialogue with God, constitutes the narrator's triumph (there is no other word). By rejecting a human world that has exiled him, he has found a divine one. In this respect, the listeners are the victims of a deceit or confidence trick. Because we doubt the veracity of the singer's tale, he manages to communicate without communicating, to elude our grasp in the very act of speaking. Our doubts and suspicions, in other words, place us, the listeners, in a position analogous to that of the townsfolk of the song. We are the human community that refuses to welcome him in. Consequently, his crime becomes our crime. By listening to it, we are infected by it. We have rejected a fellow human being, denied him charity. The singer, by contrast, is delivered from evil through his performance of abjection. Singing the song does not bind him to us; rather, it allows him to remain faithful to abandonment, the very thing that offers the possibility of grace from a divinity who, like the God of Kierkegaard's *Fear and Trembling* and Jesus in the Gospel of Luke, values the transgressive singularity of the theological over the universality of the ethical.

The performance of voice

Like the song 'I Had a Dream, Joe' (1992) on the same album, Cave's voice in 'When I First Came to Town' draws attention to itself by adopting a 'southern drawl'. There is something phoney in Cave's adopted accent, something put on. As in the plays of Luigi Pirandello, Cave's vocal performance in 'When I First Came to Town' is a performance about performance, singing that shows itself, that foregrounds its own physicality and allows the vocal gesture to appear. Even though we cannot see Cave in person, the singer is uncannily present, a spectral body penetrating our eyes through the ear. We 'see' him crooning his words, putting on a vocal show. To adopt a beautiful phrase from Barthes, the grain of Cave's voice 'sways us to *jouissance*' (Barthes 1977: 183). The timbre, cadence, melisma and rhythm of Cave's voice sensitizes us to time, and exposes the ephemeral and transient qualities of being, the fact that words come from and retreat back into the void of the body, the 'cave' of the mouth. And yet, despite that, it is precisely this awareness of simulation, this exposure of ventriloquism, that causes the listener to 'sway', and draws her/him into the uncanny space of the singer. The Slovenian philosopher and Lacanian Mladan Dolar explains:

[s]inging [...] brings the voice energetically to the forefront, on purpose, at the expense of meaning. Indeed singing is bad communication; it prevents a clear understanding of the text [...] Singing takes the distraction of the voice seriously, and turns the table on the signifier; it reverses the hierarchy – let the voice take the upper hand, let the voice be the bearer of what cannot be expressed by the words.

(2006: 30)

Cave's voice moves us precisely because we cannot always understand what he is singing about. There are moments, particularly towards the middle and end sections of the song, when his voice becomes (almost) pure body, too hysterical, all sound. When this stumbling of the signifying system occurs (who can tell without reading the lyric sheet that Cave is singing about 'juicers' and 'whores'?) the voice throws off the demand to signify, and allies itself, instead, with the music, transforming itself into an instrument in its own right, something non-human. In this 'bad communication', the listener is, to use Dolar's language, 'fascinated'; a kind of spell is put on her/him. S/he is enchanted, played on, sung. Language becomes material, pure matter, an economy of noise – vowels, consonants, tongue, breath, thorax, lungs.

In this collapse of the lyric, Cave is not communicating something deeper, a *logos* that would lie beneath the words; rather his voice is transporting us somewhere beyond the words, to a site where meaning dissolves and where self-presence is impossible (note Cave's satire of Orpheus on the title track of *The Lyre of Orpheus* (2004)). According to the philosopher Jean-Luc Nancy, music short-circuits understanding. It does so by resonating within us, by setting up an 'echo chamber' that we are immersed in and touched by: '[s]o the sonorous place, space and place – and taking place – *as* sonority, is not a place where the subject comes to make himself heard (like the concert hall or the studio into which the singer or instrumentalist enters); on the contrary, it is a place that becomes a subject insofar as sound resounds there' (Nancy 2007: 17).

If the 'sonorous place' that Nancy refers to is the space between the singer and listener, voice and ear, then to listen to music is quite literally to lose oneself, to be swept away in what the British philosopher Jonathan Rée has termed the 'oceanic indeterminacy of voice' (Rée 1999: 11). Tellingly Nancy argues that the listening subject, this subject who is displaced sensorially through the 'touch' of music, is not a philosophical subject. To an extent, he has gone beyond law, existing outside the human community: '[t]he subject of the listening or the subject who is listening (but also the one who is "subject to listening" in the sense that one can be "subject to" unease, an ailment or a crisis) is not a phenomenological subject. This means that he is not a philosophical subject, and, finally, he is perhaps no subject at all' (Nancy 1999: 21–2).

Nancy's comments disclose the ultimate perversity of Cave's dialectic of abandonment in 'When I First Came to Town', for they suggest that the object of the song is not solely to guarantee the narrator's solitude, but, more crucially, to place the listener in a similar position, to deprive us of subjectivity, our citizenship. The phoniness of Cave's voice works to unveil the inauthentic quality of all voices, to show that self-presence is impossible, a chimera, a fetish. As the popular music critic and sociologist Simon Frith has it, to listen to music is not solely to undergo passively an aural experience; it is to engage, actively and physically, in a virtual reconstruction of the sounds that enter through our eardrums. Music transforms us into mimics. We mouth and repeat the word and melodies that we hear.

Musical pleasure lies in the way we can make use of both being addressed, responding to a voice as it speaks to us (caressingly, assertively, plaintively), and addressing, taking on the voice as our own, not just physically [...] – singing along, moving our throat and chest muscles appropriately – but also emotionally and psychologically, taking on (in fantasy) the vocal personality too.

(Frith 1996: 198)

By taking on the falsity of Cave's voice, by mimicking him mimicking, and adopting his guttural crooning and hyperbolic pleading, the listener is engaged in an act of Baudrillardian simulation. We do not simply empathize with the singer; we become the Other. Frith continues, '[i]n taking on a singer's vocal personality we are, in a sense, putting on a vocal costume, enacting the role that they are playing themselves' (1996: 198). To listen to 'When I First Came to Town' is an uncanny experience. Like Artaud's theatre of the plague, Cave's song affects and infects. We assume the wretchedness and abandonment of the narrator, and, as result of that, open ourselves, against our will and understanding, to the possibility of grace, of being redeemed, like him, through a suspension of the ethical, of engaging in our own dialectic of abandonment.

In this way, we can see that Cave's performance is doubly duplicitous, a deception through deception. This exposure of falseness, the fact that Cave, in Brechtian terms, 'shows' us that he is singing, is the very thing that seduces us. In this seduction through the ear, the listener forgets – or is no longer able – to pass judgement or rationalize; s/he has lost the *logos*, the word that both joins us to the human community and, in conventional theological terms, to God. What we are left with is the voice – the senseless thing that discloses the very void at the heart of language and being. Accordingly, we are not duped by the authenticity of Cave the performer, the fact that he may actually believe in, or even have experienced, what he is singing; rather, we are duped by the inauthentic quality of the performance. The great paradox here is that this exposed falseness is what allows Cave's narrators to experience the authentic solitude that is necessary for their redemption, the touch of grace. For Cave's abject and ambivalent protagonists, to sing is not to create community or to overcome differences in some dream of reconciliation. Rather, singing is now an act that divorces us from the world of language, and engages us, physically and psychically, in what I have been calling a dialectic of abandonment. As such, we might conclude that Cave's songs are indeed religious songs, albeit ones that both negate and reverse the communitarian universalism of hymns and psalms. In them, the profound truth of religious experience is, as Kierkegaard pointed out in *Fear and Trembling*, inseparable from a performative transgression of the human world and its ethical values.

Acknowledgements

I would like to thank Professor Mike Pearson, my colleague and fellow Cave fan. In a typical act of generosity, he supplied me with the Cave lectures on CD. Thanks, too, to another colleague, Dr Paul Newland, who lent me his copy of *The South Bank Show* (2003) on Nick Cave.

References

Agamben, Giorgio (2007), *Profanations*, trans. by Jeff Fort, New York: Zone.

Barthes, Roland (1977), 'The Grain of the Voice', in *Image-Music-Text*, trans. by Stephen Heath, London: Fontana.

Broadhurst, Susan (1999), *Liminal Acts: A Critical Overview of Contemporary Performance*, London: Continuum.

Cave, Nick (1990), *And the Ass Saw the Angel*, London: Penguin.

—— (1997), *King Ink II*, London: Black Spring.

—— (1999), *The Secret Life of the Love Song and the Flesh Made Word*. CD. London: King Mob.

—— (2007), *The Complete Lyrics 1978–2007*, London: Penguin.

Cave, Nick and the Bad Seeds (1986), *Your Funeral … My Trial*. CD. London: Mute.

—— (1988), *Tender Prey*. CD. London: Mute.

—— (1990), *The Good Son*. CD. London: Mute.

—— (1992), *Henry's Dream*. CD. London: Mute.

—— (1997), *The Boatman's Call*. CD. London: Mute.

—— (2001), *No More Shall We Part*. CD. London: Mute.

—— (2004), *Abattoir Blues/The Lyre of Orpheus*. CD. London: Mute.

—— (2008), *Dig, Lazarus, Dig!!!*. CD. London: Mute.

Cave, Nick and Warren Ellis (2005), *The Proposition: Original Soundtrack*. CD. London: Mute.

Dalton, Karen (1971), *In My Own Time*. CD. New York: Paramount.

Dalziell, Tanya (2009), 'The Moose and Nick Cave: Melancholy, Creativity and Love Songs', in Karen Welberry and Tanya Dalziell (eds), *Cultural Seeds: Essays on the Work of Nick Cave*, Farnham: Ashgate, pp. 187–201.

Derrida, Jacques (1996), *The Gift of Death*, trans. by David Wills. Chicago: University of Chicago Press.

Dolar, Mladen (2006), *A Voice and Nothing More*. Cambridge, MA: MIT.

Eaglestone, Robert (2009), 'From Mutiny to Calling Upon the Author: Cave's Religion', in Karen Welberry and Tanya Dalziell (eds), *Cultural Seeds: Essays on the Work of Nick Cave*, Farnham: Ashgate, pp. 139–52.

Frith, Simon (1996), *Performing Rites: On the Value of Popular Music*, Oxford: Oxford University Press.

Hart, Carol (2009), 'Nick Cave and the Australian Language of Laughter', in Karen Welberry and Tanya Dalziell (eds), *Cultural Seeds: Essays on the Work of Nick Cave*, Farnham: Ashgate, pp. 47–64.

Hillcoat, John (2005), *The Proposition*, Century City, CA: First Look.

Jayasinghe, Laknath (2009), 'Nick Cave, Dance Performance and the Production and Consumption of Masculinity', in Karen Welberry and Tanya Dalziell (eds), *Cultural Seeds: Essays on the Work of Nick Cave*, Farnham: Ashgate, pp. 65–80.

Kierkegaard, Sören (1954), *Fear and Trembling*, trans. by Walter Lowrie. New York: Doubleday Anchor.

McCredden, Lyn (2009), 'Fleshed Sacred: The Carnal Theologies of Nick Cave', in Karen Welberry and Tanya Dalziell (eds), *Cultural Seeds: Essays on the Work of Nick Cave*, Farnham: Ashgate, pp. 167–86.

Nancy, Jean-Luc (2007), *Listening*, trans. by Charlotte Mandell, New York: Fordham University Press.

Pattie, David (2010), 'Saint Nick: A Parallax View of Nick Cave', in Karoline Grizner (ed.), *Eroticism and Death in Theatre and Performance*, Hatfield: University of Hertfordshire Press.

Rée, Jonathan (1999), *I See a Voice: Language, Deafness and the Senses: A Philosophical History*, London: HarperCollins.

Sartre, Jean-Paul (1988), *Saint Genet: Actor and Martyr*, trans. by Bernard Frechtman, London: Heinemann.

Walker, Clinton (2009), 'Planting Seeds', in Karen Welberry and Tanya Dalziell (eds), *Cultural Seeds: Essays on the Work of Nick Cave*, Farnham: Ashgate, pp. 31–45.

Wikipedia (2008), 'Katie Cruel', http://en.wikipedia.org/wiki/Katie_Cruel. Accessed 26 August 2011.

Chapter 3

'The College Professor Says It': Using Nick Cave's Lyrics
in the University Classroom

Paul Lumsden

The title of this chapter comes from the song 'Babe, I'm on Fire', the longest in Nick Cave's canon (Cave 2007: 364–74). In this song, Cave presents a litany of people and animals who all acknowledge that he is on fire, or rather that he is in love (as suggested in the refrain). Among those whom he acknowledges to profess his love is the 'college professor', preceded by the internally rhymed 'vicious cross dresser' (2007: 367). Situated in this company, a member of the teaching profession might indeed shy away from a discussion of Cave's canon if it were not such a repository of pedagogically useful distinctions. Confronted, furthermore, with Will Self's 'foreword' and Nick Cave's prefatory remarks to *The Complete Lyrics, 1978–2007,* one might be discouraged from exploring or discussing the literary merit of Cave's lyrics in an academic context (2007: ix–xii, 1–19). Will Self chastises academics who attempt to equate songwriters with poets (2007: x). Nick Cave writes of his horror and 'conflicting feelings' at finding himself, like his father, a teacher, in front of a classroom teaching the 'Love Song' (2007: 5–6). In the face of Self's admonition and Cave's discomfort, I must confess my trepidation at discussing Cave's lyrics in a university classroom; I am first a fan of Nick Cave's music, but also a university literature professor who uses Cave's lyrics in the classroom. I thoroughly enjoy listening to Cave's music and have an allegiance to it; however, I realize that not all my students will enjoy his music, particularly because it may seem to them an imposition from a teacher. Appeasing this seemingly irreconcilable and conflicting binary of fan/professor risks placing pedestrian and quixotic boundaries around Cave's irreducible subjective poetic experience and thereby subduing the unconventional romantic, rebellious impulse of his work. Nevertheless, I maintain that his lyrics are useful in a university classroom, despite the possible derision suggested by Will Self. They are replete with overt intertextual references to writers, social issues, religious yearning and scepticism, in addition to their accompanying peripatetic quest for meaning and understanding; that is, they ask the big questions relevant to nascent university students.

My chapter explores the problems and rewards of teaching the lyrics of Nick Cave in a university classroom. I will first discuss my experiences teaching Cave's lyrics, followed by an explication of 'Faraway, So Close'. I will be pointing out central themes running throughout Cave's work, all the while connecting his work with canonical writers. I will also discuss the pedagogically useful features of 'There She Goes, My Beautiful World' and 'Into My Arms' (2007: 392–4, 273–4). In my discussion, I plan to consider Nick Cave's lyrics as canonical and (dare I say blasphemously) conventional. I do not plan an exegesis of his lyrics per se, although some of this is inevitable. I want to consider what he illustrates and what he shares with the canonical writers often used in introductory literature classes. I am not discussing the biographical allusions in the lyrics, but rather how Cave takes his subjective experience and shapes it into language. I am not dismissing the salient biographies and assessments of Cave by Ian Johnstone, or Maximilian Dax and Johannes Beck, or Amy Hanson's guide; nor am I discounting Roland Boer, who writes of Cave's 'autobiographical output [as] somewhat Bible-obsessed' (Johnstone 1996; Dax and Beck 1999; Hanson 2005; Boer 2006). These Cave biographies connect his lyrics to the personal events surrounding their incarnation and appeal to the fan in me, who loves the minutiae of musical production. Likewise, Peter Webb's illuminating discussion of Cave as '[i]nfected by the seed of post-industrial punk bohemia' situates Cave's work in milieu theory (Webb 2008). Webb places Cave's work among 'social actors in a networked web of interaction and subjective understanding that is rooted in a structured field, mapped by uncovering the overlapping levels of meaning, relevance, disposition and knowledge that structure […] their lives' (Webb 2008: 105). Ultimately, the literature professor in me discourages a biographical approach to Cave's lyrics in classroom discussion, not because I am aligning my pedagogy with the formalist tradition heralded by Cleanth Brooks (and the school of New Critics), but because such an approach can diminish Cave's aesthetic expression, oftentimes broaching on authorial fallacy. I want my students to take what they learn in the classroom and apply it to their own aesthetic experience.

My university freshman students are conscripted into studying literature because it is a compulsory course; I cannot extol the merits of poetry and readily create enthusiasm for poets without some resistance or ennui. Added to this, and particularly relevant too, is the hermeneutic objective of an introductory literature course. Under the pedagogical ruse of cultivating aesthetic tastes, while acquiring an ability to critically interpret and appreciate written texts, students are wrought with disdain (usually because I have to assess their involvement and assign grades). Song lyrics, like poems, become puzzle exercises that need to be solved, rather than what Paul de Man called 'conditions of indetermination' that open up the world (de Man 1979: 51). I have used contemporary music lyrics for many years as a sneaky strategy to engage my students more closely with poetry and the written word, including lyrics by Bob Dylan, Leonard Cohen and Tom Waits (to name a few). As a feeble defence, I might add that I was a fan of Cave's music before I was a university instructor. As a fan, I enjoy the confluence of listening to the music with words. I would disdain the thought of considering the lyrics without the music; the two are married like form and content. However, by publishing his lyrics as an autonomous entity, Cave has ruptured the musical marriage. By isolating the lyrics in the classroom, I am artificially separating the polysemous expression of Cave's musical experience. A transformation takes place when the music is removed and the words stand alone to be read. Without the musical accompaniment, the lyrics become a disruptive mediation, and the power of the words becomes anterior. Students confronted with the song lyrics do not approach them, and an analysis of them, as a threat – as they do if presented with a poem. They assume the linguistic social signifiers are the usual banalities of a pop song, the effervescence of which is assumed to be without serious challenge to understanding. Most of my students do not know Nick Cave's music, and the few that do know his songs often associate them with their parents' musical tastes. Cave's lyrics, however, provide challenges that bear out rewards.

One of the problems with using Cave's lyrics in the classroom emanates from my feelings as a fan, opening Cave's lyrics to sophomoric analysis and discussion: 'what if the students don't like his music and lyrics that I love?' And even when I read them, Cave's voice is stuck in my head. Despite my trepidations and misgivings, I have used Cave's lyrics to open up my introductory literature classes because of the way he creatively combines pop music sensibilities in his lyrics with many canonical literary references to classic themes and classic structures. Even considered in isolation, his lyrics call to mind the 'theoretical indiscipline' of Jacques Attali, for whom popular music is 'prophetic' (Attali 2009: 4). It is not just the breadth of his lyrics and their range of topics that appeal to me, but I am drawn to the awareness of language in many of his song lyrics – an awareness that makes them apt specimens for critical analysis in a university literature class. Because of the perennial themes embedded in his work, Cave's lyrics provide a formidable, interesting bridge to both guide students to closer readings of texts, and to illustrate that these themes are not just the bailiwick of literature.

Using Cave's lyrics in the classroom

I have been using three of Cave's lyrics in my classroom lectures: 'Faraway, So Close!', 'There She Goes, My Beautiful World' and 'Into My Arms'. These three song lyrics cover a miniscule part of his career and their selection does not prematurely pronounce an overarching statement about Cave's work, or his 'one single poetic statement', as Martin Heidegger would suggest of poets and their poems (Heidegger 1982: 160). My choices were made as a fan, even though I presented them as a university teacher. Moreover, these three songs are embedded in themes that run through Cave's canon.

Unlike many contemporary writers who suggest that metanarrative master texts have lost their powers to convince, Cave uses the Bible as a totalizing narrative in many of his lyrics to provide certitude, albeit playfully and oftentimes ironically presented. Roland Boer argues that Cave 'moves from the Old Testament's appeal to an angry drug crazed young man to Christ's call in the New' (Boer 2006). To this oscillation, I might add that Cave combines an empirical emphasis on the tangible elements of life. As Cave tells us in the preface to his lyrics, 'I found that through the use of language I was writing God into existence. Language became the blanket that I threw over the invisible man, which gave him shape and form' (Cave 2007: 6). However, scanning through the more than 200 song lyrics contained in *The Complete Lyrics 1978–2007*, one can glean many other thematically recurring motifs. In his lyrics Cave often uses different voices (as in *Murder Ballads*) and deconstructs conventional musical forms, such as the blues and train songs. His lyrics resonate with malevolent forces and temptations of the flesh in highly crafted, poetic ways.

'Faraway, So Close!'

Consider the lyrics of 'Faraway, So Close!':

> Empty out your pockets, toss the lot upon the floor.
> All those treasures, my friend, you don't need them anymore
> Your days are all through dying, they gave all their ghosts away
> So kiss close all your wounds and call Living life a day
>
> The planets gravitate around you
> And the stars shower down around you
> And the angels in Heaven adore you
> And the saints they all stand and applaud you
> So faraway, so faraway and yet so close
>
> Say farewell to the passing of the years,
> Though all your sweet goodbyes will fall upon deaf ears
> Kiss softly the mouths of the ones you love
> Beneath the September moon and the heavens above
>
> And the world will turn without you
> And history will soon forget about you
> But the heavens they will reward you
> And the saints will all be there to escort you
> So faraway, so faraway and yet so close
>
> Do not grieve at the passing of mortality
> For life's but a thing of terrible gravity
> And the planets gravitate around you
> And the stars shower down about you
> And the angels in Heaven adore you
> And the saints they all stand and applaud you
> So faraway, so faraway and yet so close

(2007: 208)

These lyrics, which I read aloud in class, are presented in a deceptively simple stanza form, using euphonious rhyming couplets and pathetic fallacies. Hearing these lyrics, students do not associate them with music until I tell them they are song. I bring up these lyrics for the clarity of theme and because they demonstrate the distinctive craft of Cave's language. As W. H. Auden suggests of poetry in 'The Poet and the City', moreover, Cave's lyrics suggest that 'what the senses perceive [is] an outward and visible sign of the inward and invisible. But both [are] believed to be real and valuable' (Auden 2005: 379). Cave tackles the transient nature of life, its indifference to human achievement and the futility of worldly possessions. His theme is firmly rooted in a faith-based life and afterlife. The dialogue between the stanzas and the repeated, but slightly altered, refrain proposes that the seemingly irrevocably separated, the tangible and intangible, the earthly and the celestial, are actually not separated. The tone of the poem suggests a certain levity and lightness, perhaps as an attempt to assuage those incredulous to his faith-based argument. This appeasement he emphasizes in the last stanza: '[d]o not grieve at the passing of mortality/ For life's but a thing of terrible gravity' (Cave 2007: 208). Careful arrangement and repetition of words and examples create an aesthetic statement that could stand alone or as accompaniment to music.

One can easily point out themes in Cave's writing, without isolating the phases and periods of Cave's career, or suggesting musical influences. Starting with the lyrics for the songs in the Birthday Party album *Prayers on Fire* (1981), Cave evokes motifs that recur throughout his work. Along with the stereotypical self-conscious angst of a rock song, in this album alone he refers to the tangible, concrete world: water, animals and insects, nature, sex, death, love, money. Furthermore, his lyrics evoke violent inner fantasies: 'Just You and Me', for example, begins with 'First: I tried to kill it with a hammer/Thought that I could lose the head' (Cave 2007: 31). Added to this is his penchant for cultural references; in 'King Ink' he refers to Fats Domino; in 'Release the Bats' he references vampires; and in 'The Friend Catcher' he alludes to the children's tale 'The Three Little Pigs' (2007: 28, 32-3, 37). More pertinent to my discussion of his early album, however, is the consciousness of language as a theme. 'King Ink' personifies the writing process and the lyrics plead for the speaker to '[e]xpress thyself, say something loudly/AAAAAAAH!' (2007: 28). In 'A Dead Song (with Anita Lane)' Cave repeats the phrase, 'with words like' to highlight a thematic, and reflexive, importance of using words (2007: 29). What is evident in the lyrics of this first Birthday Party album, and thereafter in Cave's work, is a self-conscious awareness that he is crafting language and not just creating lyrics for songs.

Those inclinations towards self-reflexiveness, visible early in his career, are manifest in his more recent work as well. *Dig, Lazarus, Dig!!!* (2008) contains one of Cave's most obvious attempts to commingle literature into a pop song format. 'We Call Upon the Author' asks for narrative authority, of a sort – someone (an author) to provide the answers and explanations to overwhelming contemporary problems and to provide guidance on personal tastes, including how to deal with '[o]ur myxomatoid kids spraddl[ing] the streets'; the inevitability of death in a world torn between faith and science; and how to reconcile the deficiencies he feels with those who adulate him ('[w]ell I, I go guruing down the street/And young people gather 'round my feet); and how to deal with a friend who interrupts and makes a reading suggestion, only to be reminded of his own favourite poet, John Berryman (Cave 2008). In the end, a solution is obvious (his authoritative answer): '[w]ell, you know I say prolix, prolix/Something a pair of scissors can fix' (2008). That is, metaphorically speaking, cut away or edit the problems.

'Loverman'

'Loverman', from the 1994 album *Let Love In*, exhibits, perhaps, one of Cave's most obvious attempts to incorporate a self-conscious awareness of literary techniques within the construct of the song lyric. James Fenton has suggested that song lyrics, unlike poems, 'should look disappointing on the page – a little thin, perhaps, a little repetitive, or a little on the obvious side' (Fenton 2002: 115). If ambiguity, however, is a measure of the value of poetic statements, one could discount many canonical poems and poets. In 'Loverman' Cave uses an acrostic. The letters of 'loverman' are spelled out to create a message:

> L is for LOVE, baby
> O is for ONLY you that I do
> V is for loving VIRTUALLY all that you are
> E is for loving almost EVERYTHING that you do
> R is for RAPE me
> M is for MURDER me
> A is for ANSWERING all of my prayers
> N is for KNOWING your Loverman's going to be
> the answer to all of yours

(2007: 218)

Essentially an acrostic poem, or in this case, a refrain from a song lyric, is a visual element. Without the musical accompaniment, an acrostic poem aligns itself with concrete poems in which the visual typographical layout contributes to the thematic content of the poem. In 'Loverman' the refrain, repeated and altered, is used to reinforce the insalubrious lust-filled lover who aligns himself (downward) with 'a devil waiting outside your door' and imagines himself 'crawling along your floor' and eventually 'lying by your side' (2007: 218). These sentiments, of course, are not just statements pronounced by the lyrics but visually suggested by the self-consciously literary layout.

'There She Goes, My Beautiful World'

In 'There She Goes, My Beautiful World', from the Bad Seeds 2004 album *Abattoir Blues/The Lyre of Orpheus*, Cave's lyrical abilities are at the height of their powers and on full display (2007: 392–4). His scope of references is informative. He conflates environmental concerns with a plea for creative powers ('send that stuff on down to me') as he alludes to other artists and the struggles they endure in order to create (2007: 392, 394). He begins with nature: '[t]he wintergreen, the juniper/The cornflower and the chicory [...] The elm, the ash and the linden tree/The dark and deep, enchanted sea' (2007: 392). In these lyrics his quest for inspiration, combined with images of nature, is reminiscent of that of the Romantic poets and their symbols and pleas for creative inspiration (Keats' urn, Coleridge's Aeolian harp, Shelley's wind). The Romantic poets often conceived an encounter with nature (or inspiring object) as sublime; in a Kantian manner, the sublime moment occurred when the imagination, confronted by nature's brute force, ultimately conceded to the higher cognitive power, namely, reason. 'For the sublime, in the strict sense of the word, cannot be contained in any sensuous form, but rather concerns ideas of reason' (Kant 2007: 76). In other words, the imagination must acknowledge its inability to adequately grasp, perceive and convey nature's vastness. As subjects we are 'pushed to the point at which our faculty of imagination breaks down in presenting the concept of [for example] magnitude, and proves unequal to [the] task' (2007: 84). It is precisely this moment of imaginative concession mediated by reason that constitutes the sublime. The individual simultaneously recognizes the profundity of the encounter and his or her struggle to imaginatively take hold of and articulate the importance of that experience; this recognition is significant of something beyond the self, something perhaps bordering on an annihilation of the imaginative self, but which nevertheless remains a reasonably informed experience – one that allows the individual to engage imaginatively, creatively, albeit ever tempered by the rational, 'in which the mind can come to feel the sublimity of its own vocation' (2007: 92).

Kant suggests that 'the feeling of the sublime is a pleasure that only arises indirectly, being brought about by the feeling of a momentary check to the vital forces' (2007: 92). Cave seems to exemplify this kind of sublime experience or encounter, for he suggests he is willing to 'check' or subdue his own vitality in order to appease creative forces ('I will kneel […] [and] I'll ask for nothing'):

I will kneel at your feet
I will lie at your door
I will rock you to sleep
I will roll on the floor
And I'll ask for nothing
Nothing in this life
I'll ask for nothing
Give me ever-lasting life

(Cave 2007: 393)

What is more, the lyrics are constructed around images of presences and absences in his plea for creative expression and posterity – a sentiment often expressed in Shakespeare's sonnets. Here I am reminded (and remind my students) of sonnets 85 and 100 and the poet's plea to his muse for creative power: '[m]y tongue-tied Muse in manners holds her still'; '[w]here art thou Muse that thou forget'st so long,/To speak of that which gives thee all thy might?' (Shakespeare 1987: 99, 114). Cave, in the lyrics of 'There She Goes, My Beautiful World', will prostrate himself to summon his muse: kneel, lie, rock and roll. Cave is asking his muse to give him inspiration that will lead to artistic endurance, to

53

create a work of art that transcends time. This plea alludes to a further comparison with Shakespeare. Cave's lyrics, like Shakespeare's sonnet 18, plead for longevity through artistic and creative work. In his sonnet, Shakespeare writes that 'in eternal lines to time thou grow'st/So long as men can breathe or eyes can see,/So long lives this, and this gives life to thee' (1987: 32). Cave, on the other hand, truncates the sentiments of Shakespeare's sonnet 18 with '[g]ive me ever-lasting life'. Posterity for both writers involves an audience to read or to hear their work.

Even with the elimination of the extra-linguistic code of music, the song's lyrics are replete with the sound of rhyme and some verbal play but not the sophistication of the acrostics used in a song like 'Loverman': in the second stanza, for example, Cave has 'pox', 'socks', 'box' and 'rocks' (Cave 2007: 392). The playfully simple (yet imaginative) masculine rhyming quartet emphasizes that even under pain, restrictions and duress (or because of these), artists can create great works; moreover, the deliberately banal nature of the rhymes is also surely intentional in its comic quality, which undermines the portentous nature of the subject:

> John Wilmot penned his poetry riddled with the pox
> Nabokov wrote on index cards, at a lectern, in his socks
> St. John of the Cross did his best stuff imprisoned in a box
> And Johnny Thunders was half alive when he wrote 'Chinese Rocks'
>
> (2007: 392)

Furthermore, Cave evokes the senses to complement the theme of creative endeavours: sight, sound, touch and smell are all there. These senses he combines with allusions to visual artists and literary, political and religious writers.

> Well, me, I'm lying here, with nothing in my ears
> Me, I'm lying here, with nothing in my ears
> Me, I'm lying here, for what seems years
> I'm just lying on my bed with nothing in my head
>
> [...]
>
> Karl Marx squeezed his carbuncles while writing *Das Kapital*
> And Gauguin, he buggered off, man, and went all tropical
> While Philip Larkin stuck it out in a library in Hull
> And Dylan Thomas died drunk in St Vincent's hospital
>
> (2007: 392–3)

Using this poem in the classroom opens up (and introduces, perhaps) some canonical writers, and on the surface suggests a complication by doing so. Most first-year students would not know of John Wilmot (Lord Rochester) or Vladimir Nabokov (or even Johnny Thunders), but can and do surmise that in each reference there is a similar struggle to create that parallels the frustrations the speaker is complaining about in his own experience. As a teacher, one always wonders how much to explain and how much to encourage students to find out on their own to achieve understanding.

Cave's lyrics can also be illuminated through an analysis of their use of deductive reasoning. Broadly speaking, deductive arguments attempt to illustrate that a conclusion follows from a set of valid and sound premises. As an instrument of knowledge, a deductive argument is usually constructed around simple, obvious words that make assertions such as 'so' (indicating a reason or result of an action or a situation) and 'but' (indicating that something is true despite being suggested to the contrary). In 'There She Goes, My Beautiful World', for example, Cave is trying to summon his creative forces. First, he calls on nature, then the exemplum of other writers and their struggles, followed by physical prostrations ('I will kneel at your feet/I will lie at your door' (2007: 393)). Finally, he pronounces in his conclusion, '[s]o if you got a trumpet, get on your feet, brother, and blow it/If you've got a field, that don't yield, well get up and hoe it' (2007: 393). That is, the argument, via the action verbs 'blow' and 'hoe', would suggest that inspirational forces come from actions. These small but imperative words provide logical cohesion. These words and these argumentative structures are not applicable to all his songs, but they provide a guide for interpretive possibilities. In a classroom, illustrating signposts that guide interpretation does not diminish the pleasures of the lyrics nor completely explain or contain their perceived ambiguities. However, many of Cave's narrative lyrics use key words, such as 'but', 'now', 'so' and 'then' to indicate an argumentative structure.

Illustrating the argumentative features allows me to not only explore Cave, but also to evoke other canonical poems and poets who allude to and use a reasoning process in their poems. In the past I compared the structure of Cave's lyrics to the seventeenth-century poem 'To His Coy Mistress' by Andrew Marvell; how they interact was part of the comparison.

Marvell's metaphysical poem, 'To His Coy Mistress' (1681), and Cave's 'There She Goes, My Beautiful World' have pedagogically fruitful argumentative similarities. Marvell playfully structures his poem according to a hypothetical syllogism. Using deductive logic, he subjunctively writes: '[h]ad we but world enough, and time [...] But at my back I always hear [...] Now therefore, while youthful hue' (Marvell 2006: 543). Marvell's argument is used for the purposes of gaining the physical pleasures of seduction; as he writes, 'let us sport us while we may' (2006: 543). Cave's argument in 'There She Goes, My Beautiful World' is not a plea for carnal love, but for poetic inspiration. Even though the tenors of the poems are dissimilar, and without suggesting Cave is a metaphysical poet, students can be led to appreciate the importunate nature of the speakers and their language. Moreover, both writers playfully draw attention to language in their rhymes: Marvell rhymes 'lust' and 'dust', while Cave manages to bring together 'Das Kapital', 'tropical', 'Hull' and 'hospital' into one stanza (Cave 2007: 393). Once these connections are established for students, other contrasts can be illustrated.

'Into My Arms' and deductive logic

Deductive logic brings together two of Cave's favourite topics – God and love. The lyrics of 'Into My Arms' exemplify how Cave disregards many of the problems associated with postmodern representation and its suspicion of metanarratives, such as the Bible. This song's theme is not usually a popular classroom topic (at least in my part of the world); faith is a personal issue rarely brought up for critical analysis without irony or tension. Like the abrupt openings used by a poet like Donne (in a poem like 'The Flea', which I will address shortly), this song makes one of Cave's strongest assertions about love:

> I don't believe in an interventionist God
> But I know, darling, that you do
> But if I did I would kneel down and ask Him
> Not to intervene when it came to you
> Not to touch a hair on your head
> To leave you as you are
> And if He felt He had to direct you
> Then direct you into my arms
>
> Into my arms, O Lord
> [...]
> Into my arms
>
> And I don't believe in the existence of angels
> But looking at you I wonder if that's true
> But if I did I would summon them together
> And ask them to watch over you
> To each burn a candle for you
> To make bright and clear your path
> And to walk, like Christ, in grace and love
> And guide you into my arms
>
> Into my arms, O Lord
> [...]
> Into my arms
>
> But I believe in Love
> And I know that you do too
> And I believe in some kind of path
> That we can walk down, me and you
> So keep your candles burning

And make her journey bright and pure
That she will keep returning
Always and evermore

(2007: 273–4)

Cave counterpoints religious faith with the act of wooing. Of course other equally important elements contribute to augment the beauty of the lyrics of this song, such as the repetition of 'into my arms' and indubitably, one might add, the music that accompanies them. I stress, however, the argumentative structure of the lyrics: he follows an approximate syllogistic structure. Excluding the repeated refrain, the first two choruses begin with a negative assertion or premise, followed by two qualifying statements: 'I don't', '[a]nd I don't', and 'but':

Major premise: 'I don't believe in an interventionist God'
Minor premise: 'And I don't believe in the existence of angels'
Conclusion: 'But I believe in love'

(2007: 273)

Again, Cave's lyrics (and in this case the topic of love) open up the possibility of comparison with many other canonical writers. John Donne, although using a witty, preposterous conceit in 'The Flea', seizes the reader's attention with the lines, '[m]ark but this flea, and mark in this/How little thou deniest me is' (Donne 2007: 98). He uses a tri-part structure to make his plea for love, alluding blasphemously to religious matters in the process. Of course, Cave is not pleading for love or using the same tone in his lyrics as Donne is in his poem. Nevertheless, broadly applying a logical structure to Cave helps to construct meaning. This meaning implied structurally plays with the outward and the visible and the inward and invisible and thereby, in the process, conflates faith with love to represent his desires for physical assurance: '[t]hat she will keep returning/Always and evermore/Into my arms, O Lord' (Cave 2007: 274). From negative assertions ('I don't believe in an interventionist God [...] And I don't believe in the existence of angels'), Cave hopes for a positive resolution (2007: 273). Again, this evokes a comparison to a Shakespeare sonnet. In sonnet 130, 'My mistress' eyes are nothing like the sun', Shakespeare uses a rhetorical trope of negative comparisons to suggest the opposite of his desires. After listing what his mistress is not (nothing like the sun, no roses in her cheeks, never like a goddess), he turns to state that she is incomparable because she is real and not a construction of poetic metaphors, or 'any belied with false compare' (Shakespeare 1987: 144).

Cave's lyrics do not necessarily fit into a postmodern paradigm with its relativistic sense of contextuality and self-referentialism, or 'adlinguisticity' to quote from Jean Francois Lyotard (1983: 329). Cave is not pandering to postmodernism's dismissal of totalistic concepts. He is not recycling as much as he is working with universal, transcendent themes and ideas within the rock lyric medium – but even the use of these themes and ideas is elusive and nonconformist at times. 'Faraway, So Close!', 'There She Goes, My Beautiful World' and 'Into My Arms' renew venerable themes and reengage canonical writers, thereby making them useful in the university classroom. However, if one considers, for example, the sound differences between the ballads of *Abattoir Blues* and the grungy, abrasive sounding (but nonetheless enjoyable) *Grinderman*, one quickly grasps that Cave does not want to be pigeonholed into a particular sound.

Conclusion

To conclude, I am not trying to be reductive and simplify Cave's lyrics to suggest that he only has merit at rudimentary levels in university classes. Rather, I am trying to demonstrate that he has usefulness that opens up many possible lines of inquiry relevant in university classrooms. Not just for his use of the natural world reminiscent of the Romantic poets, nor his use of the Bible, or even his autotelic argumentative structures that present images of presence and absence, do I include Cave's work as part of my syllabus. Cave's lyrics 'consistently challenge [his] hearers with [...] fundamental artistic problems about the human condition', unlike much popular music (Cousland 2005: 129). My students responded favourably to discussing Cave's lyrics and music in part because his lyrics (at least the ones I have presented) help to erase the boundaries between popular culture and literary studies, and thereby, illustrate a relevancy in both. Cave's music and lyrics were not to the liking of all my students, but studying his lyrics allowed even those who thought his music antiquated to make and find connections between what we study in the classroom and the world of culture outside of it. As a university teacher, I believe his lyrics are becoming more pedagogically relevant with each new work. And as a fan, well, at least I get to read (and sometimes listen) to his lyrics in the classroom, which I enjoy, even if my captive audience may not.

References

Attali, Jacques (2009), *Noise: The Political Economy of Music*, Minneapolis: University of Minnesota Press.

Auden, W. H. (2005), 'The Poet and the City', in Jon Cook (ed.), *Poetry in Theory 1900–2000*, Oxford: Blackwell, pp. 377–84.

Boer, Roland (2006), 'Under the Influence? The Bible, Culture and Nick Cave', http://www.usask.ca/relst/jrpc/art12-nickcave-print.html. Accessed 26 August 2011.

Brooks, Cleanth (1975), *The Well-Wrought Urn*, New York: Harcourt.

Cave, Nick (2007), *The Complete Lyrics 1978–2007*, London: Penguin.

Cousland, J. R. C. (2005), 'God, the Bad, and the Ugly: The Vi(t)a Negativa of Nick Cave and P.J. Harvey', in Michael J. Gilmour (ed.), *Call Me the Seeker: Listening to Religion in Popular Music*, London: Continuum, pp. 129–57.

Dax, Maximilian and Johannes Beck (1999), *The Life and Music of Nick Cave: An Illustrated Biography*, Berlin: DGV.

de Man, Paul (1979), 'Shelley Disfigured', in Harold Bloom (ed.), *Deconstruction and Criticism*, New York: Continuum.

Donne, John (2007), *John Donne's Poetry*, ed. by Donald R. Dickson, New York: Norton.

Fenton, James (2002), *An Introduction to English Poetry*, New York: Farrar, Strauss and Giroux.

Hanson, Amy (2005), *Kicking Against the Pricks: An Armchair Guide to Nick Cave*, London: Helter Skelter.

Heidegger, Martin (1982), *On the Way to Language*, New York: HarperCollins.

Johnstone, Ian (1996), *Bad Seed: The Biography of Nick Cave*, London: Abacus.

Kant, Immanuel (2008), *Critique of Judgement*, trans. by James Creed Meredith, London: Oxford University Press.

Lyotard, Jean-Francois (1983), 'Answering the Question: What is Postmodernism', in Ihab Hassan and Sally Hassan (eds), *Innovation/Renovation: New Perspectives on the Humanities*, Madison: University of Wisconsin Press, pp. 329–41.

Marvell, Andrew (2006), 'To His Coy Mistress', in John P. Rumrich and Gregory Chaplin (eds), *Seventeenth-Century British Poetry*, London: Norton, p. 543.

Shakespeare, William (1987), *Shakespeare's Sonnets and a Lover's Complaint*, London: Oxford University Press.

Webb, Peter (2008), 'Infected by The Seed of Post-Industrial Punk Bohemia: Nick Cave and the Milieu of the 1980s Underground', *Popular Music History* 3.2, pp. 103–22.

Chapter 4

A Beautiful, Evil Thing: The Music of Nick Cave and the Bad Seeds

David Pattie

'More News from Nowhere', the last track of *Dig, Lazarus, Dig!!!* (2008), the last Nick Cave and the Bad Seeds album (at least at the time of writing), has a rhythmic, harmonic and melodic structure that is, one might say, hallowed by association. The verses detail the journey of an unnamed narrator, modelled on Odysseus, whose struggles to 'get back home' are constantly interrupted and disrupted by the people he meets en route; musically, the song is based on a simple I–IV chord progression, with a slight variation (III–V) in the chorus. The melody is similarly simple; it seems designed to draw attention away from itself to the words – an interpretation reinforced by Cave's characteristically clear, performative vocal style. Everything about the track conspires to encourage the listener to place the song squarely in that long tradition of songwriting inaugurated by Bob Dylan; simple chords, simple melodies, a simple harmonic structure, all there to support complex poetic lyrics.

Except that this simple, stripped-back music is not the first thing that we hear. Before the music begins, an atonal electronic drone, sounding like nothing so much as the sea in a shell, has already started up: it persists throughout the song, a disruptive backing to the intentionally plain musical foreground described above. There are elements of a recognizable musical template in the sound; something in it suggests the scraping of violin strings (although this might be something I personally read into the sound; it is a fair guess that it has been produced by Warren Ellis, whose main instrument is the violin). Inescapably, this persistent noise colours our reaction to the rest of the track: as Paul Hegarty notes, it forces us to take account of it:

> [n]oise is not the same as noises. Noises are sounds until further qualified (e.g. as unpleasant noises, loud noises, and so on), but noise is already that qualification; it is already a judgement that noise is occurring. Although noise can occur outside of cognition (i.e. without us understanding its purpose, form, source), a judgement is made in reaction to it. Noise is then something we are forced to react to, and this reaction, certainly for humans, is a judgement, even if only physical.
>
> (Hegarty 2007: 3)

This is a good description of the way that this troubling sound operates within the framework of the track. It cannot be reconciled with any other element within the sonic landscape of the music; it does not swell or fade; nothing about it suggests a cadence that will be resolved as the track progresses. It is simply there; not loud enough to dominate, not quiet enough to be ignored. It demands a reading, but does not suggest what that reading might be.

In a Pitchfork interview in 2008, Cave discussed the recording of *Dig, Lazarus, Dig!!!*. For this album, the group consciously attempted to rework their music: some of the elements that had marked out previous Bad Seeds albums – the piano, for example – were eschewed (to take, as Cave put it, 'the stateliness' from the group's sound) (Masters 2008). He also pointed out that Warren Ellis, a member of the group since 1994, did not play the violin at all during the recording sessions. When asked what part Ellis played on the album, Cave replied

[w]ho knows what Warren does, really? [laughs]. He's usually off crouching in the corner working with his various instruments and things, some of which we don't even know what they are. He'll often make loops that we base songs around, or that get added to the songs. Sometimes he'll send me a loop as an mp3 and I'll use that to write a song around.

(Masters 2008)

An interesting answer, it seems to suggest that, in the composition of the music, two separate sound worlds operate – the band recording the music, and Ellis operating his machinery, connected to, but not integrated with, the rest of the group. Moreover, it suggests that these two separate sonic worlds (the world of music, and the world of noise) are not blended seamlessly together in the process of composition; rather, they are placed side-by-side – juxtaposed, rather than fused.

This process also echoes, interestingly, Cave's description of a formative musical experience in 2003:

I lost my innocence with Johnny Cash. I used to watch the Johnny Cash Show on television in Wangaratta when I was about 9 or 10 years old. At that stage I had really no idea about rock'n'roll. I watched him and from that point I saw that music could be an evil thing, a beautiful, evil thing.

(Cave 2003a)

What always strikes me about this quote is the bareness of the comparison: the music is beautiful and evil – those two terms, in opposition, without too much in the way of romantic shading or ambiguity. Given the early identification of The Birthday Party and the Bad Seeds with Gothic rock in the 1980s, it would seem that this opposition maps on to the music that Cave and his band make in an entirely predictable fashion. After all, the idea of beauty in evil is perhaps the Gothic's defining cliché (whether we are talking about Dracula's brides – or Dracula himself for that matter – or the various emo-goth vampires in *Twilight* and its numerous offshoots).

However, it is hard to argue that this is what Cave does, either in his music or his lyrics. Just as the words of the songs are hard to type (what character is Cave adopting, and what is his relation to that character?), so the music does not normally attempt to create the kind of dissonant, alienated decadence one might more commonly associate with The Cure or The Sisters of Mercy. Rather, the music the Bad Seeds produce sometimes seems to have been cobbled together from a range of disparate elements – the blues, country, rock, what Cave in an interview has called the classic American song tradition, the European avant-garde, industrial music and more recently digital sampling (MacLennan 1993). What is more, it is periodically disrupted, as the example above suggests, by moments of dissonance; feedback, atonality or, more subtly, by sonic elements which seem simply out of place – for example, 'Far from Me' on *The Boatman's Call* (1997) juxtaposes its well-crafted melodic line against a harsh violin line, played by Warren Ellis.

These elements are not present in every song: sometimes they arise from the juxtaposition of tracks. A personal favourite is the opening of 'The Curse of Millhaven' from *Murder Ballads* (1996): after the lush orchestration of 'Where the Wild Roses Grow', 'The Curse of Millhaven' begins with what can only be described as the sound of the Bad Seeds being thrown down a flight of stairs. Sometimes, as in the stretch of albums from *The Boatman's Call* in 1997 through to *Nocturama* in 2003, these elements are downplayed, almost to the point of disappearing altogether. However (and as both *Dig, Lazarus, Dig!!!* and the Grinderman albums would seem to attest), the possibility of disruption, of the unexpected, or the just plain uncontainable is one of the defining features of Cave's and his band's sound: if nothing else, the presence in the Bad Seeds of Blixa Bargeld (from 1983 to 2004) and Warren Ellis (who first played with the group in 1994) would seem to reinforce the importance of an unconventional approach to composition and instrumentation in Cave's work. How, though, can we account for the peculiar nature of the relation of noise and harmony in this music? To go back to the opening example: the chords and the drone do not fit together. It is not only that they do not belong to the same genre: they do not fit within the same sonic universe. And yet it works: *Dig, Lazarus, Dig!!!* was, financially and critically, one of Cave's most successful albums. How can we begin to think our way through this odd mixture of melody, harmony and noise?

Theorizing noise

When Cave's first band, The Birthday Party, came to record their second album, *Junkyard*, in late 1981, they were determined to produce something that declared the gaping chasm between their music and the mainstream. To do this, they chose a rather conventional method; they went straight for a sonic assault:

[Tony Cohen, the album's producer] would always endeavour to make the guitar sound as distorted and abrasive as possible. 'We made a tunnel out of corrugated iron around an amp and put mikes on to the iron itself [...]. The noise was so bad it made the fillings pop out of your mouth. A really vicious sound ... We mistreated things very seriously. We put contact mikes on cymbals. The things only last for three minutes before they're blasted to bits because it's so loud.

(Johnston 1996: 97)

In doing this, the band was travelling down what was already a very well-worn track, stretching, it could be argued, all the way from The Kinks' use of overdriven amps on 'You Really Got Me' to the mix of electronica and white noise on Fuck Buttons' *Tarot Sport* (2009). Noise, in the sonic framework of a number of popular music genres, signals freedom, the breaking of restraint, and the manifestation of a profoundly rebellious spirit that animates the musicians (think, for example, of the samples and cut-ups used by Public Enemy on *It Takes a Nation of Millions to Hold Us Back* (1988)). As the Bad Seeds guitarist Blixa Bargeld once put it, in relation to the music he produced with Einstürzende Neubauten:

[m]usic shouldn't stop with musicianship, we are changing the areas of what is known as music, when there is no limit to what is music, no difference between music sounds and noise, when you can't find anything that isn't an instrument, then a point is reached where there is no analysis. Then, when noise is music, there would be a social progress.

(Bargeld, in Shryane 2011: 106)

We have here a clear dialectic – noise is freedom, music (at least as it is conventionally imagined) is restraint.

At this point, a strand of popular music history and a strand of popular music theory rather neatly coincide. We find a version of the dialectic described by Bargeld in Paul Hegarty:

[n]oise is negative: it is unwanted, other, not something ordered. It is negatively defined – i.e. by what it is not [...] but it is also a negativity. In other words, it does not exist independently, as it exists only in relation to what it is not. In turn, it helps structure and define its opposite (the world of meaning, law, regulation, goodness, beauty, and so on).

(2007: 5)

And behind Hegarty (and behind a number of other academics who employ variations on the same basic idea – see, for example, Cobussen (2005), Damai (2007), Kohl (2007) or Mattern and Salmon (2008)), there is Jacques Attali; and, in particular, *Noise: The Political Economy of Music* (1985). Attali's text has proved massively influential: it posits that the evolving opposition between harmony and noise in music is tied in to wider changes in western society – in particular the operation of the market in capitalism. Simply put, Attali's genealogy of music begins in the medieval marketplace, and in the opposition between Carnival and Lent. Echoing Mikhail Bakhtin, who read Carnival as an archetype of subversion and Lent as an archetype of control, Attali sees the medieval Carnivalesque marketplace as a place of non-hierarchical sound, which is slowly and gradually regularized as capitalism comes to replace other types of economy. According to Attali, music under capitalism is, like so much else, part of an industrial process, which favours repetition over originality:

> [l]ittle by little, the very nature of music changes: the unforeseen and the risks of representation disappear in repetition. The new aesthetic of performance excludes error, hesitation, noise. It freezes the work out of festival and the spectacle: it reconstructs it formally, manipulates it, makes it abstract perfection. This vision gradually leads people to forget that music was once background noise and a form of life. Repetition communicated an energy. Repetition produces information free from noise.
>
> (Attali 1985: 106)

It is not that noise can entirely be eliminated: this is not quite what Attali means by a system free from its influence. Rather, freedom from noise means that noise has been tamed utterly, subjected to authority, made to operate along strictly codified lines. For Attali, noise is an inherently violent disruption of social peace: this violence must be tamed, and converted into something more amenable to those who wish order above all else: 'the whole of traditional musicology analyses music as the organisation of controlled panic, the transformation of anxiety into joy, and of dissonance into harmony' (1985: 27).

If we were to read the Bad Seeds' music against the term that Attali proposes as an antidote to the industrialization of music, we would soon find ourselves stretching the argument somewhat. The idea of 'composition' – the unrepeatable organization of sound produced by ever-changing collectives, designed to re-introduce as far as is possible the relation between the *jongleur* and the market place – does not really fit their work (even though there are some common features: the Bad Seeds' line-up has changed radically since 1983, and at least two of the musicians in the group have an idiosyncratic approach to instrumentation and performance). The Bad Seeds are bound up in the operations of the music industry, and Cave has acquired the kind of star status that Attali condemns as an integral part of the whole deadening process of repetition. However, as I have noted above, the Bad Seeds have never followed the path marked out by conventional musicology (and, it is worth saying, by other noisy bands and artists: by the time we reach *Avalon* (1982), Roxy Music's rough edges are entirely smoothed away, My Bloody Valentine's second album takes the harshness out of the dense waves of feedback that characterize their first album, and so on). The Bad Seeds, it could be said, have made a career as much from the transformation of joy into anxiety as they do from the transformation of extreme experience into musically assimilable forms.

So, the unstable dialectic that I have identified in the Bad Seeds' music seems to be at least partially accounted for, if we tie it to the ostensibly similar dialectic outlined by Attali. The band employs dissonance as a way of removing their work from a deadening mainstream musical culture; they might sometimes produce music that sounds as smooth, as harmonically and melodically conventional, as Attali might expect from a band operating under capitalism's rules, but there is always the possibility that, in some form or other, the forces of noise will break through and reassert themselves. I must admit, though, that I do not find this argument particularly convincing. First of all, Attali's work on noise is subject to the same general critique as Bakhtin's work on Carnival: the forces of misrule operate, but they do so within a framework determined by the forces of order. In other words, Carnival only operates under the same set of rules as Lent; they both, in their various ways, serve the power that Carnival is supposed to unseat. Similarly, Attali's writing on noise, it has been pointed out, fails because the capitalist system that appears to suppress dissonance actually, in practice, finds a way to assimilate it and to make it pay:

> [n]oise appears to critique the prevailing cognitive and social habits of modernity – what T. W. Adorno named identity thinking – by providing concrete and particular art objects that demand attention and jar us from one-dimensional life. Noise sounds, for a moment, like a true alternative not only to contemporary music but to a whole way of thinking through abstract generalisation and living through commercial mediation. Understood in this way, noise makes sense. Once noise is no longer inscrutable, however, it is assimilated into popular culture and becomes a commercial novelty. The blatant contradiction of the commodification of noise gives rise to a second order of critique wherein noise parades its uselessness and occasions reflection on the tortured existence of art in modernity, the ubiquity of identity thinking, and the relation between use and exchange value. This ironic endgame for noise, however, is itself absorbed by consumer culture and noise lives on as but another cool, extreme product.
>
> (Smith 2005: 44)

This is an inescapable paradox: the very features that make noise unassimilable make it marketable. After all, a small niche audience is still an audience, waiting to be sold the latest in rebellious musical extremity. Masonna (the Japanese avant-garde noise artist Smith uses as his main example) might produce music that is as violently dissonant as Attali might wish; however, at the time of writing, his music is available on Amazon, just like Sonic Youth, Sunn 0))) and everyone else (the Amazon customer review of Masonna's CD *Inner Mind Mystic* (1996) includes the telling line, 'If you like Melt Banana, Merzbow, Boredoms type recordings this may well suit your tastes').

Secondly, Attali's argument only applies to the Bad Seeds if we conveniently forget that, for Cave at least, harmony and melody are not simply musical qualities that cry out for subversion. A 1993 conversation with Cave's fellow Australian musician Grant McLennan produced the following interesting exchange:

McLennan: In the days of the Boys Next Door the songwriting was, for want of a better word, traditional. When the band deconstructed to the brilliant noise of The Birthday Party, that tradition went out the window. Now we find that you are back with form and melody.

Cave: I'm like you in that I'm very interested in classic songwriting, creating songs that have a classic feel to them. I mean, I don't think either of us are really concerned about doing anything that's new, or breaking new areas of music. We're far more interested in writing purposeful and soulful and well-constructed songs, and, as you go, you get more tools to be able to do that.

(1993: 61–2)

Further on in the same interview, Cave seems to dismiss the more raucous, dissonant parts of his output as stemming from nothing more radical than his own musical incompetence:

When I can't find a neat and nice chord progression, I can always just bang out a song on one chord and scream over the top and have the Bad Seeds play dramatic instrumentation around that and it can still be a successful thing. I couldn't play you any of my songs (laughs). I mean, if you asked me to play one on the piano, I couldn't. I write them, I give them to the band and they learn them and play them. I wouldn't have a clue how they go after that.

(1993: 63)

However, if this were a true indication of his favoured career path, Cave would be churning out album after album of stately piano ballads: and, as we have seen, that simply is not the case. Perhaps something else is happening in the fabric of Cave's music: something that is not resolvable in terms of the dialectic outlined by Attali. To understand it, we need to look at the balance of musical forces within the Bad Seeds themselves – and in particular, at two iconic members of the band – the Bad Seeds' former guitarist Blixa Bargeld, and their current violinist/multi-instrumentalist, Warren Ellis.

Blixa Bargeld: 'Tupelo'

According to Ian Johnston, Cave first met Blixa Bargeld in June 1981, after a Birthday Party gig at the Paradiso in Amsterdam; Cave, the biography notes, was instantly impressed by Bargeld's appearance – the German musician was thin and gaunt (indeed, some pictures of the period show him looking positively emaciated). Bargeld for his part was impressed by Cave: 'well, I knew nothing about The Birthday Party or their music but I instantly liked it', he told Johnston (Johnson 1996: 142). However, Cave was not drawn to Bargeld because he would make an interesting looking addition to any future live work. There was something else: something in Bargeld's approach to making music, which was to prove far more amenable to the kind of music that Cave went on to produce in the 1980s and 1990s. When he met Cave, Bargeld was already gaining some fame (or perhaps notoriety would be a better word), as a founder member of Einstürzende Neubauten – a Berlin group, whose performances had already gained a reputation for a violently assaultive stage show (they used sledgehammers and drills, for example). When conventional instruments were used, they were radically reconfigured – guitars were placed on the floor and played horizontally: they were also played with (amongst other things) bows and electric razors.

When Bargeld began to play guitar in the Bad Seeds, however, his approach was initially a little more conventional. On 'In the Ghetto' (the first single Nick Cave and the Bad Seeds released in 1984), he plays the kind of upward slide guitar swoop that would not have been out of place on the original. However, such moments of conventional harmonic embellishment were always counterpointed by other, more abrasive guitar parts: on 'From Her to Eternity', on the Bad Seeds' first album, Bargeld contributes an unpredictable, assaultive repertoire of scratches, squeaks and feedback over the one-note vamp of the song. As Bargeld himself has said, his role in the Bad Seeds was unusual, given the sonic experiments he conducted with Neubauten, and given his publicly declared hatred of the symbolic place of the guitar in rock music. He told Ian Johnston that

> I thought it was a good decision to play guitar because I claimed my hatred for playing guitar in several interviews [...] [It's] probably good to play an instrument out of hatred of what other people do with it rather than play [...] I tried to do everything differently. I didn't have any effects pedals, apart from one somebody built me as a total anti-effect pedal, which cut on and off the signal. No reverb, no middle frequencies, no bass frequencies, only treble and a bottleneck slide.
>
> (Johnston 1996: 142–3)

This answer might position Bargeld in the same musical universe as The Birthday Party in their final incarnation.

The apparent contradiction between 'In the Ghetto' and 'From Her to Eternity' might be simply explained as demonstrating the difference between Bargeld confined and Bargeld set free. The truth, though, is rather more ambiguous. An article in *Guitarist* called Bargeld 'the Anti-Guitarist'; he told the magazine that he wanted to find a way into guitar playing without playing guitar:

> [t]o me playing any instrument is a thinking process [...] I'd consider myself to think more like a singer. I come up with an idea for what to play on the guitar due to the value of how much sense it makes in a singing context [...] one of the things I've always disliked about playing the guitar are the connotations in reference to masculinity.
>
> (Reid 1997: 151–4)

Bargeld, in other words, did not simply approach the guitar in the way that the Barbarian hordes approached Rome: the instrument was to be used to create music – but music that resisted, as far as possible, the guitar's conventional musical vocabulary. He provides neither a relentless rhythmic drive to the Bad Seeds songs nor heroic guitar fills and solos. His function in the Bad Seeds is analogous to the sample that Warren Ellis provides as the backdrop to 'More News from Nowhere'; he provides the music with what might be termed a nagging sense of sonic disturbance. The other band members have a rather more conventional approach to their musical roles: they construct arrangements (usually under the aegis of Mick Harvey, a talented multi-instrumentalist, and a fixture in the Bad Seeds from 1983 to 2009) that rely on the usual mixture of instruments found in a rock band, and those instruments are dealt with more or less conventionally, even when the music itself is discordant (as in 'The Carny', or 'Scum'). Bargeld, however, moves from harmonic consonance to atonal disruption within the framework of individual tracks, and his place in the arrangement of the tracks never seems entirely fixed – as though what he does is always just on the point of disrupting the sonority of the music.

For example: the track 'Tupelo' opens the Bad Seeds' second album, *The Firstborn is Dead* (1985). Lyrically, it conflates the lives of Elvis, Jesus and Euclid Eucrow (the antihero of Cave's first novel *And the Ass Saw the Angel*); musically, it is one of the tracks where, in Cave's rather dismissive description, he 'just bangs on one note and screams over the top' (although this by no means accounts for the evocative sonic landscape the arrangement conjures up). Bargeld's place in this landscape, however, is a very interesting one. His approach to the guitar might be idiosyncratic, but it does fit the song; someone playing slide guitar, of whatever kind, will find what they do fitting into a track that borrows from Bo Diddley and Delta Blues. When his guitar comes to the fore (in the quiet section, beginning on the line 'oh go to sleep, my little children'), Bargeld plays a series of disconnected notes, which do not fit either the rhythm, the key or the melody of the track. They might momentarily pull the listener's attention away from Cave's lyrics; as such, they function as noise – as a subversion of the musical framework of the track. However, it is a subversion of the track that also fits the track's atmosphere: the notes might be jarring, but they come from a slide guitar – the type of guitar playing one might expect in the blues. The live version of the track (on *Live Seeds*, from 1993) makes this paradox more apparent: Bargeld's guitar is further forward in the mix; it conforms a little more closely to the conventional idea of the slide in country and blues (it accents climaxes, provides atmospheric glissandi, and so on). But it also produces feedback, glitches and atonal roars; to go back to the terms of the dialectic identified by Paul Hegarty above, it functions both as noise and as music – both confirming and disrupting the track's sonority. Or, to borrow the terms Cave applies to Johnny Cash, it is simultaneously beautiful and evil: beautiful because it fits the atmosphere of the track, and evil because it always seems on the verge of incipient musical chaos.

Warren Ellis: 'Dig, Lazarus, Dig!!!'

Bargeld left the Bad Seeds in 2003: although his statements at the time stressed that the departure was not motivated by personal or artistic differences with Cave and the rest of the band, it was no secret that his dislike of the more conventional tropes of rock and pop had served to distance him from the rest of the band. Indeed, looking at the Bad Seeds' output at the turn of the twenty-first century, it was easy to see reasons for Bargeld's discontent. It is not that *No More Shall We Part* (2001) and *Nocturama* (2003) are consistently weak albums (although in retrospect Cave himself seems rather unimpressed by them: in one interview, he refers to them, but gets the titles of the albums confused) (Bartlett 2004). They are, though, far more conventional than previous releases: in Emma McEvoy's rather dismissive phrase, Cave seemed to have 'entered the world of ego-psychology', leaving the disturbing and disturbed musical landscapes of his earlier work behind (McEvoy 2007: 89). In retrospect, this seems to have been a passing phase. From *Abattoir Blues/The Lyre of Orpheus* (2004) onward, the Bad Seeds' music grew steadily more raucous: the *Abattoir Blues* double album contained tracks that harked back to the group's earliest days ('Fable of the Black Ape' could sit alongside 'The Carny'; 'Hiding All Away' has the kind of distorted harshness that one might find on *Tender Prey* (1988)). However, these disruptions take place in a musical environment that owes far more to the chord structures and instrumental forces of rock music than previous albums.

In a Salon interview at the time of *Abattoir Blues*' release, Cave spoke of Bargeld's departure, and the impact this had on the music the band made:

[h]e was such a significant presence in my adult life [...] That he's not around, there's just a big hole there. At the same time, we were moving towards something that was less ironic in nature, and he was very much about playing the guitar in a non-guitar way. You know, that I have this sort of foreign instrument in my hands, and I'll make the best of it that I can. Whereas, if, in a way, Warren has replaced Blixa to a degree, and filled that hole, Warren doesn't play music in that way. He plays it in the opposite way, without any irony, and with a real love of rock 'n' roll and noise.

(Bartlett 2004)

Warren Ellis had first played on a Bad Seeds album in 1994, providing some of the violin parts on the tracks 'Do You Love Me? (Part 2)' and 'Ain't Gonna Rain Anymore' on *Let Love In* (1994). Although at this stage the parts Ellis added were melodically and harmonically contiguous with the arrangements, the violin tone he used was not the lush, singing tone that tends to be the default setting whenever strings are used in rock music. Frequently, his playing was as harsh (if more conventionally harmonic) as Bargeld's. The DVD *God is in the House* (2003) includes a striking performance of 'Oh My Lord' (from *No More Shall We Part*) (Cave 2003b). Ellis spends the first part of the song crouched foetally in front of the drum kit. Bargeld, during the same section, does nearly nothing at all: he stands, arms by his sides and the guitar hanging limply around his neck, providing backing vocals on the chorus and nothing else. When the song moves into the first of three instrumental breaks, Ellis and Bargeld spring into life (in Ellis' case almost literally: he rises to his feet and stands for a moment with his bow posed theatrically above his head). Both musicians play a series of ascending notes, sliding across each interval – and they do so facing each other, toe to toe. The harshness of Bargeld's guitar, and the distortion applied to Ellis' violin, make it in practice impossible to distinguish the instruments from each other.

When (as Cave notes above) Ellis took on Bargeld's role in the Bad Seeds, he did so from a position that was far more amenable to the idea of rock music as authentic expression. However, this did not mean that his approach to playing, composition and arrangement was any less idiosyncratic, or that his approach to his main instrument was any less unconventional. Ellis' range of influences is wide; in one interview, he mentioned that his current listening included Neil Young, Alice Coltrane, John Coltrane, Shostakovich, Beethoven, Arvo Pärt, Bob Dylan, Van Morrison, Bach, Felix Lajko, Miles Davis, Bartok, Stravinsky, AC/DC and Led Zeppelin. When asked in the same interview why he chose to play rock music on the violin, he replied that

[w]ell, I always disliked violins in rock music, and if the truth be known I probably still do. I was asked to play a show with a friend 15 years ago, and I put a guitar pick-up on with a rubber band, and have continued to play electric till this day. I don't know how people reacted – I was too busy trying to play, and dodge the cans.

(Stupar 2006)

This answer echoes Bargeld's comments about approaching the guitar with hatred, rather than love. Both musicians worked with other bands before their time in the Bad Seeds, and both continued to do so when they had joined Cave's band (Ellis' trio, The Dirty Three, produced music that moved between rock, folk and free improvisation: they supported Sonic Youth on tour during the 1990s). Both also developed an approach to playing their instruments that could be described (with a fair amount of understatement) as non-traditional. Ellis runs his violin through effects pedals, radically distorting the sound; he plays it like a guitar, picking out lead-lines with his fingers; he has recently branched out, playing mandolin, small-scale guitars, or manipulating effects pedals to create unpredictable bursts of sound; and, as in 'More News from Nowhere', he provides digital samples against which the songs run.

The title track of *Dig, Lazarus, Dig!!!* provides a good example of Ellis' relation to the music the Bad Seeds now produce. The track, like 'Tupelo', has a simple musical structure, based around a chord sequence that would not be out of place on a blues track: Cave's vocals are half-spoken, half sung, locking tightly into the accompanying music on the lines 'I don't know what it is/But there's definitely something going on upstairs'. Ellis' presence is a lot more immediately obtrusive than Bargeld's: from the beginning, we are aware of an undertow of distorted noise and feedback that runs, more or less unimpeded, through the track. Unlike Bargeld's, Ellis' playing is more conventionally expressive: for example, the lines 'I can hear my mother wailing/And a whole lot of scraping of chairs' are accompanied by sound bursts (generated by a heavily distorted violin, played as though it was a guitar), which illustrate the wailing and scraping the lyrics describe. However, even though Ellis fulfils one of the basic requirements of the soloing musician in rock – he provides fills that punctuate and illustrate the track – what he does is excessive: the fills constantly threaten to overwhelm the rest of the music, rather than sitting comfortably in the background, they threaten to become the foreground. When Ellis – again on violin – provides a lead line, it once again fits the mode of rock instrumentation more neatly than Bargeld's slide guitar: it sounds for a second like a heavily distorted but quite conventional guitar solo – and yet it uses an arpeggio, which does not sit entirely comfortably with the harmonic structure of the rest of the song. Once again, the line conforms to the musical framework the rest of the band sets down, but threatens to go beyond it. It threatens, in other words, to convert a known musical structure into noise: but it never quite makes good on that threat. In Ellis' playing, as in Bargeld's, the dialectic between music and noise – between what is thought of as beautiful (because consonant) and evil (because dissonant) – remains unresolved.

Conclusion

I have written elsewhere on a curious feature of Cave's performances: they seem to be, in the terms laid out in Slavoj Zizek's *The Parallax View*, parallax in nature – that is, they are composed of incommensurate performative choices that are not reconciled as the performance develops (Pattie 2010; Zizek 2006). As Zizek puts it:

> [t]he standard definition of parallax is: the apparent displacement of an object (the shift of its position against a background), caused by a change in observational position that provides a new line of sight. The philosophical twist to be added, of course, is that the observed difference is not simply 'subjective', due to the fact that the same object which exists 'out there' is seen from two different stances, or points of view. It is rather that, as Hegel would have it, subject and object are inherently 'mediated', so that an 'epistemological' shift in the subject's point of view always reflects an 'ontological' shift in the subject itself.
> (2006: 17)

Zizek identifies the operation of the parallax as a key part of the process of interpretation: it is not that a hierarchy operates, in which new readings supersede old ones, but that it is possible to hold two or more readings of the same event, the same idea, or the same artefact, within the same interpretive framework without necessarily allowing those meanings to collapse into a final interpretation of the whole. In relation to Cave's and the Bad Seeds' music, this seems to me to be a far more fruitful approach to the interplay of noise and music than anything which stems from Attali (whose work, as I have said, has become the default theoretical conduit through which the discussion of noise in popular music is filtered). The problem with applying Attali to the Bad Seeds is that Attali argues for a socially accepted hierarchy (music beautiful, noise evil) to which the Bad Seeds' music does not conform: but he then posits a process ('composition') through which this harmful dialectic can be resolved. It could be said that the very reason for the impact of the Bad Seeds' music is that it actively resists the resolution of the dialectic between noise and music: in particular, the roles of two musicians in particular – Bargeld and then Ellis – would seem to be precisely the production of musical moments that actively resist full incorporation, either in the ultimate subversion of music by noise, or the resolution of noise within music. The music they and the band produce remains a beautiful, evil thing: neither one nor the other (and also, neither one because of the other), but both together, operating from two different stances but incorporated within the same pieces of music.

References

Attali, Jacques (1985), *Noise: The Political Economy of Music*, Minneapolis: University of Minnesota Press.

Bartlett, Thomas (2004), 'The Resurrection of Nick Cave', *Salon*, 18 November 2004, http://dir.salon.com/story/ent/feature/2004/11/18/cave/index.html. Accessed 18 November 2008.

Cave, Nick (2003a), 'I Saw Music Could Be a Beautiful, Evil Thing, While My Parents Shifted Uncomfortably', *The Guardian*, 13 September 2003, http://www.guardian.co.uk/world/2003/sep/13/arts.artsnews1. Accessed 11 July 2011.

Cave, Nick and the Bad Seeds (2003b), *God is in the House*. DVD. London: Mute.

Cobussen, Marcel (2005), 'Noise and Ethics: On Evan Parker and Alain Badiou', *Culture, Theory and Critique*, 46: 1, pp. 29–42.

Damai, Puspa (2007), 'Babelian Cosmopolitanism: Or Tuning in to "Sublime Frequencies"', *The New Colonial Review*, 7: 1, pp. 107–38.

Hegarty, Paul (2007), *Noise/Music*, London: Continuum.

Johnston, Ian (1996), *Bad Seed: The Biography of Nick Cave*, London: Abacus.

Kohl, Paul R. (2007), 'Reading Between the Lines: Music and Noise in Hegemony and Resistance', *Popular Music and Society*, 21: 3, pp. 3–17.

MacLennan, Grant (1993), 'Nick Cave: Interview', *Juice Magazine*, March 1993, pp. 60–3.

Masters, Marc (2007), 'Grinderman Interview', http://pitchfork.com/features/interviews/6577-grinderman/. Accessed 26 August 2011.

Mattern, Shannon and Barry Salmon (2008), 'Sound Studies: Framing Noise', *MSMI*, 2: 2, pp. 139–44.

McEvoy, Emma (2007), '"Now, who will be the witness/When you're all too healed to see?" The Sad Demise of Nick Cave', *Gothic Studies*, 9: 1, pp. 79–89.

Pattie, David (2010), 'Saint Nick: A Parallax View of Nick Cave', in Karoline Gritzner (ed.), *Eroticism and Death in Performance*, Hatfield: University of Hertfordshire Press, pp. 224–41.

Reid, J. (1997), 'Devil's Advocate', *Guitarist*, August 1997, pp. 151–4.

Shryane, Jennifer (2011), *Blixa Bargeld and Einstürzende Neubauten: German Experimental Music*, Aldershot: Ashgate.

Smith, Nick (2005), 'The Splinter in Your Ear: Noise as Semblance of Critique', *Culture, Theory and Critique*, 46: 1, pp. 43–9.

Stupar, Taisija P. (2006), 'Q&A with Warren Ellis of Dirty Three', http://www.beat-a-go-go.com/story/2006/5/6/9246/53330. Accessed 26 August 2011.

Zizek, Slavoj (2006), *The Parallax View*, Cambridge: MIT.

PART II

Murder Ballads

Chapter 5

'Executioner-Style': Nick Cave and the Murder Ballad Tradition

Nick Groom

'**D**eath is not the end' – or is it? *Murder Ballads* has the highest body-count of any Nick Cave and the Bad Seeds album: some 65 men, women and children (and a dog) get murdered in various ways over the album's duration, averaging more than one per minute. Previously, Cave had tended to identify with criminals as victims – either on the run ('Wanted Man') or being punished ('The Mercy Seat') (Cave 2007: 114–16, 137–40). In *Murder Ballads*, however, the killing hardly stops, and we welter in the blood of mass murder rather than travelling the brimstone way of vengeance and guilt, mercy and repentance that characterizes previous Bad Seeds albums.

Why is this? And why was *Murder Ballads*, released in 1996, the most successful album by Nick Cave and the Bad Seeds, reaching eight in the United Kingdom, three in Australia, and five in Germany – at least until *Dig, Lazarus, Dig!!!* (2008)? Was it simply the inclusion of a few duets with more mainstream stars (PJ Harvey, Shane MacGowan and most notably Kylie Minogue) or are there deeper reasons? David McInnis places *Murder Ballads* in the tradition of Thomas De Quincey's essays 'On Murder, Considered as One of the Fine Arts' (1827–54), noting the similarities between De Quincey's aestheticization of murder and Cave's stance, particularly in his reworking of 'Stagger Lee' (McInnis 2006: 117–38). Arguing that De Quincey develops a model of the crooked sublimity of murder and suggesting preoccupations in the gendering of both victims and the scene of the crime, McInnis concludes that there is a continuity between the two, revealing 'the very distinct and enduring legacy of Romantic aesthetics and motifs in contemporary culture' (2006: 117–38; Marcus 1977: 75-9). Doubtless; but as will become clear, *Murder Ballads* (and as it happens De Quincey's 'Murder' essays) are actually part of a far older tradition, in particular the urban murder ballad tradition. What – if anything – does this reveal about the album's success?

The murder ballad tradition

The 'murder ballad' tradition is as old as the ballad tradition itself. By 'ballads' I do not mean the degraded 'power ballads' of modern rock – lush AOR played on acoustic instruments that crescendo to a melodramatic guitar solo. Indeed, many songs that describe themselves as ballads are just pop songs – Bob Dylan's 'Ballad of a Thin Man', for example, may be many things but it is not technically a ballad. And not all of Nick Cave's murder ballads are actually ballads; alluding to an influential reworking of the ballad tradition published two centuries earlier, Wordsworth and Coleridge's *Lyrical Ballads, with a Few Other Poems*, the collection should perhaps really be called *Murder Ballads, with a Few Other Songs*. So for the purposes of the present discussion, the ballad tradition is an English-language poetic and musical style first recorded in the fourteenth century. It has thrived in Britain in oral and published forms since the sixteenth century, and through migration subsequently spread to parts of North America – notably the Appalachian Mountains – and (much later and mixed with other forms) to Australia. Although the tradition was largely superseded in Britain during the nineteenth century by music hall, it was by then already in the process of being energetically rescued and recorded by antiquarian song collectors such as Walter Scott and James Hogg, Francis James Child, Sabine Baring-Gould, Cecil Sharp (who made notable collections in the Appalachian region), A. L. Lloyd and Alan Lomax. In the twentieth century the ballad tradition was thoroughly revived and reinvented and incorporated into blues, rock, and of course folk music (Newman 2007: 185–228). Nick Cave is just one of the many recent students of this tradition, following both the anonymous singers who were responsible for the tradition, and the middle-class scholars who, after a fashion, preserved it. And Cave has admitted as much, saying of 'Stagger Lee', for example: '[t]he reason why we did it, apart from finding a pretty good version of it in this book [a collection of the folk poetry of black hustlers], was that there is already a tradition. We're kinda adding to that' (White 1996).

Ballads are narratives told in simple rhyming four-line verses – usually iambic and anapæstic quatrains in a rising rhythm. They are traditionally sung, either unaccompanied or with folk instruments such as the fiddle or hurdy-gurdy, the musical line tending to be a repetitive refrain. Traditionally, words and music were seldom mutually dependent; rather, there was a shared canon of simple and familiar tunes that could be inflected in different ways, and so printed ballads (broadsides) were often sold as being 'a new song to an old tune'. (Interestingly, the Bad Seeds improvised their version of 'Stagger Lee' in the studio, recording it in just 15 minutes (White 1996)). Moreover, in the eighteenth century the ballad became recognized as a literary genre that could be read privately as well as performed publicly, and the form thereby achieved a degree of respectability at fashionable London theatres. Ballad narratives were used as sources for plays, and some enterprising writers would string together popular songs with their own compositions to produce ballad operas. This proved to be an enduring format: John Gay's *The Beggar's Opera* (1728) was the basis for Brecht and Weill's *Threepenny Opera* 200 years later (1928), and is effectively a forerunner of musicals today.

Traditional ballads cover a range of subjects: the exploits of legendary heroes such as St George and King Arthur, episodes in British history (particularly military and maritime actions), domestic events from seduction and marriage – often ending badly – to carousing and making merry. In other words, ballads are about singing, drinking, fucking and killing. Killing: ballads seem particularly suited to recounting tales of outlaws and crime, particularly murder, and while it may be tempting to conclude from this that long narratives in simple verses favour the black-and-white moral structure of crime narratives, ballads are often surprisingly amoral (Groom 1999: 59). This is in part because they functioned as a medium of news, and reports of lawlessness then (as now) made good copy. But such balladic reportage did not merely consist of warnings to the population in general about criminals at large, or accounts of felons brought to book as a reminder of the authority of the state. Criminals were often themselves popular folk heroes. The most obvious example was, doubtless, Robin Hood, but other notable outlaws include the trio Adam Bell, Clym of the Clough and William of Cloudesley, and so ballads were an important part of the culture of the lower labouring classes, and tales of the adventures of maverick heroes and arguably lovable rogues (*hoodlums* might be a better word for them) were understandably popular and provided a template for later bad man ballads.

There is more to this, however, than ballads offering a contained little rebellion against those in power. It is worth bearing in mind that the Robin Hood of the ballad tradition is not the Robin Hood of the BBC TV series, or the fey 'Robin of Sherwood' of the 1980s, or Errol Flynn, or the aristocratic Earl of Loxley of the romantics and Pre-Raphaelites, or even Russell Crowe and Ridley Scott's mud-spattered Robin Longstride. The Hood of the ballad tradition is an unemotional, brutal, ruthless, cold-blooded killer. The early ballad 'Robin Hood and Guy of Gisborne', for example, is centred on a bloodthirsty duel between the two men. They fight for two hours before Gisborne is slain. Hood then decapitates his adversary, pares off Gisborne's face, and leaves his head on a stick as a warning. The ballad then concludes on a note of incongruous jollity when Robin Hood frees Little John from the Sheriff of Nottingham, and John revenges himself on his captor by shooting him in the arse.

Yet the barbarity with which Hood treats Gisborne's corpse is horribly sinister, and remains in the memory:

Robin pulled forth an Irish kniffe,
And nicked Sir Guy in the fface, [i.e. cut]
That hee was neuer on a woman borne
Cold tell who Sir Guye was

(Child 118, st. 42)

Even his mother will not recognize the butchered skull. This savagery is shocking, particularly in the bucolic setting of the forest (now revealed as a pitiless wilderness), but it also forms a symmetry with the savagery of the state. The penalty for killing the king's deer, the crime of choice of Robin Hood and his Merry Men and literally their meat and drink, was nothing so common as simple hanging: it was blinding and castration. Being captured would ensure the execution of this ghastly punishment; Hood's response was to show Gisborne that he would not be the one to lose face.

This, then, is the source for twentieth-century narratives such as 'Stagger Lee'. Nick Cave:

I like the way the simple, almost naive traditional murder ballad has gradually become a vehicle that can happily accommodate the most twisted acts of deranged machismo. Just like Stagger Lee himself, there seem to be no limits to how evil this song can become.

(White 1996)

Indeed, the exact and intimate violence that Hood inflicts on Gisborne is characteristic of ballads of revenge, particularly when dealing with adulterous or murderous women. In 'Old Sir Robin of Portingale', the young wife of the elderly Sir Robin plots with her lover to kill him. They are overheard by a page who duly warns the old man. When the lover arrives at night, leading a gang of thugs, Sir Robin is ready: he beheads the lover and the gang flees (the page, incidentally, has his arm lopped off in the confusion). The wife arrives to find her lover decapitated. Old Sir Robin, however, has not finished, and proceeds to carve her up:

> Hee cutt the papps beside her brest,
> And bad her wish her will;
> He cutt the eares beside her heade,
> And bade her wish on still.

(Child 80, st. 29)

Having hacked off her nipples and ears, that last quip, '[a]nd bade her wish on still', is particularly chilling.

Lord Barnard treats his wife in a similar fashion when he catches her in bed with Little Musgrave. First he eviscerates the naked Musgrave, then he mutilates his wife as she prays over the body of her lover, again by coring her breasts; there is also a hint that he has circumcised or otherwise genitally mutilated her as well:

> He cut her paps from off her brest;
> Great pitty it was to see
> That some drops of this ladie's heart's blood
> Ran trickling downe her knee

(Child 81(A), st. 26)

This verse is usually left out of recordings (Fairport Convention, 1969/1970).

Thwarted love is a bloody business too. Lord Thomas loves the Fair Ellinor, but is enticed by the riches of the 'browne girl' (or 'nutbrown maid' – so called for her hair) as she has houses and land. Thomas marries the 'browne girl' but invites Ellinor to the wedding whereupon he rashly declares his love for her. The 'browne girl' (who, like some feral force, is never named) stabs Ellinor; the blood flows from her, she goes pale and dies in Thomas' arms. Thomas shows no mercy to his new wife:

> He cut off his brides head from her shoulders,
> And he threw it against the wall

(Child 73(D), st. 18)

They had not even left the church.

These are not ballads of some simple black-and-white morality; these are ballads of no morality. In 'Edom o' Gordon', the traitor Gordon and his gang engage in a capricious spree of wanton pillage and attempted rape. They barrack a fortified house, threatening the lady there and trying to force their way in as her husband is away. Eventually they set the place on fire. As the smoke rises the children cry and the lady's daughter jumps from the battlements to save herself; she is killed out-of-hand by Gordon who leaves the house burning. The lady's husband returns too late to save his family. And that is it: he gets no chance to exact revenge. In comparison, the precise slaughter of Cave's songs 'Where the Wild Roses Grow' and 'The Kindness of Strangers' seems positively affectionate (Cave 2007: 250–1, 256–7).

A well-known example in the tradition might be 'The Children in the Wood', with which William Wordsworth was familiar. It is still sung and performed in pantomime today, where it is often combined with a debonair Robin Hood and Maid Marian subplot; a version of the ballad was collected from the Copper family in 1963. The usual story consists of the babies straying into the wood, getting lost, and dying, whereupon the robins of the wood gather around them to sing a requiem. But in fact these versions owe more to sentimental Victorian music hall songs than to the English ballad tradition. The traditional ballad has a much more detailed – and darker – narrative. It tells how the parents of two children fall terminally ill. Before they die, they leave money for their soon-to-be orphaned children to be raised by their uncle. Within a year, the uncle is plotting to kill them, and to that end hires two thugs. The thugs take the children into the woods but then squabble among themselves. Hope is raised (for the children at least) when the milder of the two thugs kills his partner-in-crime and leads the children away. This respite, however, is short lived. Mild thug then goes off to get bread, but does not return; the two babes wander around the woods, lost; they die of starvation; mild thug, meanwhile, is arrested for his pains and executed for robbery. In some versions the wicked uncle dies in jail; in other versions, however, he receives no retribution and even prospers. And perhaps the memory of this dark tale, an anti-Eden, lies behind 'Song of Joy' and its own invocation of Milton's *Paradise Lost* and the 'red right hand': the avenging hand of God as the incitement to civil war (Cave 2007: 243–5; Milton, II l.174).

Evidently the world described by such traditional ballads is unremittingly flesh and bone. There is no redemption. Death is not presented as an escape or transcendence, it is not a form of sacrifice – it is merely a crushing reassertion of the material nature of reality. This is not to say that there are no ghosts in this world, just that what ghosts there are have either a horrid corporeality about them and are walking accounts of their own decomposition, or are premonitions of death or temptations to die – such as 'The Unquiet Grave' or, indeed, 'Lovely Creature' (2007: 248–9). In 'Sweet William's Ghost', for instance, a ghostly lover visits a girl; when his ghost leaves she dies. Likewise, dreams only offer enigmatic glimpses of the scene of death. Fair Margaret and Sweet William (stock names) are lovers, but, like Lord Thomas, William resolves to marry another. It is an unwise choice. Margaret dies and her ghost haunts William, manifesting itself as grotesque dreams:

I dreamt my bower was full of red swine,
And my bride-bed full of blood

(Percy's Reliques, iii. 123)

It may be that 'swine' here should be 'wine', but 'swine', with the hint of the possessed Gadarene swine and the delayed decoding of the tainted bridal bed as a harlot's sty, is much more menacing, uncanny even. Whatever the case, William visits Margaret's corpse to make amends, kisses her, and dies himself.

Ballads are clearly obsessed with the body. By dwelling on narratives of sex, rape, torture, mutilation, dismemberment, decapitation, death, and even in some cases cannibalism, bodies are laid bare, made explicit, unravelled or undone or unmade – and thereby made to speak. The suffering body is locutionary, and it is articulated by song. Ballads give voice to the body as it dies. Beauty, honour, mercy and vengeance are not inherent in the body, but are introduced by refrains that anatomize the body, by a performance that shapes a body. In a sense, then, the body is sacrificed to poetry – whether the body is one's own or that of one's enemy (Groom 1999: 51). As Michel de Certeau puts it:

> [t]he undone body was a precondition of the speech it sustained up to the moment of death; in the same way, this undone speech, split apart by forgetting and interpretation, 'altered' in dialogic combat, is the precondition of the writing it in turn supports. That speech makes writing possible by sinking into it. It induces it.

(de Certeau 1968: 78)

It is perhaps worth pointing out that alongside ballad culture, which they were instrumental in preserving, eighteenth- and nineteenth-century antiquarian collectors were also fascinated by the 'death song' motif of primitive literary cultures. The 'death song' was supposedly a self-sung epitaph, the most famous being that of the Viking chieftain Ragnar Loðbrog. Although clearly a literary convention, the idea that bodies can sing themselves across the threshold of life and death is a powerful theme in myth and legend. Song here is a form of transit, a way of moving between worlds – or rather, a way of leaving this world, a way of going. The song – literally an *air* – is precisely not corporeal. No physical trace of it will remain: it is evanescent, lost in the very moment of utterance.

The proximity of ballads to death songs is evident in the often problematic position of the narrator. Many ballads are told in the first person from the perspective of the protagonist. In such cases, the singer sings of his or her own death. In the ultra-violent ballad 'Titus Andronicus's Complaint', for example, which was either a source for Shakespeare's hellish play or an attempt to cash-in on its success, the first-person narrative creates an extraordinarily eerie effect as the litany of betrayal, rape, mutilation, cannibalism and mass murder reaches its climax in suicide: '[a]nd then myself: even soe did Titus die' (Percy's *Reliques*, i. 209). Titus is master of his own destiny and able to revenge himself on his enemies. In contrast,

Jane Shore's ballad tells her sordid tale of sexual degradation that ends with her dying in a sewer, the 'common shore', a vale of shit – her very name reveals her miserable fate:

> Within a ditch of loathsome scent,
> Where carrion dogs did much frequent
>
> (Percy's *Reliques*, ii. 257)

'Jane Shore' is told in the first person – as is the execution of Alice Davis, *The Unnaturall Wife* (1628), for stabbing her husband to death. Such a voice adds the glamour of authenticity to the narrative: it is an impossible first-person account through the very eyes of the one witness who saw exactly what happened – the perpetrator. Alice Davis speaks from beyond the grave – or rather, because as a felon she would have no grave, hers is the voice of the damned, accompanied by the fires of Hell – fires that are prefigured by her method of execution:

> And being chayned to the Stake,
> Both Reedes and Faggots then
> Close to my Body there was set,
> With Pitch, Tarre, and Rozen
>
> (*Pepysian Garland*, 283–92)

(Women condemned to public execution were nearly always burnt at the stake rather than hanged, ostensibly for reasons of decorum: the hanged body tended to evacuate its bladder and bowels under the shock of death.)

This is strong stuff, and contemporary singer-songwriters meddling in the darkness of murder ballads cannot do so lightly. The lyrics are literally a 'burden', the stuff of Gothic nightmares. And Nick Cave co-opts all the rancid aesthetics of the tradition in the mere title of his album. Murder ballads – ballads about killing – are peculiarly intense examples of the visceral violence of the ballad form, well suited to modern retellings.

There is a further reason for physical preoccupations being acutely pertinent to murder ballads, which also binds them to the preoccupations of contemporary audiences. Crime writing became particularly popular at the end of the seventeenth century as a textual supplement to the spectacle or drama of public hangings, and souvenir ballads sold at these events were extremely popular. Such ballads would recount the crimes and confessions of the felon about to be hanged – and none were more popular than murderers. It is in fact worth pointing out that execution was not reserved for murderers. They only accounted for about 10 per cent of those executed. The vast majority fell foul of the 'Bloody Code', which permitted the death penalty for major crimes such as forgery and rape, but also minor offences of petty theft and crimes against property such as vandalism (Emsley 1987: 203, 209–12; Linebaugh 1991: 80; Hay 1975: 22, 43).

As historians have noted, the gallows scaffold at Tyburn was like a stage: the condemned man would often dress for the occasion (usually as a bridegroom in anticipation of embracing death), give speeches and utter fitting final words (Linebaugh 1975: 112). In one way, this was a theatre of morality in which the criminal represented a particular occupation, class or social background, age, and so forth (Emsley 1987: 214–15; Linebaugh 1991: xx). But like the popular theatre, it was also the scene for dissent and carnival: large crowds, drinking and singing, and mixing with prostitutes and the criminal classes. Public hangings were also, ironically, notorious for pickpocketing – a misdemeanour that could itself land the perpetrating miscreant on the gallows (Laqueur 1989: 305–55).

It might therefore be more apt to consider public executions as a sort of festival, a sacrificial ritual (Bataille 1997: 287). The execution was literally the moment of truth – the defining point at which existence became non-existence. If a murder was open to interpretation in the courtroom, execution itself was final: it certainly could not be argued away after the event. Place, time and date of death – all the variables that make murder elusive – were in the case of execution fixed by the court. Act, evidence and sentence all came together in one absolute and exterminating instant, irreversible and unrepeatable – and in complete symmetry with the state of the victim. Spectacle and representation were briefly obliterated by the unforgiving nature of reality. And as the sacrificial victim was 'launched into eternity', he gave the congregation of the counterculture a glimpse of the other world. The gallows was a sort of portal and the body could be a conduit for truth – indeed, the body parts and vital fluids of hanged men were reputed to have supernatural properties: mandrakes, for example, were supposed to grow beneath gallows from the semen ejaculated by a criminal in the spasms of death. The hanged man was at the brink of reality. What lay beyond: was death the end?

Sacrifice 'essentially turns its back on real relations'; the world at the end of the hangman's rope is, as Georges Bataille has suggested, 'contagious and its contagion is dangerous [...] what is started in the operation of sacrifice is like the action of lightning: in theory there is no limit to the conflagration' (Bataille 1992: 44, 53). In theory, there is no limit and the sacrificial logic could deluge the real world; in practice, however, it can only last a few seconds before the twitching body at the end of the rope completes its 'funny ride' and hangs still. Reality recedes and is once again masked by spectacle and representation.

The murder ballad is an echo of the sacrificial revelation of execution. Popular true-crime writing (what in the eighteenth century eventually became the popular series of *Newgate Calendars*, forerunner of later sensationalist genres that survive in rude health today) presents its narratives as salacious and gruesome and threatening and amoral as murder ballads. The aim of crime writing is strangely disruptive: to prove the truth of what is not permitted and cannot be allowed – to prove, if you like, the incapacity of the law. And at the height of the ballad tradition, in attempting to describe indescribable crime, to explicate the inexplicable, crime writing resorted not to moral allegories or predestinarian theology, but to a determinedly forensic analysis. In other words, accounts of crimes were as visceral and as obsessed with the physical as were murder ballads themselves.

So we have all the gory details of murders committed: headless bodies, bodiless heads, disembowelled corpses – these are clearly not accidents.

> they found her in a shed belonging to the house, with her throat cut from ear to ear, her stomach cut down throughout like a sheep, and her bowels and heart taken out and put into a tub.
>
> (Groom 1999a: i. 135, i. 343)

One unidentified head was actually put on display in case anyone recognized it:

> [o]n Wednesday, March 2, 1725–6, about break of day, one Robinson, a Watchman, found a man's head (which appeared to be newly cut from his body) and a bloody pail near it […] the Church-wardens offered it to be washed, and the hair to be combed; which being done it was set upon a post for public view, to the end, that some discovery might be made.
>
> (Groom 1999a: iii. 23)

We are back to the fascination with describing dismembered bodies: the whole legal process was, as it were, an act of re-membering:

> looking at the water, [he] perceived the toe of a boot above the surface; upon which he got a pole with a hook on the end of it, took hold of it, and raising it a little higher, perceived above the upper part of the boot, a scarlet stocking, and afterwards found it to be a man's body.
>
> (Groom 1999a: i. 29–30)

It is perhaps no surprise that the art critic Ralph Rugoff has described the 'scene of the crime' as a site of uncanniness:

> [c]rime scenes present us with both a surplus and a dearth of meaning. They are full of the resonance of inexplicable dread and destruction. At the same time they can appear stupidly banal and vacuous. As we enter the terrain of the crime scene, we enter a world in which meaning seems overwhelming in its presence yet strangely insubstantial. […] This anti-space is haunted.
>
> (Rugoff 1997: 25)

Peter Wollen has observed that '[t]he scene of the crime is a fertile site for fantasy – morbid, fetishistic, and obsessive' (Rugoff 1997: 24). As the crossroads where sex and violence, loss and strife, death and torture – the whole basis of psychoanalysis – may all meet, crime writing could hardly be anything else.

This haunting or uncanniness extends to the whole description of a crime scene and the objects within it: everything is accounted for in minuscule and excessive detail, the most mundane item could have a profound significance or carry a lethal secret. In other words, '[b]lood – the crucial fact of existence – makes the world of pots and pans uncanny' (Groom 1999a: i. xxv). There is too much potential meaning everywhere. As Michel Foucault argues, this heightened sense of perception or sense of hyper-significance affected (and indeed still affects) the whole style of crime writing by making the everyday perpetually exceptional (Foucault 1982: 204). Such a superfluity of unspent meaning can only be controlled by making the scene of the crime a physical reality, not a symbolic space – a place of verifiable empirical fact, and, as it transpires, a place distinctively urban. Urban spaces are contained environments that can be measured and accounted for and described – surveyed, if you like – in ways that do not work in non-urban spaces, such as meadows, or the sea. Clarity cannot be controlled in the same way in these non-urban places – it disperses and the scene becomes supernatural, threatening in a different way – but urban spaces can be defined in the same ways that crime writing and ballads delineate the dark materiality of the world. Hence the urban murder ballad is a sort of degree zero or absolute point of material space.

The most renowned urban murder ballad of the seventeenth and eighteenth centuries is probably 'George Barnwell'. The first part of this long tale is told in the first person: Barnwell describes how he takes up with a cash-strapped whore, Sarah, whom he visits regularly for sex. Barnwell starts stealing to fund his sexual appetite, and is caught, but manages to take refuge in Sarah's lodgings. To solve their money problems, Barnwell suggests they murder his uncle. Barnwell visits his uncle, stays with him, picks his moment, and then 'beat[s] his brains out of his head' (Percy's *Reliques*, iii. 239 [part ii]). They take the money and live happily ever after – until the money runs out. Sarah then shops Barnwell, who escapes and puts the blame on her. Sarah is caught and condemned to death; Barnwell is then recaptured himself, and he too is hanged.

This ballad of prostitution, thieving, murder, betrayal and execution has all the grisly bodily detail of traditional murder ballads, but also a deal of empirical information: precise sums of money are given, there is an exact time scale, and a covetous materiality – a handkerchief, for example, is described as being '[a]ll wrought with silk and gold' (Groom 1999a: xvii). It could be read as a miniature epic narrative – an urban epic, stripped down, pared to the bone. The crimes of George Barnwell and Sarah eclipse the trade and industry of the city, the political ideologies of improvement and opportunity. The city is now a place of annihilation, and this annihilation can be endlessly replayed, resung as a perpetual memento mori. Crime writing and urban murder ballads present the city as a visceral space on the verge of inevitable extinction.

In the twentieth century such murder ballads crossbred with blues and other folk forms. Alan Lomax, for example, made many field recordings of what he called 'bad man' ballads that reflected the American myths of the outlaw and desperado. These were not only of wild-west gunslingers like Jesse James, Robin Hoods of the time, but also often from an African-American perspective – such as 'Po' Lazarus'. Lomax himself pointed out that some of these derived from old British sources: 'Railroad Bill', for example, is based on the eighteenth-century ballad 'Willie Brennan'. Others have gone through various incarnations: Almeda Riddle was recorded in 1959 singing 'Hangman Tree', her version of the traditional 'Hanging Tree' ('Maid Freed from the Gallows', Child 95), which was recast a few years later when it was taken up by Led Zeppelin as 'Gallows Pole' (1970; Page and Plant 1994, 2004). A year later, Led Zeppelin recorded another American ballad, 'When the Levée Breaks', based on a ballad by Kansas Joe and Memphis Minnie from 1929. Listening to the recordings of the 1920s and 1930s, however, it is clear how little this strand of American folk and country has influenced Nick Cave's treatment of ballads, which owes far more – by luck or design – to the English collectors and 1960s–70s folk rock reworkings.

'O'Malley's Bar'

And so to 'O'Malley's Bar', the archetypal Cave murder ballad (Cave 2007: 260–5). The killer speaks directly to us: his very first words are a declaration of identity and being, 'I am': 'I am tall and I am thin' (2007: 260). His voice has the grain of authenticity, shifting between a curt, objective, observational realism and the inarticulate utterances of something bestial: '[h]uh! Hmmmmm', '[m]mmmmmmmmmm' (2007: 260, 261). He walks into a bar in a town, a bar he knows well. He gives us pointless, protracted, dreamlike precision over two verses when ordering a drink. Time slows in the fecundity of detail: 'I sniffed and crossed myself' (2007: 260). All this evidence and witnessing is of course characteristic of urban crime narratives. The killer is also physically disembodied – '[m]y hand decided that the time was nigh' and his dick feels 'long and hard' – as well as being mentally disembodied (2007: 260). This does not indicate that he is some sort of supernatural being – on the contrary, these are acts of self-alienation. The killer is outside of himself: he imagines his physique, admiring his height and presenting a preening self-portrait as he pulls the trigger. He has slicked back black hair 'like a raven's wing' and muscles 'hard and tight' (2007: 264). He is a figure in a book, or in a film, or of course in a ballad: '[w]hen I shot him, I was so handsome/It was the light, it was the angle' (2007: 260). This is 'executioner-style'.

The glasses jangle. The killer reports his own speech, but uses a more confiding, colloquial register when he speaks directly to the listener, describing Mrs O'Malley and Siobhan in eccentric detail, detail that gradually resolves itself into a suppressed religious iconography. The killer sings – he is composing his ballad in the very instant of murder, the separation between representation and reality dissolves. 'I sang and I laughed' as victims are decapitated by gunshot ('[I] blew his head completely off') or have their skulls stoved in ('with an ashtray as big as a fucking big brick') or spill their 'bowels out on the floor', and minute instances of materiality and mortality seep into the account in moments of panting and coughing (2007: 262, 263). He declares his name – although not to us, the listener. Or does he? Just as the song's composition overlaps with the events it depicts, so the protagonist (who is himself a performer and composer) overlaps with the performer and composer Nick Cave. Possibly. The point is that the ambiguity or the very possibility of identification further dissolves the gap between representation and reality – the gap that murder and execution are so keen to close. This identification is perhaps strengthened by the killer watching himself in a mirror – as if Cave is teasing us to hear the ballad as a reflection:

> Well, I caught my eye in the mirror
> And gave it a long and loving inspection
> 'There stands some kind of man', I roared
> And there did, in the reflection

(2007: 264)

Finally, the police surround the bar and the killer has one bullet left. His body reforms, returns to normality – '[m]y hand it looked almost human' (2007: 265). The killer is approaching an epiphany of being and identity, his own execution, but he fails to seize it – leaving us with the problem of a potentially unreliable narrator.

Nick Cave's lyric clearly has many murder ballad motifs, but is also innovative in describing the killer's deranged state of mind. In the first-person narrative we have not simply an account of exactly what happens, but also an increasingly otherworldly reading of the carnage – the references to the Madonna, the martyred St Sebastian, angelic wings, blinding light, floating, and, in an alternative version, invisibility: 'O'Malley he looked right through me' (2005). The killer is apparently engaged in a theological experiment investigating moral culpability and free will. The result of this experiment is that his gun speaks to him – first in the deafening bangs of extermination, then in silence with a question mark: 'a query-mark of cordite' (Cave 2007: 264). That is enough to break the killer's will. He leaves his own epic unfinished – he does not even manage to finish counting his victims. We do not know whether or not death is the end. Resolution is instead left to the legal system.

Murder Ballads

Nick Cave takes the voice of the murderer in other ballads and songs here too – 'Lovely Creature', 'Where the Wild Roses Grow', 'The Curse of Millhaven' and as direct speech in much of 'Stagger Lee', while in 'Song of Joy' he is the sole survivor of slaughter (and possibly the perpetrator too), and in 'Henry Lee' is the victim when PJ Harvey takes the first-person lead. He is continually narrowing the distance between subject and singer. ('Henry Lee' supposedly derives from 'Young Hunting' (Child 68) – if so, it is a very pared down version of a supernatural ballad that includes cruentation (a corpse bleeding in the presence of its killer) and a querulous bird. In Nick Cave's version, it actually contains more elements of 'The Jew's Daughter' (or 'Sir Hugh', Child 155), in which a young boy,

Hew, is stabbed, drained of blood, disembowelled, and thrown down a well, which he then haunts plaintively (Percy's *Reliques*, i. 32). This anti-Semitic story dates to the thirteenth century; it was still being sung in 1950. The gendering of the female voice is discussed by McInnis).

Other tracks on the album display a comparable level of detail by turns mundane and horrific: a sleeping bag, electrical tape, 'Warning' signs, a six-by-five shack, children butchered, oral rape, a head sawn off and left in a fountain. But there are no executions. Most of Nick Cave's killers in *Murder Ballads* escape, only two are arrested – and at least one of these, Loretta, ends up in an asylum. So again, resolution is left to the legal system, to a place beyond the end of the ballad, outside the text.

This is quite different from the murder ballad and true-crime traditions Cave is drawing on. It may be because when the Bad Seeds recorded *Murder Ballads* Cave was already the laureate of 'The Mercy Seat' and so did not wish to repeat that searing first-person confession (the album *Tender Prey* also includes a first-person hanging in 'Up Jumped the Devil' as well as the murder pact of 'Deanna') (Cave 2007: 141–3, 144–6). But there is perhaps another reason for these characteristic changes, changes that effectively shift the entire literary and ballad tradition into a world governed by legal institutions and moral values rather than one oblivious of the law and humanity. Indeed, they may even help to explain why people bought *Murder Ballads* and how it resonated with its audience.

The abdication of authority to a power beyond the murder ballad narratives, signified by the police sirens in 'O'Malley's Bar', or just the 'they' who discover the corpse of Mary Bellows in 'The Kindness of Strangers', is a refusal to allow closure (Cave 2007: 265, 256–7). These ballads remain open, remain fugitives themselves, with the implied possibility that justice will be meted out sometime in the future: death is not the end of the story – we have not got there yet – these narratives are still unwinding. Law and order are coming, but only after the last notes of the songs have died.

I wonder whether this struck a chord in Britain, where it was felt that there was still unfinished business following one of the most highly publicized celebrity murder trials of the twentieth century: in October 1995 OJ Simpson was acquitted of murdering his former wife Nicole Brown Simpson and her friend Ronald Goldman. The album was released in February 1996. In that same month the IRA renewed its terrorist attacks on the British mainland with the Canary Wharf bomb. The worst, however, was to come: a month later Thomas Watt Hamilton walked into Dunblane Primary School in Scotland armed with four loaded handguns. Sixteen schoolchildren and one adult died in the massacre before Hamilton shot himself.

Could these events accidentally account for the success of a collection of songs that left justice hanging? Somewhere between the killings, between a high-profile premeditated assassination, the inexplicable mass-murder of young children and ongoing, anonymous, indiscriminate bombing campaigns, *Murder Ballads* could perhaps offer some sort of consolation.

References

Anon. (2001), 'Babes in the Wood' ['The Children in the Wood'] (Roud 288), *Come Write Me Down: Early Recordings of the Copper Family of Rottingdean*, Topic. First recorded 1963.

———— (2007), 'Billy Lyons and Stack O'Lee' (Roud 4183), on *People Take Warning: Murder Ballads and Disaster Songs, 1913–1938*, Tompkins Square. First recorded 1927.

———— 'Fair Margaret and Sweet William', Child 74 (Roud 253), Percy's *Reliques*, III. ii. 4.

———— 'George Barnwell', (Roud 546), Percy's *Reliques*, III. iii. 2 (second part).

———— 'Jane Shore', Percy's *Reliques*, II. ii. 25.

———— 'Jew's Daughter, The', Percy's *Reliques*, I. i. 3 ('Sir Hugh', Child 155), ('Little Sir Hugh', Roud 73), on *Classic Ballads of Britain and Ireland*, The Alan Lomax Collection, Rounder, *Folk Songs of England, Ireland, Scotland and Wales*, vol. ii. First recorded 1950.

———— 'Little Musgrave and Lady Barnard', Child 81(A) (Roud 52), on *Classic Ballads of Britain and Ireland*, The Alan Lomax Collection, Rounder, on *Folk Songs of England, Ireland, Scotland and Wales*, vol. i. First recorded 1958.

———— 'Lord Thomas and Fair Annet [Ellinor]', Child 73(D) (Roud 4).

———— 'Maid Freed from the Gallows' ['Hangman Tree' (2000)], Child 95 (Roud 144), on *Bad Man Ballads: Songs of Outlaws and Desperadoes*, The Alan Lomax Collection, Rounder, *Southern Journey*, vol. v. First recorded 1959.

———— 'Old Sir Robin of Portingale', Child 80 (Roud 3971).

———— (2000), 'Po' Lazarus', on *Bad Man Ballads: Songs of Outlaws and Desperadoes*, The Alan Lomax Collection, Rounder, *Southern Journey*, vol. v.

———— 'Robin Hood and Guy of Gisborne', Child 118 (Roud 3977).

———— 'Titus Andronicus's Complaint', Percy's *Reliques*, I. ii. 11.

———— 'Unquiet Grave, The', Child 78 (Roud 51).

———— 'Unnaturall Wife, The' ['The Lamentable Murther, of one Goodman Dauis, Locke-Smith in Tutle-streete, who was stabbed to death by his Wife, on the 29. of Iune, 1628. For which Fact, She was Araigned, Condemned, and Adiudged, to be Burnt to Death in Smithfield, the 12. of Iuly 1628'], *Pepysian Garland*, 283–92. See also sequel 'A Warning for all Desperate Women' (1633).

———— 'Young Hunting', Child 68 (Roud 47).

Bataille, Georges (1992), *Theory of Religion*, trans. by Robert Hurley, New York: Zone.

———— (1997), 'Hegel, Death and Sacrifice', in *The Bataille Reader*, ed. by Fred Botting and Scott Wilson, Oxford and Malden: Blackwell, pp. 279–95.

Beier, A. L., David Cannadine and James M. Rosenheim (eds) (1989), *The First Modern Society: Essays in English History in Honour of Lawrence Stone*, Cambridge: Cambridge University Press.

Cave, Nick (2007), *Complete Lyrics 1978–2007*, London: Penguin.

Cave, Nick and the Bad Seeds (2005), 'O'Malley's Bar', on *B-Sides and Rarities*, Mute. Three-part version recorded for Mark Radcliffe Show session, BBC Radio 1 (1996).

de Certeau, Michel (1968), *Heterologies: Discourses on the Other*, trans. by Brian Massumi, Manchester: Manchester University Press.

Child, Francis J. (ed.) (1882–98), *English and Scottish Popular Ballads*, 5 vols, London: Sterns, Son, and Stiles.

De Quincey, Thomas (2009), *On Murder*, ed. Robert Morrison, Oxford: Oxford University Press. Originally published 1827-54.

Dylan, Bob (1965), 'Ballad of a Thin Man', on *Highway 61 Revisited*, Columbia.

Emsley, Clive (1987), *Crime and Society in England: 1750–1900*, London and New York: Longman.

Fairport Convention (1969/1970), 'Matty Groves' ['Little Musgrave and Lady Barnard'], on *Liege & Lief*, Island/A&M.

Foucault, Michel (ed.) (1982), *I, Pierre Rivière, having slaughtered my mother, my sister, and my brother …: A Case of Parricide in the 19th Century*, trans. by Frank Jellinek, Lincoln and London: University of Nebraska Press.

Groom, Nick (1999), *The Making of Percy's Reliques*, Oxford: Clarendon Press.

—— (ed.) (1999a), *The Bloody Register*, 4 vols, London: Routledge. First published 1764.

Hay, Douglas (1975), 'Property, Authority and the Criminal Law', in Douglas Hay, Peter Linebaugh, John G. Rule, E. P. Thompson and Cal Winslow (1975), *Albion's Fatal Tree: Crime and Society in Eighteenth-Century England*, Harmondsworth: Penguin.

Hay, Douglas, Peter Linebaugh, John G. Rule, E. P. Thompson and Cal Winslow (1975), *Albion's Fatal Tree: Crime and Society in Eighteenth-Century England*, Harmondsworth: Penguin.

Laqueur, Thomas W. (1989), 'Crowds, Carnival and the State in English Executions, 1604–1868', in A. L. Beier, David Cannadine and James M. Rosenheim (eds) (1989), *The First Modern Society: Essays in English History in Honour of Lawrence Stone*, Cambridge: Cambridge University Press.

Led Zeppelin (1970), 'Gallows Pole', on *Led Zeppelin III*, Atlantic.

—— (1971), 'When the Levée Breaks', on untitled fourth album [*IV*], Atlantic.

Linebaugh, Peter (1975), 'The Tyburn Riot against the Surgeons', in Douglas Hay, Peter Linebaugh, John G. Rule, E. P. Thompson and Cal Winslow (1975), *Albion's Fatal Tree: Crime and Society in Eighteenth-Century England*, Harmondsworth: Penguin.

—— (1991), *The London Hanged: Crime and Civil Society in the Eighteenth Century*, Harmondsworth: Penguin.

McInnis, David (2006), '"All Beauty Must Die": The Aesthetics of Murder, from Thomas De Quincey to Nick Cave', *Traffic* 8, pp. 117–38.

Marcus, Greil (1977), *Mystery Train: Images of America in Rock 'n' Roll Music*, London and Sydney: Omnibus.

Milton, John (1971), *Paradise Lost*, ed. by Alastair Fowler, London and New York: Longman.

Newman, Steve (2007), *Ballad Collection, Lyric, and the Canon*, Philadelphia: University of Pennsylvania Press.

Page, Jimmy and Robert Plant (1994), 'Gallows Pole', on *No Quarter*, Atlantic/Fontana [*Unledded* DVD, 2004].

Percy, Thomas (ed.) (1996), *Reliques of Ancient English Poetry*, 3 vols, ed. by Nick Groom, London: Routledge/Thoemmes Press. First published 1765.

Rollins, Hyder E. (ed.) (1922), *A Pepysian Garland: Black-Letter Broadside Ballads of the Years 1595-1639, Chiefly from the Collection of Samuel Pepys* (1922), Cambridge, MA: Harvard University Press.

Roud Folk Song Index, http://library.efdss.org/cgi-bin/home.cgi. Accessed 27 May 2011.

Rugoff, Ralph (1997), *Scene of the Crime*, Cambridge, MA and London: MIT.

Wordsworth, William and Samuel Taylor Coleridge (1991), *Lyrical Ballads, with a Few Other Poems*, ed. by R. L. Brett and A. R. Jones, second edition, London: Routledge. First published 1798.

White, Nick (1996), 'Stagger Lee: NC Interview and List', http://www.bad-seed.org/~cave/info/songs/mb_staggerlee.html. Accessed 27 May 2011.

Note

Ballads are quoted from 'Child' by number and stanza; the Roud number is also given where available. Some texts are unique to Percy's *Reliques*, in which case they are quoted by series, book and number, and one appears in *A Pepysian Garland*. Contractions have been silently expanded and are not indicated by italics or other typographic conventions. Note that the account of ballads draws on Groom (1999), *The Making of Percy's Reliques*, pp. 43–60; the account of early crime writing is derived from Groom (1999a), *The Bloody Register*, vol. i, i–xxxiii.

Chapter 6

In Praise of Flat-out Meanness: Nick Cave's 'Stagger Lee'

Dan Rose

Is it better to have a nightmare than no dream at all?

If one is an entrepreneur in the illicit drug trade and assaults prostitutes for leisure, it is not art. However, if one casts these actions in song, whether autobiographical or fiction, then art it can be. The point of this chapter is not to chart how one can move between these two disparate points, but why one would want to engage with the art that would result. More to the point, what do more extreme forms of art do for us and might that have a value? Contemporary aesthetic theory is becoming quite adept at describing what art does to us. It uses neurological models, brain imaging and brain-based metaphors to explain the ways art plays us like an instrument (see Skov 2009). Some 'neuroaestheticians' tout the use of exaggeration and emotional hyperbole as a major component of how art affects us. Examples of how art plays on our natural wiring towards the world and how it provides a more concentrated experience of what we are wired to anticipate can be easily found in the current literature (see Ramachandran 2011). More extreme art, art that engages in narrative or images that are disturbing, violent or jarring, certainly plays on concentration and exaggeration. It moves us by its hyperbole. Its historical ubiquity bears witness to some utility, if only through the notion that for a behaviour (in this case listening to a specific form of art) to reoccur it must serve an adaptive purpose.

Nick Cave is a master of the disturbing narrative and chronicler of the extreme, though he is also certainly capable of a subtle romantic vision. He does much to the listener who enters his world. His take on the Stagger Lee mythos, the song appropriately titled 'Stagger Lee' on his even more appropriately titled album *Murder Ballads*, is a perfect distillation of extreme art, particularly of the brand of folk/blues-soaked song Cave has made his own. 'Stagger Lee' tells the tale of a psychopath who, after being thrown out of his home by a girlfriend, kills one man for no apparent reason then forces another man into a sexual act before killing him, while that same man's prostitute girlfriend is forced to watch. 'This Little Light of Mine' it is not. Cave has said he was attracted to the Stagger Lee mythos because of its capacity to accommodate 'the most twisted acts of deranged machismo' and 'just like Stagger Lee there seems to be no limits to how evil this song can become' (White 1996). Better yet, he states that the song has no real meaning, that it was not 'man made' but a 'gift from the gods' (1996). In fact, for Cave, Stagger Lee's atrocious behaviour has nothing to do with anything but 'flat-out-meanness' (1996). A 'gift' of 'flat-out-meanness' by an artist is an interesting thing and makes for an interesting kind of art. This sort of extreme art seems to be increasingly more common. Death metal and gangster rap are both forms of music that reflect a variant on (not so) new kinds of 'flat-out-meanness'. Stagger Lee is alive and well, or, at least, his cousins proliferate in the present culture. Again, Cave has built his song on a long line of art that continues to flourish and moves the listener through extreme acts of violence.

Theodor Adorno wrote that 'we do not understand art, art understands us' (Adorno 1998: xi). Cave's gift, one that has been passed down for generations, understands us in what I hope to show are some hidden and vital ways. Most importantly, Cave has an at least innate understanding of what the listener needs. This understanding can be reduced to the idea that we are closer than we are wont to admit to the human predators and human prey that populate the stories and songs of the extreme art we consume. This proximity to the murder ballad is not just a desire but a psychological need to be predator, prey and witness. We have met Stagger Lee and he is us.

The aforementioned neurological models are both in vogue and useful in understanding how art moves us. Psychoanalytic theory provides potential answers to what use art imbued with 'flat-out meanness' might provide the listener. In the pages that follow a detailed exploration, through several psychoanalytic lenses, of Cave's 'Stagger Lee' will provide a specific map for both the hidden needs the song fulfils and the means by which art such as this does the fulfilling. In effect, the assumption is that the song reflects our hidden cognitive and affective needs for artistically rendered 'meanness' because, no matter how far Cave pushes the evil, it is in reality much closer to what each of us experiences every single day. In essence, we live a continuous murder ballad and some forms of art make survival more possible or at least life more endurable. The key is in the unconscious thinking or, better yet, waking dreaming such art allows us.

History of the hustler

Before diving into theoretical waters a brief detour into history is necessary. Stagger Lee, or any of the variations of his name (Stackerlee, Stagolee, etc.) that appear throughout the various songs that summarize his exploits, was probably based on an actual murder by a man named Lee of Billy Lyon in 1895 (see Roberts 1983). There are some who counter that the character Stagger Lee existed long before the flesh and blood Lee and his reported murder of Lyon occurred (see Brown 2003). Regardless, the actual event has been twisted and stretched to fit the changing needs of many a performer and audience.

It is important to note that Nick Cave's lyrics for the song 'Stagger Lee' are not his own. 'Stagger Lee' is, at best, borrowed. Most of the lyrics are taken by Cave from a 'toast' delivered by the 'black hustler' 'Big Stick' in 1967 (White 1996). These lyrics may have had quite a long life before 'Big Stick'. What is also important is that, in some sense, Cave edited the lyrics in such a way that downplays some of the more graphic, especially scatological, elements. Extreme as the song is, it could have been worse.

Regardless of the specific historical facts, what is most significant is the transformation of the historical Lee into the archetypal Hustler. Broadly defined, the Hustler is a character based on the exploits of real hustlers and pimps that represents some form of assertion in the face of societal oppression, the king of the underground. Be he pimp or simple criminal, his (and he is always male) exploits reflect the assertion and triumph of the oppressed, be he of a minority culture or of lower social status. That Stagger Lee arose from the urban African-American experience is no coincidence. The history of slavery, dispossession and the breaking apart of families, resulting in the loss of fathers and stability, created the perfect storm for the expression and creation of the Hustler archetype. He is more than mere trickster. He is the embodiment of the assertion of the self in the face of pervasive shame and trauma. He is older than Stagger Lee and newer than Tyler, the Creator, though both are characters that assert the same self needs, the need to feel some sense of control, self-worth and attachment in a world that is hostile to the self. This might also illuminate the connection between the image of the Hustler or pimp and its appeal to the adolescent. In an optimum developmental stage for shame and the struggle for acceptance, the dream of the Hustler has no small use. Though it may seem to trivialize the history that gave birth to the Hustler and in turn Stagger Lee, oppression and tumult are the order of everyday living in the world. We recycle history in the present as we move through the here and now.

The murder ballad as lullaby

If contemporary aesthetics informed by neuroscience offers explanations of how art affects us, contemporary psychoanalytic theory offers a potential map of what it does for us. In effect, psychoanalytic theory offers a means to tie Stagger Lee's history, as well as the murder ballad backdrop he inhabits, to its uses in the present. There is a long history of the exploration of art through psychoanalytic theory, beginning at the very origin of psychoanalysis with Freud (see Freud 1997). One can sum up a major tenet of Freudian thinking by stating that art provides an outlet for the impulses that civilization does not allow. The individual experiences secondary gratification through singing along to symbolized violence, thereby discharging his impulses in a safe and societally mandated fashion. Though this is certainly a component of the uses of art, it is wedded to a less postmodern view of the self, a vision of a solitary self that is assuaged by art so as to wear the yoke of civilization with more ease and therefore not the same discontinuous self as reflected (or, better yet, refracted) in contemporary psychoanalytic theory.

At present, one of the dominant psychoanalytic schools of thought, at least in the United States, is interpersonal psychoanalysis (see Aron and Harris 2005). Broadly defined, it is a model that posits the therapeutic encounter as co-constructed through the dance and/or collision of both participants. The emphasis is squarely on mutual influence. Philip Bromberg is a major intellectual engine of the movement. Bromberg views the self as multitudinal, a shifting set of self-states that are co-created in the collision with objects both internal and external (see Bromberg 2001). To Bromberg, the you that exists while chatting with co-workers by the water cooler ceases to exist when the friends disperse. The self is Legion, it is bounded by developmental history, yet fluid enough to be co-created and contained by present object relations.

Psychoanalytic theory offers various complementary (or often competing) narratives that explore the birth of the self, fluid and changing as it may be. Attachment theory, in particular, explains the means by which the pre-wired impulse for generative connection and the external maternal object available to meet these needs create a dialectic that engenders selfhood (see Schore 1994). Others are necessary for their impact and the generative results of this impact. With its notion of the nursery as a war zone, rife with envy, lust and violence, Kleinian and Neo-Kleinian psychoanalytic theory afford a strangely commensurate picture of the world to that which Cave paints with 'Stagger Lee'. The self is born in struggle, driven by lack and torn by internal forces generated by the natural failures of the maternal object. The Neo-Kleinian Christopher Bollas argues that an individual's first encounter with an object of art is in the form of the maternal object, with all subsequent aesthetic experiences built on this primal experience (see Bollas 1978). If so, then this view affords a connection between the earliest forces that inspired our growth and the very art objects we consume in the present.

Bollas also offers another important construct to help illuminate the utility of 'Stagger Lee'. Bollas speaks eloquently of the 'unthought known', the guiding thoughts and internalized experiences that implicitly direct our movement through the world and have not been (and sometimes cannot be) put into language or symbolized (see Bollas 1987). Much of the war that birthed the self is unthought and merely lived as the self moves through the day.

Finally, Wilfred Bion theorizes a specific cognitive and affective process that allows us to make use of the impact of our day as we move through it (see Grotstein 2009). Unthought narratives of our birth may guide us, but we are in turn affected and potentially changed by the world that we navigate. Bion speaks of the need to 'dream' or 'digest' the emotional collisions and dances that occur as we interact with objects and the others that populate the world through which we move. If Cave's 'Stagger Lee' is in one way a birth narrative, a story of how we come to be and the 'flat-out meanness' that our birth engenders, it also offers us an art object, a means to facilitate the digestion of our daily birth, the self-states born of the impact of an other.

In summation, the self is born in struggle and is rife with internal conflict fed by the external world, a world first borne by the maternal object. The self maintains a fluidity, is in a sense continually re-born and recreated by subsequent encounters with others and objects (sometimes song objects). These impacts require some form of processing or 'dreaming', at least to the degree that they engender emotional impact, an impact made more eventful as they touch on the primal impacts implicit in the birthing of our self. As I hope to make clear in the line-by-line reading to follow, Cave's 'Stagger Lee' is the perfect narrative to encompass the history of that birth, illuminate the continuous murder ballad that is our daily life, engender its own generative impact, and allow us a chance to dream.

Oedipus in rat-drawn shoes

The song begins:

> It was back in '32 when times were hard
> He had a Colt 45 and a deck of cards, Stagger Lee
> He wore rat-drawn shoes and an old Stetson hat
> Had a '28 Ford, had payments on that, Stagger Lee

(White 1996)

This is how Big Stick's toast began, with only a few minor adjustments, the most significant being the forceful punctuation of each second line with Stagger Lee's name. The name use is like an evocation, an affirmation of selfhood, a declaration of being despite any potential obstacle. The continued recitation of Stagger Lee's name alerts us to the centrality of selfhood in the discourse. The references to the gun and the cards are visible signs of his hustlerhood and a set of badges indicating his outsider status. He is a gambler and a dangerous man. The shoes, hat and the lovely addition of a not-so-new car, one he still does not own, place Stagger Lee in some continuum between everyday debt and poverty. He is, if not quite on the skids, no success, and certainly not the high rolling Stag he may pretend to be. He is in a place of vulnerability, yet self-declarative. The narrative tone is set.

The narrative is augmented by the musical backdrop. There is an almost martial element to the music. It is deliberate and incessant, as if to mimic the sound of a man walking with a steady, determined footfall, undeterred by the things in his way. The two main instruments that accentuate this drivenness are – first – a wonderful bassline that is sinewy, part footfall and heartbeat. It literally drives the song. The other element is an atonal guitar that scrapes out a rhythm. It seems foreboding, a bit like the scratching of a branch stirred by an ill wind. Combined, the determined footfall and the ill wind foreshadow the collision with other people to come, signalling the threat of Stagger Lee himself as he moves, projectile-like, towards self-reclamation. One could argue that we are all similar missiles, moving through the world unconscious of the predatory nature of our drive and need for connection.

With this small and telling autobiographical sketch, Stag is made real. Each of us, as we awaken, is in turn awakened to our failings, the things we owe and a self worn by history and fate. We wear that history differently throughout the moments of the day, especially in those moments where our feelings are made manifest. Stag, at least in this initial part of the song, may not be so different from any of us, be it in the majority or minority, businessman or hustler. It is the self prior to the impact of the other.

The song continues and gives us the first narcissistic impingement:

> His woman threw him out in the ice and snow
> And told him 'Never ever come back no more', Stagger Lee

> So he walked through the rain and he walked through the mud
> 'til he came to a place called 'The Bucket of Blood', Stagger Lee

(White 1996)

In these lines the narrative takes flight and establishes the murder ballad as birth narrative. Stagger Lee is expelled by a woman. Much as the infant must leave the maternal orbit, so Stagger Lee moves into the world. The Oedipal overtones are evident too, though Stagger Lee has no obvious father with whom to identify or to blame. Thus drifting, he leaves that orbit vulnerable, and as will be clear, enraged.

Again, are we not like Stag in our own leaving the maternal orbit? Each of us has been 'thrown', to some degree, into 'the ice and snow' of attachment loss, be it our earliest with the maternal object, such as Klein would have it, where bottle or breast is not forthcoming and lack is first made real, or our most recent conflict with a loved one. All relationships, even the most secure, have shadows of such loss in the daily rupture and repair of attachment. Nothing disturbs narcissistic equilibrium like being 'dropped' by a loved one or, in fact, any human being. Each 'drop' initiates a potential for rage and restitution. Again, as Bollas would have it, the mother is the first art object. We approach all subsequent art through this historical lens. Here is the primal impingement given to us through the frame of an art object. Both Stag and ourselves are primed by this, made vulnerable to any subsequent loss by this first and engendering primal loss and fated to find some means to solve it, be it through rage or whatever else.

Again, the incessant drive of the music propels Stagger Lee through the elements that act as obstacles and mirror his own inner state. He is the primal self driven by initial lack, formed, as all selves are, in the maternal orbit and forced into the world of objects – into a world that will feed a multitudinal self. His destination is appropriate as well. 'The Bucket of Blood' occurs throughout toasting and folk idioms (see Wepman, Newman and Binderman 1986). It seems to hint at the blood that must be spilt in restitution as Stag moves towards the venting of his rage.

> He said, 'Mr Motherfucker, you know who I am', and the barkeep said
> 'No, and I don't give a good goddamn' to Stagger Lee
> He said, 'Well bartender, it's plain to see
> I'm that bad motherfucker called Stagger Lee, Mr Stagger Lee'
>
> The barkeeper said 'Yeah, I've heard your name down the way
> And I kick motherfucking asses like you every day, Mr Stagger Lee'
> Well all those were the last words that the barkeep said
> 'cause Stag put four holes in his motherfucking head

(White 1996)

Here Stag receives his first collision with the world of objects and subsequently commits his first murder. If the first blow is primal, even necessary for the birth of the individual, the second is a challenge to the self born through that primal blow. Stag asks for affirmation of his power, a reflection of his strength in the eyes of the barkeep, and is at first denied. The gender of his denier is most significant. A male is both potential rival and father figure. If female rejection is a blow to the self that Stag answers by leaving, the barkeep can experience an answer directly fuelled by narcissistic rage, a rage present before the encounter but fuelled by his lack of affirmation and challenging Stag. Here is the Oedipal murder of the father. The continued lyrical and musical punctuation of Stagger Lee's name again serves to heighten Stag's need for affirmation and assertion. Unheeded, unheralded, Stag responds in narcissistic rage. The four holes (excessive and signalling the need to discharge more than lead) suffice.

Stag's response is extreme and shocking. This is most likely the point and one can imagine that in toasts of old, the audience would respond with gasps and laughter. Such a response would, among other things, signal recognition. Even in the subtlest meetings with the other, we look for the mirroring and reflecting this other provides. When denied or challenged we either crumble, assert ourselves internally (our own inner musical punctuation) or respond with external or internal violence. For most, this is a murder in effigy in which the other survives. We use internal bullets and secretly hope for the survival of the other, that those bullets will be accepted and given back to us in the form of understanding, even love. Like the audience for those old toasts, we gasp in the telling and secretly long for the freedom to shoot.

Just then in came a broad called Nellie Brown
Was known to make more money than any bitch in town
She struts across the bar, hitching up her skirt
Over to Stagger Lee, she's startin' to flirt with Stagger Lee

(White 1996)

Nellie Brown's entrance signals an important turn in the narrative. Stagger Lee is now an object of desire. In live versions of the song (e.g., Cave sings 'she's starting to hurt' after the phrase 'starting to flirt') Nellie's desire is even painful in its intensity (Cave 2004). Here lies another power of the Hustler, to be irresistible, a magnet to the opposite sex. To be irresistible, even better to be painfully so, creates a quick fix to any narcissistic injury and binds the self through power over an other. Nellie wants him, and to be wanted, if only for a fleeting instance, shores up a damaged self. Both singer and listener can bask in the glow of the sexual champion, selves vicariously affirmed. Much as the self is first forged in the gleam reflecting us in our mother's eye, here, as in all romantic encounters, the initial romance between mother and child is echoed. In the initial moments of our birth into the world we endure lack, while we are rewarded later by romantic return.

In this instance, we can also see the damage significant collision or excessive lack does to attachments, especially potentially sexual ones. This is hardly Jane Austen territory, where the dance with another is subtle or sophisticated and suggestive of less primal spaces. Instead we have attachment needs associated with pain and a love object denigrated as prostitute and dog. A potential love/sexual object, by its mere appearance, is a collision of sorts and a stirring of conflictual self-states, stirring old losses and warded-off attachment needs. This is attachment reduced to its most primal, reflecting the damage of past attachment history. In some psychoanalytic circles, Nellie would be considered a part object (see Kernberg 1994). Her denigration and pure desire make her an object to be used, shrunk to the size of something that merely satiates. A woman as equal would not, maybe could not, feed the same need.

However, even in this simple encounter, our day-to-day connections are mirrored in grotesque miniature. In our moment-to-moment fluctuating sense of self, as the vicissitudes of the day generate our sense of ascendance or decline, we need something to make us forget how old the Stetson hat is and our car payments. In that moment of decline, that place when we most feel the squeeze of those rat-drawn shoes, a Nellie-like object's desire (maybe Internet porn, where an airbrushed eye or genital beckons) provides temporary polish for those same shoes.

With these lines the stage is more fully set and we head towards the final collision with an other:

> She saw the barkeep, said 'O God, he can't be dead'
> Stag said 'Well, just count the holes in the motherfucker's head'
> She said, 'You ain't look like you scored in quite a time
> Why not come to my pad? It won't cost you a dime, Mr. Stagger Lee'
>
> (White 1996)

Stag's response to Nellie's exclamation is low, if ghoulish, comedy. In toasts of old, this would surely elicit laughter. It also signals his power. His masculinity is affirmed, both through the nature of the deed and the degree to which it was done. One gunshot has much less cred than four. Nellie's response is a free gift. Others pay, but not Stag. Again he is affirmed through the measure of his deed and the power of his charisma. He has got power, old hat be damned. He can get sex he does not have to pay for, be it in real currency or the emotional currency required in the give and take of relating to whole objects, and that is a prize indeed.

In this interaction there is a small window into the motivations of both everyday and grander violence. Be it the promised virgins in an afterlife that motivate mass murder and suicide or the notice and notoriety of the much simpler face piercing, both reveal underlying attachment motivations. Stag illuminates how the broken self demands greater reparation through action, how wounds are given so payment can be received, and how sweet this is when the cost is waived. There is a scale to this. In most of our lives, the objects are less denigrated and the actions that elicit the gift of being noticed are less severe.

The narrative speeds towards its conclusion with the creation of the triangle:

'But there's somethin' that I have to say before you begin
You have to be gone 'fore my man Billy Dilly comes in, Mr Stagger Lee'
'I'll stay here till Billy Dilly comes in, till time comes to pass and
Furthermore I'll fuck Billy Dilly in his motherfucking ass', said Stagger Lee

(White 1996)

Though the concept is less relevant in contemporary psychoanalytic circles, Freud had a point when he focused on the Oedipal triangle. Three is a world beyond two. Billy Dilly gives Stag a focus for his 'meanness', a foil for his rage. His mere presence initiates the fourth and final impingement. Not only does he promise an Oedipal victory (he gets Nellie), he also vows to sexually assault Billy as well. What better way to assert power and dominance than through forcible sodomy? This is the true result of an Oedipal victory, the anger and loathing that results from a collapse of the triangle, what should be a binding of impulses through societal prohibitions by a paternal third. Stag's 'meanness' is unbridled by authority, by any law.

Connecting this 'meanness' to the everyday may seem difficult. Few consciously allow such fantasies to fill their heads. Within the space of unconscious processes, I would argue otherwise. In fact, all three points on the triangle have unconscious relevance, each allow the listener a place to elaborate experiences unconsciously, to think them without being known. An important point here is that we may at least reluctantly identify with Stag or even Nellie, but we are Billy too – and here lies the real power in this narrative, here we can truly process an experience we are likely to repress or shy from metabolizing. We may rightly defend, if only through avoidance or repression, against knowing vulnerability to domination and possibly even desire to be so dominated, to maintain an illusion of self-cohesion and efficacy. However, we must dream all sides of the triangle to move through the world of real relationships, as Cave allows us (forces us?) to do here.

At this point Cave makes his first real detour from the Big Stick lyrics. The details of Stag's sexual encounter are omitted, as well as some serious scatological detail involving coitally induced flatulence. Maybe this was too much, even for Cave? No one would accuse him of shying away from difficult material. I suspect that from Cave's perspective the omitted passage took away from the conclusion to come and softened the impact of the climactic, disturbing events with toilet humour. Instead, he adds a line from a completely different song to start the next couplet, a line taken from Snatch and the Poontangs' song 'Two Time Slim' (White 1996). This seems to take away the possibility of Nellie and Stag consummating their sexual desires. It implies that Stag's motivation is not sexual, but dominating and aggressive. It is less about pleasure and more about assault.

'I'm a bad motherfucker, don't you know, and I'll crawl over
Fifty good pussies just to get one fat boy's asshole', said Stagger Lee
Just then Billy Dilly rolls in and he says, 'You must be
That bad motherfucker called Stagger Lee'. 'I'm Stagger Lee'

(White 1996)

Cave's inclusion of this line is telling. It reveals a new level of pure 'meanness'. Billy recognizes Stag, doing what the bartender did not do. It is not enough. The accumulation of all past affronts, a history of collision and lack, must fuel Stag's rage.

In the listener, this must stir new levels of unconscious aggression and subsequent fear of being aggressed. Stag states that he would stop at nothing to dominate another male. The two words 'fat boy' – shades of the 1972 film *Deliverance* – reveal a level of domination, of usurping a vulnerable other, made more vulnerable by being a child and the softness implied in obesity (Boorman 1972). Stag would pass up 50 possible attachments, if only part object connections, for the chance to assert his self in a transgressive act. To defile a man, the Father, and God Himself, is a desperate transcendent act, something only a broken self could both wish for (this can be done by all) and act on (this requires a Stagger Lee to act out, or at least a Nick Cave to tell the tale).

'Yeah, I'm Stagger Lee, and you better get down on your knees and
Suck my dick, 'cos if you don't you're gonna be dead', said Stagger Lee
Billy dropped down and slobbered on his head
And Stag filled him full of lead – oh yeah

(White 1996)

This recognition stirs Stag to ascend the pinnacle of 'meanness'. The demand for fellatio in this instance seems also a demand for ultimate control of the object, an other, as literal and symbolic receptacle of projected vulnerability and need. Once these are projected and owned by the other, the object is destroyed. Meloy describes a similar pattern with psychopaths who commit compulsive acts of violence (see Meloy 1998). The other is brutalized, humiliated and the psychopath is momentarily transformed during the act, made whole and invulnerable as he destroys the other. The victim contains the projected vulnerable parts of the aggressor and for a brief moment those parts are destroyed with the victim. This is the ultimate act of creating an inner equilibrium by a tortured self, or at least, a mental event that is played out in unconscious fantasy by the normal but tortured.

The listener is again allowed to experience three parts of the triangle. He or she is simultaneously the dominant Stag, the subservient Billy and the silent witnessing Nellie. He or she is the object destroyed and the destroyer. The listener is also the horrified, stimulated witness, moved either by the horror or the adrenalin. A certain unconscious equilibrium is allowed the listener. In pantomime, in sonic effigy, we watch the ultimate goal of our narcissism-fuelled rage attained. We are satiated and allowed to exit the song, no longer murderer, victim or spectator. Our hands are clean and we are the better for our fantasized transgressions.

One more important point. Cave's final lyric, 'oh yeah', seems to signal the end of language, the end of symbolization, the point at which meanness shatters any possible confinement by words. The music reinforces this. Up until now the music has provided an incessant push towards climax. Here it finally explodes into near cacophony. What sounds like a violin (it is not credited in the recorded version, but clearly there in most concert versions) competes with Bad Seed Blixa Bargeld's scream, creating a piercing moment. The song bursts and so does the narrative. It is the end of words, the place where unthought knowns cannot be captured and symbolized. It is the point where dreaming stops, even with nightmares. We are awakened to a truth that cannot be dreamed. This truth seems connected to the very transgressive transcendence afforded by the song. What if we committed the ultimate act of meanness? Instead of a balanced, if torn, self we would have – what?

Here the recorded song ends. In concert (in his 2004 tour backed by female singers, adding a perverse Gospel touch and adding to the Hustler's sexual power to captivate the backup sirens), Cave incorporates lyrics from a version of the song in which Stag goes to hell to confront the Devil (Cave 2004). Even the Devil is no match for Stag as he inevitably 'fills him full of lead', just as he penetrated and subdued other male/father figures. I prefer the recorded version, as its climax seems the natural end to 'flat-out-meanness'. However, in concert, the song is a group sport, and the dreamers are many. It is possible this ending provides a better conclusion for that setting. We are saved from the wordless horror of the real by comedy and Stag's ascendance to some form of Godhood. It seems to say, 'don't worry, it was a joke after all'.

Praise God for meanness

The song (and performance) Nick Cave and the Bad Seeds gives us is a nightmare, of sorts. But, as I hope to have shown, nightmares can be useful too. There is an everyday nightmare in the shadows, a burden of suffering we face in the simplest moments as we move through our day. Self-states are generated through our impact with objects that create these fleeting, unthought shadows. Murder ballads in any form (I would include gangster rap, death metal and other transgressive tunes in this boat) provide a means for us to process this; dream it, if you will. This does not tame meanness or do what I think Cave was hinting at when he disparaged the notion that art objects like 'Stagger Lee' are man-made (White 1996). Everything has a context, exists in a web connected to a multitude of things. Everything that reoccurs in art and discourse has a purpose, is a working through of something. Just writing that moves dangerously closer to the rationalizing of meanness, robbing it of its power by rendering it mundane. Some psychoanalytic writers stress that an aesthetic experience requires an unmediated immersion into the art object (see Spitz 1989). I suspect to receive the gift that nightmares afford us, we must in some way struggle against the tendency to render them mundane, to mediate the aesthetic impact by explaining away what shocks and moves the listener.

Cave himself seems to revel in singing nightmares. His career is dotted with blood-soaked artistic peaks. Prior to his more recent project Grinderman, Cave took a more romantic turn after *Murder Ballads,* his music stepping away from the 'meanness' into a more personal, emotional space. Some might grumble that he has lost this need for 'meanness', been tamed and is now just a performer. I think this is wishful thinking, a way of arguing him away and the nightmares he brings, or to simply bemoan the fact that his art takes him away from just being a spinner of nightmares. Not to psychoanalyse Nick Cave, but (it is psychoanalytic cliché to say that any sentence that starts with no or not is a way to do the thing without having to own it), there is something gained by the singer in bringing nightmares into the world or revelling in vicarious 'flat-out-meanness'. One could go for the obvious and point out that his father was a man of words (an English teacher) and died at a key point in his life. Maybe Cave is building a bridge to his father in songs like this, lacing them with anger and transgression in the hopes of some answer, be it recognition, damnation or restitution? The loss of a father demands nothing less from a child and these demands are insatiable, even in song. The Oedipal dynamics seem clear in the song, and Cave chose to record it as an 'afterthought', something that every psychoanalyst knows signals words unbidden, uncensored and closer to the truth (White 1996). But then, I am not going to psychoanalyse Mr Cave.

There are also cultural components only hinted at by what I write. The Stagger Lee narrative arose from African-American folklore and bears the stamp of a people torn by slavery and oppression. In that sense, Stagger Lee is the embodiment of wounded but unbroken human will. There are even larger cultural contexts. There seems a growing ubiquity to violence and sexual violence, at least in western culture as the rise of gangster rap and sadism in film (horror movies abound with 'torture porn') seem to imply. It has entered the public discourse in a way that is historically significant. It seems to be no longer repressed. The bar on transgression has been raised as well. I could speculate that both a broadening of awareness coupled with an increasingly, possibly overly empathic society (at least, that is what right-leaning politicians might argue as they rail against the 'socialist nanny state') requires bigger nightmares for balance. The demand from society to be happy may generate longer shadows. This might also signal a consequence of the need for 'meanness' in a post-patriarchal world. If our fathers are gone or, as in 'Stagger Lee', they are ill-equipped to deal with violence (the barkeep) or simply rendered passive (Billy), then we need Stagger Lee and his ilk even more to plumb the depths and speak our unthought knowns. Praise God for meanness.

References

Adorno, Theodor (1998), *Beethoven: The Philosophy of Music,* ed. by Rolf Tiedemann, trans. by Edmund Jephcott, Palo Alto, CA: Stanford University Press, p. xi.

Aron, Lewis, and Adrienne Harris (2005), *Relational Psychoanalysis, Vol. II: Innovation and Expansion*, Hillsdale, NJ: The Analytic Press.

Bollas, Christopher (1978), 'The Aesthetic Moment and the Search for Transformation', *The Annual of Psychoanalysis*, 6, Madison, CT: International Universities Press, pp. 385–94.

—— (1987), *The Shadow of the Object: Psychoanalysis of the Unthought Known*, New York: Columbia University Press.

Boorman, John (1972), *Deliverance*, Burbank, CA: Warner Brothers.

Bromberg, Philip M. (2001), *Standing in the Spaces: Essays on Clinical Process Trauma and Dissociation*, London: Routledge.

Brown, Cecil (2003), *Stagolee Shot Billy*, Cambridge, MA: Harvard University Press.

Cave, Nick and the Bad Seeds (2004), 'Stagger Lee', live performance (Brixton 2004) uploaded to YouTube on 13 February 2008, http://www.youtube.com/watch?v=IYyl78qQPVI. Accessed on 7 July 2011.

Freud, Sigmund (1997), *Writings on Art and Literature*, Stanford, CA: Stanford University Press.

Grotstein, James S. (2009), 'Dreaming as a "Curtain of Illusion": Revisiting the "Royal Road" with Bion as Our Guide', *International Journal of Psychoanalysis*, 90, Oxford: Wiley, pp. 733–52.

Kernberg, Otto F. (1994), *Internal World and External Reality: Object Relations Theory Applied*, New Jersey: Jason Aronson.

Meloy, J. Reid (1998), *The Psychopathic Mind: Origins, Dynamics and Treatment*, New Jersey: Jason Aronson.

Ramachandran, V. S. (2011), *The Tell-tale Brain: A Neuroscientist's Quest for What Makes Us Human*, New York: Norton.

Roberts, John W. (1983), 'Stackolee and the Development of a Black Heroic Idea', *Western Folklore*, 23, University of Colorado, Boulder, pp. 179–90.

Schore, Allan N. (1994), *Affect Regulation and the Origin of the Self: The Neurobiology of Emotional Development*, Hillsdale, NJ: L. Erlbaum.

Skov, Martin (2009), *Neuroaesthetics (Foundations and Frontiers of Aesthetics)*, Amityville, NY: Baywood.

Spitz, Ellen Handler (1989), *Art and Psyche: A Study on Psychoanalysis and Aesthetics*, New Haven, CT: Yale University Press.

Wepman, Dennis, Ronald Newman and Murray Binderman (1986), *The Life: Lore and Folk Poetry of the Black Hustler*, Los Angeles, CA: Holloway House.

White, Nick (1996), 'Stagger Lee: NC Interview and List', http://www.bad-seed.org/~cave/info/songs/mb_staggerlee.html. Accessed 7 July 2011.

PART III

Film and Theatre

Chapter 7

'You Won't Want the Moment to End': Nick Cave in the Theatre, from *King Ink* to Collaborating with Vesturport

Karoline Gritzner

This chapter explores Nick Cave's distinctive compositions for the theatrical stage. To date, Cave has composed the music and song lyrics for a stage adaptation of Franz Kafka's novella *Metamorphosis* (2006), a production of Georg Büchner's modernist classic *Woyzeck* (2005), and Goethe's *Faust* (2010). All of them were performed by the Icelandic physical theatre company Vesturport Theatre. In what follows, I will examine the extent to which these theatre productions are informed by Nick Cave's music aesthetic, discuss Cave as an experimental playwright, and touch on the theatrical nature of his music and live performances.

Nick Cave is one of popular culture's iconic figures and a remarkably multitalented artist. As musician, singer-songwriter and frontman of various rock bands (The Birthday Party, Bad Seeds and Grinderman), his music career has spanned over three decades. He is also the author of two novels (the acclaimed *And the Ass Saw the Angel* and *The Death of Bunny Munro*), has written screenplays (for *Ghosts ... Of the Civil Dead* (1988) and *The Proposition* (2005)), various film soundtracks (most recently for the screen adaptation of McCarthy's *The Road*), and taken small acting roles in films. In recent years he has also developed a penchant for collaborative work in the theatre, in particular with Vesturport Theatre, who were awarded the prestigious European Theatre Prize in 2010.

Cave's music, one could argue, is permeated by a distinctive theatrical sensibility. Textually, many of his song lyrics contain stark and dazzling poetic imagery and dramatic storytelling features, such as the haunting presence of an authorial voice, which may appear seductive or aggressive, self-questioning and self-exposing, in intense dialogue with the listener or in self-absorbed melancholic solitude. As songwriter, musician and live performer, he has developed a style and creative vision that is eclectic and complex, ranging from the pleasure-pain expressivity of his early Gothic excesses (in the 1980s), to crooning religious love songs (1990s and 2000s), to the fantastical, autobiographical, absurd and hilarious (featuring in his more recent work with Grinderman). Whilst much of his music is expressive of a range of heightened emotions and abounds with themes of obsessive love, violent sex, murder, death, eroticism and the allure of evil, there is also a distinct religious sensibility to be found in his work, a longing for redemption, grace and peace. His brand of rock music might be described as romantic in an emphatic sense: a musical expression of 'dangerous emotions', to borrow a phrase from the American philosopher Alphonso Lingis, which is tinged with a tragic sensibility and affirms the irrationality of love and the power of desire as creative and healing but also (self-) destructive forces (Lingis 2000). Like all romantic art, this music and the poetic imagination that informs it draw us closer to the unknown, inexplicable and extraordinary dimensions of life.

In live concert the expressive power of Cave's music and lyrics is heightened by the dialogic presence of a participating audience and Cave's performance. David Pattie has recently drawn attention to the creation of Cave's stage persona as a dramatic, obscure, self-conscious but also playfully ironic character (Pattie 2010: 224–41). The scenographic dramaturgies of his live shows often include the creation of floating shadows and colours, which add depth and layering to the stage space and give visual emphasis to Cave's movements.

Nick Cave, playwright of the 'real thing'

A more direct engagement with theatre emerged when Cave, after a number of contributions to the world of film, began to compose stage soundtracks and song lyrics for the Icelandic company Vesturport Theatre, in collaboration with his band member Warren Ellis. This was, however, not the first of Cave's direct encounters with the world of theatre. Cave wrote 50 one-act plays between 1980 and 1981, ten in collaboration with the American punk jazz and experimental rock singer-songwriter Lydia Lunch, and 40 on his own ('Hans' 2007). One of them, *Main Kelly and Me on a Bender*, was performed live by Lydia Lunch with The Swans at the White Columns gallery in NYC in May 1983 and recorded on the various artists' compilation album *Speed Trials* (Homestead Records, 1984). The other plays have so far remained unperformed. During this time Cave was working with The Birthday Party and developing a distinctively visceral energy in his songwriting, influenced by his studies of the 'brutal and jealous and merciless' Old Testament God. Cave says: '[s]o it was the feeling I got from the Old Testament, of a pitiful humanity suffering beneath a despotic God, that began to leak into my lyric writing. As a consequence my words blossomed with a nasty, new energy' (Cave 1997: 138).

His experimental work as a playwright is worth drawing attention to because it is yet another example of his wide-ranging literary talent (as has been evident, apart from the poetry of his song lyrics, in his novels and various essays). Entitled *Ugly Is as Ugly Does or The Dance of the 50 Cancers*, the plays are conceptions for an Artaudian theatre of cruelty, or a theatre of revenge, understood in a literal sense: they abound with physical violence, sadistic and masochistic urges, animalistic copulation, murder, excessive drinking, indecent slang, erotic and vulgar poetry ('Hans' 2007). Some of these plays were later published by Cave in *King Ink* (Cave 1988).

There is a distinctive preoccupation with self-mutilation in the context of religion, for example in *The Five Fools*, in which a 50-year-old priest cuts off his own fingers, one by one, as punishment for his sins. Cave's interest in the Old Testament narratives is also evident in his pared-down theatrical rendering of *Salomé*, which is divided into the scenes 'The Seven Veils', 'Dialogue with the Baptist', 'Salomé's Reward', 'The Chop' and, finally, 'The Platter'. The dialogue is a mixture of high-blown, archaic rhetoric: 'JOHN THE BAPTIST: Get thee behind me, Satan! A single strand of your hair would pollute the sacred Jordan river', and vulgar language: 'SALOMÉ: Suit yourself, dick breath!' (Cave 1988: 71).

The handful of plays that are set in the context of car racing and car maintenance is also distinctive. *Garbage Hearts*, for example, is composed of a short scene of quick copulation followed by a few words *'up against the garbage dumpster'*: 'GIRL: [*Pulls away*] I'm late for work and I am a waitress in a truck shop. What about you? BOY: [*In blue jeans and a t-shirt, turns his face to light*] Nothing' (Cave 1988: 60). In addition to engaging a range of gender stereotypes, the self-performances in these theatrical contexts of cars, sex and speed draw attention to language and evoke a consciousness of mortality. *Golden-Horn-Hooligan* is a monologue performed on the bonnet of a *'big-golden-hot-rod-car'*:

> I am Golden-Horn Hooligan. [*He rolls the words in his mouth*] Golden … Horn … Hooligan … I've got a girl, best on the track, dark eyes and a sweater saying Golden-Horn-Hooligan and a red dress that goes swish-swish when she walks and I got Pope-Panther, my car, fastest and leanest around […] But I'm feeling something now, something strange when I'm driving that circle … hot breath on the back of my neck […] saying, 'FLY' or … or maybe 'DIE', and sometimes I hear 'SPEED' and then it gets to sounding like 'BLEED' or 'FAST' that becomes 'LAST' that becomes 'GOLDEN-HORN-HOOLIGAN … THIS IS THE LAST'
>
> (Cave 1988: 61)

Cave's experimental attitude is most striking in those short plays that are entirely made up of stage directions, which confront the performer and the audience's imagination with the physically impossible. The action of *Gun Play #3*, for example, consists of a man and a woman spinning and stumbling around on the stage until the woman *'makes a gay little bee-line toward the young man'*, who in turn *'jams a Colt 45 into her mouth and blows off the back of her head'* (1988: 57). All of this to the cheerful tune of 'Pretty Woman'. In Cave's original manuscript, this play is entitled *Spin the Bullet* and forms the first part of the trilogy *Silent But Deadly* ('Hans' 2007). It was subsequently published as *Gun Play # 3* in *King Ink* (Cave 1988: 57).

Another example of extreme physical action is found in *Untitled (mutilation)*, which is part of the *Silent But Deadly* trilogy:

> [a]t three appropriate moments throughout performance, a sickly green light illuminates, for 10–15 seconds, an ACTOR stript [*sic*] from the waist up. This should look not unlike the demonic apparitions of skeletons, monsters etc. one sees on the Ghost Train, spook houses, etc. at fun fairs. Using broken glass, scissors, screwdriver, powerdrill or any other instrument that is traditionally associated with violent self-abuse the man, in an upright position, mutilates himself. THIS MUST BE THE REAL THING. (no cheap theatrical tricks, o.k.)
>
> ('Hans' 2007)

The explicit emphasis on 'real' performance as opposed to 'fake' theatricality belongs to the discourse of Live Art and Body Art, which emerged in the 1960s and 1970s. Performance artists' critique of representation and their rejection of theatrical illusion led to experiments with the live body (often the artist's own body) as a direct medium of expression. Live art performance tends to employ and explore the body as artistic material, for example as a canvas in the blood-letting performance work of Franko B, or in Orlan's post-cosmetic surgery performances. (For a discussion of body art with references to the work of Orlan, see Amelia Jones (1998). For documentation of the work of Franko B, see Lois Keidan and Stuart Morgan (2000)).

With strikingly similar intentions, Cave's theatre experiments also explore the 'explicit body in performance' (Rebecca Schneider), and in doing so they challenge our imagination and the dominant social norms. Drawing on the Freudian concept of the uncanny, Schneider speaks of the 'threat of literality' inherent in transgressive body performance. 'If the threat of literality is relative to the fear of the uncanny, then for the patriarchal imagination there is nothing more literal and threatening to the prerogatives of the Symbolic Order than the sight (seeing back) of the female genitalia' (Schneider 1997: 82).

The explicit and transgressive nature of these texts is akin to the Gothic excesses expressed by Cave in recordings such as The Birthday Party's *Mutiny!* and the Bad Seeds' *From Her to Eternity* (1984). Cave's confrontational aesthetics during this period emphasize expression and affect: a darkly surreal, insatiable imagination unsettles the audience with images and visions of danger, excess, violence and explicit sexuality.

Cave's early experiments with the medium of theatre, albeit not realized in actual productions, should nevertheless be considered as significant, if eccentric, contributions to a distinctive theatrical sensibility, which he has more recently continued to develop in his collaborative work with co-band member Warren Ellis. The music and lyrics they contributed to Vesturport Theatre productions contain many recognizably Cavean aesthetic qualities, combining motifs of romantic love, excessive emotions and visceral sensuality with dark humour, melancholy longing and moments of spiritual darkness.

For many decades, Cave has explored the love song as a powerful musical form that has the potential to make the listener sensitive to the contradictory forces of love, the tensions between pleasure and pain, loss and longing, and love's capacity to transform ordinary reality into something extraordinary, akin to the sacred. The love song, according to Nick Cave, brings us closer to God: 'ultimately the Love Song exists to fill, with language, the silence between ourselves and God, to decrease the distance between the temporal and the divine' (Cave 2007: 11). An interest in the sacred and the divine has been central to Cave's artistic vision for many decades.

Even the violent eroticism of his short plays contains religious dimensions; like most of his music in the 1980s, they are inspired by themes and ideas of the Old Testament, especially its presentation of God as a jealous, menacing and vengeful force. As Cave explains in his talk 'The Flesh Made Word', his early music and songwriting for The Birthday Party was inspired by the 'cruel and rancorous God' of the Old Testament (Cave 1997: 138). When he began his period of romantic songwriting, Cave's sacred vision became mellower and less explicit, more melancholy and religious than raw and sexual. Cave's sacred vision is, as Lyn McCredden has argued, 'the inescapable, incarnate force of the divine', and his songs, in typical Christian fashion, evoke the bodily appearance of the divine – 'the word made flesh' (McCredden 2009: 170). But Cave also shows how the spiritual essence of the body is manifest in its erotic, violent and poetic form. Music and theatre provide suitable mediums for the performance of Cave's romantic sacred vision, which embraces the contradictions of human passion, the intractable connections between pleasure and pain. As will be discussed below, the tragic sensibility of his love songs, their melancholic tone and contradictory fusions of joy and pain are also manifest in his collaborations with Vesturport Theatre.

Woyzeck – 'Everybody knows that everybody dies, but me'

Vesturport's *Woyzeck* had its premiere at the Barbican Theatre, London, in October 2010. Their adaptation of Georg Büchner's nineteenth-century masterpiece, left unfinished due to the poet's early death, brings into focus the key elements of this tragic tale of love, deception and murder. In this version, the play's anti-hero, Woyzeck, is a disadvantaged,

Figure 1: Marie and the Drum Major in Vesturport's *Woyzeck* (Photo: Eddie Jonsson).

abused, poor and mentally unstable factory worker who struggles to keep down a job to support his lover Marie and their child. Marie begins an affair with the better-looking and financially more successful Drum Major (in this production a factory owner). Woyzeck is distraught and murders her in a fit of jealousy before committing suicide by drowning. The play's dramaturgical juxtapositions between the main characters' deceptively plain language, reified appearances and outbursts of intense emotionality are heightened by the production's physical approach to characterization, space and movement. Where expression falters, verbal language is superseded by the irrational violence of extreme physical action. The production emphasizes the anti-hero's isolation and confusion by separating him from a chorus of factory members and other citizens, and Cave's music and lyrics emphasize his loneliness, alienation and longing: repetitive chants of the chorus implore the anti-hero to transgressive action. Büchner's original play already envisions the inclusion of powerful musical elements in the famous dance scene during which Woyzeck encounters his rival. The production effectively heightens the existential and dizzying weight of this scene through the use of repetitive musical themes and the endless twisting and turning of bodies outside and inside a big glass-fronted pool of water that dominates the stage space. The production's key element is water, which functions in turn as a medium of cleansing, lovemaking, danger and death. After having murdered Marie, Woyzeck submerges her body in the water – which turns red – before he drowns himself. Woyzeck's anger and frustration, the mental and physical exhaustion, which shows on his tortured body, his entrapment and desperate attempt to understand – all these facets are suggested primarily in physical and musical terms.

Vesturport's adaptation is characterized by an extreme physicality (bodies swimming and being drowned in water; the use of ropes on which actors swing, suspended over the heads of the audience; fights between Woyzeck and the Drum Major). The darkness of the story's universe is underscored by the use of dim lighting, grey shadows, blue colours and Cave's haunting, melancholy musical score, which creates an atmosphere of danger, violence, seduction and hopeless longing. The key songs express the play's conceptual leitmotifs: love, suffering, death and a sense of tragic inevitability. At one point Woyzeck sings a waltz, accompanied by a choir of workers:

O Marie O Marie
Life is full of trouble and woe
O Marie O Marie
It is everywhere you go
O Marie O Marie
It is in the falling snow
O Marie O Marie
It's in the ebb and in the flow

And I know that life goes on, dear
And I know that life goes on and on

And I know that life goes on, dear
And I know that you are the only one

(Büchner 2005: 25)

Cave's soundtrack is lyrical and elegiac for the most part, making effective, haunting uses of the waltz rhythm and the single violin (expressing solitude and tender longing). Poignantly simple, repetitive lyrics underscore the romantic and sensitive, sad moments in the play (e.g., when Marie is given a bunch of red roses by the Drum Major and Woyzeck arrives with his small, less impressive collection of plain wild flowers – this is the tragic moment of realization that he has lost the only love of his life). An entertainer performs another melancholic song. Again, it expresses an existentialist, world-weary attitude that nevertheless contains aspects of resistance or at least wilful ignorance (rejection of the reality of one's own death):

In this world we can't abide,
We know we all must die
Everybody knows why.

Everybody knows
Everybody sees
That everybody dies
But me.

The day has come
For all to swing high
You'll think you're the one
That will never die.

Everybody knows
And everyone agrees
That everybody dies
But me

(Büchner 2005: 30)

The production also contains a number of songs which are performed in the theatricalized style of live rock concerts. Immediately following Woyzeck's woeful 'O Marie', the arrival of the Drum Major is announced with flash lighting, loud music and the performer appearing suspended in the air, swinging on a rope above the stage and reaching out towards the auditorium. The actors who accompany him wear stylish black suits and dark sunglasses, as does the seducer himself, who in his performance imitates Cave's distinctive vocals. He literally appears like a dark angel from above and captures everybody's attention, especially Marie's: she seems mesmerized and deeply impressed by the man's powerful (and flashy) entry. The lyrics, electric guitars and relentless drum beats establish a raw, gothic, highly energized atmosphere reminiscent of songs such as 'Tupelo' from the album *The Firstborn is Dead* (1985):

DRUM MAJOR (*Singing.*)
I am the Drum Major!
Come gather around!
A better Drum Major
Will never be found!

I ride on the thunder!
I pound on my drum!
When I spin my big baton
All the little girls come!

ALL (*Singing.*)
He is the Drum Major! White gloves and high hat!
With a rat-a-tat! A-rat-a-tat! A-rat-a-tat-tat-tat!

(Büchner 2005: 26)

In keeping with the play's emphasis on human suffering and the visceral sentiments of Cave's rock music, the production's performance style foregrounds sexual pleasure and physical pain. The love scene between Marie and the Drum Major is, unsurprisingly, given elaborate emphasis and creates heightened tension. The Cavean dark seducer, the Drum Major, entices Marie with his low voice and suave sounds and movements, and she joins him in song in an emotional expression of love. This love duet is given a central place in the play and brings to mind some of Cave's statements about the love song as a vehicle for transformation and communication with a higher power that connects those who are in love (see Cave 2007: 1–19). The affair offers them a temporary escape from the mundane daily grind that the workers, especially Woyzeck, have to contend with in this hell of soul-destroying labour.

One also detects a comic theatricality in this particular love song and scene. The Drum Major performs a magic trick for Marie as he makes two big white roses appear from the water, lifts them out and uses them as microphones in his performance of the love song. He occupies the stage by swaying like a loved-up predator, a sex god, the eternal seducer, and even strips down to his underpants in a comic-heroic gesture of total abandon for his beloved object of desire. Marie joins in this romantic, musical love duet, and they consummate their carnal passion in the water tank, on the same spot where later on Marie will succumb to Woyzeck's possessive mad-struck and deadly embrace – his extreme, desperate gesture of (broken) love. The love song, even its melodramatic rendering in this particular scene, also reminds us of the inescapable pull of human desire and passion, the circle of love, life

Figure 2: Marie's death in Vesturport's *Woyzeck* (Photo: Eddi Jonsson).

and death, which science cannot explain (in both the play and the production the Doctor appears as a grotesque, idealistic, 'mad' type).

'The Flesh Made Word'

Sacred theatre is a theatre that wounds, as Carl Lavery has compellingly argued with reference to the work of Jean Genet (Lavery 2007: 127–50, 192–3). It evokes an aesthetic experience of spatial and temporal dislocation. The driving force of sacred theatre is the principle of uncertainty and ambiguity, which encroaches upon consciousness and disrupts the ego's epistemological certainties. Theatre produced in this vein creates shock effects, startling images, sounds and movements that produce powerful responses in the spectator. Cave's music produces similar effects and, one could argue, thereby engages the listener in an experience of the sacred; he uses music as a means to make God's presence felt in the secular world, as he argues in his lecture on the love song (Cave 2007: 1–19). Many of his love songs are indeed invocations of the divine; a good example being 'Into My Arms' on the album *The Boatman's Call* (1997). Linked to the sacred is an experience of theatricality, as Lavery suggests:

[t]his focus on presence and absence, on being there and elsewhere, is an intensely theatrical experience, and to that degree 'the ontology of performance' might well be an 'ontology of the sacred': the thing that binds actors, audiences and spaces together – the thing, that is, which wounds us.

(Lavery 2007: 192)

The emotional intensity of Cave's poetry and songs is given added emphasis in the context of theatrical performance. As Lyn McCredden has pointed out, in Cave's work the sacred is not opposed to, but intrinsically intertwined with, the profane, with the 'human dimensions of flesh, erotics and violence', and in the materiality of the theatre his lyric writing seems to find a natural home (McCredden 2009: 167). But theatre always provides more than a straightforward translation of words and ideas into images and movement, of ideas into flesh or concepts into rhythms. Cave reverses the central principle of Christian spirituality, that of incarnation ('the word made flesh'), into 'the flesh made word' and thereby articulates the phenomenological basis of his own aesthetic practice. The flesh, the body and its sensations and emotionality, coins the 'word' (the poetic image), which in itself is an embodied aesthetic figure. This is also how language operates in the theatre. However, the theatrical image or figure harbours within it an exaggeration: that which is shown gives expression to a 'more', an excess to the appearing image. Art, the aesthetic expression, insists on this 'more than'; it is what constitutes art's ontological difference from life, from empirical reality, whilst of course establishing a relationship to the world. (See Adorno on the notion of 'more than' as a central aesthetic quality and effect (Adorno 1997: 78)).

In his essay 'The Flesh Made Word', Cave describes his relationship to art in the following terms: 'art had the power to insulate me from the mundanity of the world, to protect me' (1997: 137). In Cave's view, the creative imagination is literally 'God-like' and can be perceived both as a defence against the world and as a creative channel for the divine; the notion that in a spiritually empty world God's presence is kept alive in art and in love is central to Cave's music where love and eroticism often feature as a redemptive force: 'God is gone. We got to get a new one/Not lock Him down in cathedrals and cages/I found the eternal woman/The fire that leapt from Solomon's pages' (2007: 298).

Rock performance à la Cave

Vesturport's productions include live rock performances where the characters are transformed, on stage, into rock singers and musicians, the lead actor often modelled on Nick Cave himself. These are interesting moments in these productions because they change the theatre event into a live rock music event for the duration of the song, after which the theatrical illusion of the plotline is resumed. As David Pattie argues, with reference to Simon Frith's work on popular music (and touching on the relation between music and identity):

a good rock performance must contain a central contradiction – that it must be '4 real', both constructed and authentic, both theatrical and spontaneous; but that the theatrical, constructed elements of the performance always exist in opposition to that which is authentic and spontaneous, while at the same time those theatrical elements are subsumed within the spontaneity of the event.

(Pattie 1999)

The precise moments at which the theatrical narrative turns into a live rock music performance in each of the productions are revealing. In *Woyzeck,* the rock music event coincides with the effectively staged appearance of the seducer, the Drum Major. His exaggerated masculine energy and stylized sex appeal are emphasized in the rock performance during which he literally flies into the performance space on a swing suspended from the ceiling, thus occupying maximum space and attention for the audience below (the other characters and the spectators in the auditorium). Our gaze turns upwards to greet this spectacular, ironic performance by the irresistible Don Juan of love and rock music. This is also the moment where the live rock music performance (clearly carefully constructed and choreographed) produces an effect of authenticity which, I would argue, stems from its unpredictable, spontaneous occurrence as a meta-theatrical rupture of the plot development. The insertion of a live rock music event within the larger theatre event that is *Woyzeck* is a comment on the play's preoccupation with the question of the 'real' as it is experienced by the narrative's central characters Woyzeck and Marie. We are reminded of Cave's precocious instruction, 'no theatrical tricks, o.k.', from his experimental playwriting during the 1980s. Cave's music adds to the theatre performance a dimension of authenticity and spontaneity which, as Pattie suggests, the audience accept as something that is simultaneously staged (aesthetically constructed) yet '4 real'.

Metamorphosis: 'Could he really be an animal, if music affected him so deeply?'

Vesturport's *Metamorphosis* opened at the Lyric Hammersmith, London, in September 2006. In accordance with their signature performance style, Vesturport's adaptation of Franz Kafka's novella uses a physical theatre approach to embody the themes of surprise, horror and abjection. A family's ordered, bourgeois normality is suddenly disturbed one day when the son of the house, the conscientious travelling salesman Gregor Samsa, begins to notice strange changes in his body. He fails to get up to go to work in the morning, which comes as a shock to the family. He starts speaking a language they do not understand and his voice hurts their ears. Gradually, his transformation into a strange kind of insect becomes a nightmarish reality for all concerned. In the production, the metamorphosis from human to animal is suggested in terms of distortions of space, body and movement. The stage setting consists of a two-tier structure, with a living room on the ground level and Gregor's bedroom on the upper level. In his room, which becomes a dreadful no-go area for the family members, the furniture is

Figure 3: The stage setting of Vesturport's *Metamorphosis* (Photo: Eddi Jonsson).

arranged in such a way as to offer a top-down perspective. Gregor's body language and movements take on insect-like features: he jumps from furniture to furniture, crawls on the walls and ceiling, suspends himself and swings, performing in the typical company acrobatic style. Vesturport thus effectively capture the irruption of an alien, uncanny, grotesque force into the predictability of daily life. Being hurled into a Kafkaesque world of abjection, transformation and insecurity, the central question becomes what it means to be human.

Walter Benjamin's interpretation of Kafka focuses on the importance of the gesture in the novelist's work (Benjamin 1999: 108–35). In stories such as *Metamorphosis* it is the 'animal gesture' that performs a kind of fictional ambiguity and dramatizes a collapse of boundaries. Kafka was, as Benjamin states, interested in man's condition of exile – from the world as well as from his own body (1999: 122). Man's disconnection from the world around him and even from his own body may create a longing for salvation or at least for some kind of transformation or mystery, which opens up before the self like a secret and a question. Music plays a central role in this process and it is part of the narrative of the novella as well as the theatrical adaptation.

Gregor's sister's musical talent, which is in danger of going to waste as a result of the family's entirely materialistic ambitions, remains a focus, inspiration and concern for Gregor. Music seems to carry him through his dejected condition where he has to contend with vicious verbal abuse (he is referred to as 'vermin') and repeated physical attacks. When his sister finally begins to play the violin again, Gregor is mesmerized by the sound and interprets it as a sign of hope, which might at last help him to come to terms with his transformation. But in fact this pure moment of bliss tragically coincides with his deterioration – his body is shaking vigorously, he is literally in the process of dying, yet captured by the beauty of her music. This bittersweet moment of musical pleasure creates a temporal shift, or crack, in the narrative and the play's action. It invites the invisible figure of the infinite to appear and suggests, after Schlegel, that 'music is most of all longing' (Bowie 2007: 92).

'Could he really be an animal, if music affected him so deeply? He felt as if he were being shown the way to that food he so longed for without knowing what it was' (Kafka 1981: 136). The emotional power of this scene is evoked by Cave and Ellis' melancholy string composition. Most of the soundtrack for the production takes the form of atmospheric background music, which supports the melancholy pain that Gregor experiences yet is unable to articulate. Through music the 'way to the unknown', which the novella's narrator refers to, is given a conceptual and emotional expression. The family's decision to 'get rid' of the creature by refusing him food is radical but disturbingly explicable in the context of their growing fear of social exclusion and may be, as hinted at in the production, a sinister manifestation of fascist tendencies.

Eventually Gregor, who has become fully aware of other people's aversion to him, commits suicide by hanging himself. Whilst this is experienced as a relief for his parents and sister, the audience are left with a sense that Gregor's suffering and death are an allegory of the fate that awaits other people who are labelled as 'social vermin' in totalitarian societies. Upon encountering the dead body, the play's nuclear family decide that they need time alone 'as a family'. A 'ditch outside town', crawling with rats, is suggested as a possible resting place for the body; and finally the decision is made to let the past be and venture out into nature. Kafka writes: '[a]fterwards the three of them left the flat together, which was something they had not done for months, and took the tram out into the country. They had the carriage to themselves, and it was full of warmth and sunlight' (1981: 145).

David Farr and Gísli Örn Gardarsson's sensitive adaptation fills the last moments of the play with visually sumptuous images of vibrantly colourful flowers, to suggest the family's outing to a beautiful garden outside of town. This garden takes shape in what used to be Gregor's prison-like room, but now becomes a visual depiction of their new dreams and hopes for the future, embodying the daughter's tranformation into a beautiful young woman who is confident about the future. This highly theatrical metamorphosis of the dark room into a paradisal flower garden is underlined by the haunting melodies of Cave and Ellis' music, a tender song with Cave's lyrics about butterflies and daffodils. The show ends with the image of the daughter on a swing in front of a backdrop of flowers, her proud parents next to her, throwing flower petals in the air. The flowers fall down gently onto Gregor's body, which has been dropped into the lower half of the set. He is now a dark shape limply hanging on a red rope, eerily echoing the youthful body on a swing on the upper level, which is bathed in beautiful colours.

Cave's songs, like 'People Ain't No Good' (1997), often speak about the falseness and corrupt nature of the world, and the particular use of music in this final scene enhances the contradictory double-nature of the image: a sacrificed body in darkness juxtaposed with the hopeful spirits (or dangerous delusions) of a re-united bourgeois family. Gregor, like many of Cave's own fictional characters, has struggled but finally come to terms with his alienation from other people; and music, again, functions as a medium in this tragic process of overcoming. If one can speak of a metaphysical thrust in Cave's music, it is a metaphysics experienced as a result of a return to bodily reality and one's surrender to the magnetism of sensation. In Cave's music, the imagination only takes flight (reaches beyond the real) as a result of this return to the flesh. Redemption can also only be imagined as involving either the acceptance of death or the love of the other: as an uncompromising and far-reaching experience of the world, not as a Gnostic rejection of it.

Faust : 'You won't want the moment to end'

More recently, Vesturport, Cave and Ellis took on Goethe's famous 1808 play about the transient nature of all earthly appearance and man's desire to discover the meaning of existence. The premiere of Vesturport's production of *Faust* was at Reykjavik City Theatre on 15 January 2010. They performed their show at the Young Vic in London in September and October 2010.

Being self-consciously set in the theatre (Goethe's play contains a prelude in which a director, poet and spectator engage in discussions about theatre), it is also a comment on the theatricality of life, the many masks people wear and the roles they perform, wittingly and unwittingly. As Goethe wrote:

> All things corruptible
> Are but a parable;
> Earth's insufficiency
> Here finds fulfilment;
> Here the ineffable
> Wins life through love;
> Eternal Womanhood
> Leads us above

(1959: 288)

This seems to be an apt summary of Cave's objectives and the effects of his music in the elusive present moment, the 'here and now', which the theatre event draws attention to. Goethe's masterpiece is the perfect dramatic text to undergo a Cavean treatment, as Vesturport's production shows. Central to Goethe's tragic drama is Faust's energetic pursuit of self-knowledge and self-exploration in varying contexts of danger and crisis; his obsession

Figure 4: Faust and his tempters in Vesturport's *Faust* (Photo: Grimur Bjarnason).

with Gretchen, which leads to moments of ecstasy and pain in equal measure; his pact with the devil and his moral transgressions. Employing the passionate energy and tender longing of Cave and Ellis' music, Vesturport bring into focus all of these elements whilst also adding an important layer of grotesque, comic and evil action.

Set in an old people's nursing home on Christmas Eve, Vesturport's adaptation tells the story of Johann, a retired actor who has played all of the stage's best-known dramatic characters, except for the iconic role of Faust. Despairing of life and full of regret for lost opportunities, the old man is about to commit suicide when he is interrupted by a trio of dark spirits from the underworld: the wisecracking Mefisto and his devilish company, who tempt him back to life with their promise of manifold earthly pleasures. Mefisto offers him the most exquisite experiences possible in exchange for Johann's soul when he dies, on Johann's condition that he would surrender himself only when the experience is so intense that he wishes to stay in the moment forever.

If to the fleeting hour I say
'Remain, so sweet though art, remain!'
Then bind me with your fatal chain,
For I will perish in that day.

'Tis I for whom the bell shall toll,
Then you are free, your service done.
For me the clock shall fail, to ruin run,
And timeless night descend upon my soul

(Goethe 1949: 87)

Vesturport's Mefisto agrees, slyly predicting that '[y]ou won't want the moment to end'. Having signed the pact in blood, Johann is encouraged by the devils to 'say goodbye to your old self and hello to life' and undergoes a magical transformation of body and soul: he has become a young Faust and thus begins a (theatrical) dreamlike journey of experience and sensation.

Structurally, Vesturport's retelling of *Faust* shows a number of literary influences, namely Jorge Luis Borges' short story *The Secret Miracle* and Bulgakov's magical realist novel *The Master and Margarita* in which the plot also appears as a dream-like experience and the reader is left uncertain as to the 'reality' of the characters' experiences. As with *Woyzeck* and *Metamorphosis*, the company's approach to adaptation incorporates Cave and Ellis' soundtrack to draw out the emotional force of certain visual and poetic images, physical movements and spatial rhythms. Faustian desire is shown in action, and a lot of it bears the imprint of Cave's aesthetic and lyric imagination: the relentless search for new experiences, the erotic longing, the excessive need for self-transformation, the transgression of moral and social limits, and ultimately the readiness to come face to face with evil. The search for love and happiness can never be satisfied; it goes on and on and on to the dizzying, explosive rhythms of Cave's rock music scores, especially in the Walpurgis-night scene involving Mefisto's chorus of witches and other malicious spirits.

The spirit world in *Faust* is evoked by actors swinging above the stage and auditorium on a huge suspended net. Vesturport's signature acrobatic style is crucial to the success of this production and Cave and Ellis provide a soundtrack that colours the scenes in an almost cinematic style. There are only two occasions where the audience's attention is self-consciously drawn to the music. One of them is the rock concert performance in the Walpurgis-night scene in which the characters become musicians and background singers, supporting a frontman who is modelled on Cave's stage persona himself. The song is entitled 'I am Evil' and is performed with explosive energy, stark lighting and colour effects.

The other key moment of heightened musical and theatrical force is the love scene between Faust and Gretchen in which both actors perform a gentle, romantic dance in the air, suspended on ropes swinging from the ceiling. Their floating movements and loving embraces are accompanied by a simple, melancholy melody on piano and strings. This is the leitmotif of the whole production, Cave's sacred love song, which is briefly introduced at the beginning of the performance and then re-occurs at specific moments throughout the play. It captures the emotional intensity and melancholy tenderness of the lovers' encounter without the need for words, because words cannot express it, suggesting at once the power and fragility of this moment of romantic union. Faust's brief awareness of what seems like eternal bliss can only be captured in music and, as one of the dark spirits predicts: 'love will hunt you down'.

Figure 5: Love dance in the air in Vesturport's *Faust* (Photo: Grimur Bjarnason).

Robert Eaglestone says of Cave's music that it paradoxically expresses the 'inexpressible mysteries we find in the world' (2009: 149). The theatrical projects that Cave has collaborated on are based on literary and dramatic source texts that already contain strongly Cavean sentiments, as has been argued here. Ultimately, it is the source texts' spirit of romanticism and Kafka's surrealism that communicate so powerfully with Cave's artistic vision and imagination. Cave's music and lyrics add a crucial third perspective to these plays, one that reaches further into the unknown than text, spectacle, movement and spatial exploration could achieve on their own. Music produces sensations that reach beyond representation and meaning, beyond any reductive literal rendering of experience or figurative depiction. Essentially, Cave's music – at times imploringly tender or violently arresting – enhances the theatrical event by turning it into an experience of intensity that makes us sense what Deleuze and Guattari call affect: 'the effectuation of a power of the pack that throws the self into upheaval and makes it reel' (Deleuze and Guattari 2004: 265).

(I would like to thank 'Hans' for access to a selection of Cave's unpublished plays, and Vesturport Theatre for providing the production photos.)

References

Adorno, Theodor W. (1997), *Aesthetic Theory*, trans. by Robert Hullot-Kentor, London: Athlone.

Benjamin, Walter (1999), *Illuminations*, trans. by Harry Zorn, London: Pimlico.

Bowie, Andrew (2007), *Music, Philosophy, and Modernity*, Cambridge: Cambridge University Press.

Büchner, Georg (2005), *Woyzeck*, adapted by Gísli Örn Gardarsson, lyrics by Nick Cave, London: Oberon.

Cave, Nick (1988), *King Ink*, Black Spring.

—— (1997), 'The Flesh Made Word', *King Ink II*, Black Spring Press, pp. 137–42.

—— (2007), 'The Secret Life of the Love Song', *The Complete Lyrics 1978–2007*, London: Penguin, pp. 1–19.

Deleuze, Gilles and Félix Guattari (2004), *A Thousand Plateaus: Capitalism and Schizophrenia*, London: Continuum.

Eaglestone, Robert (2009), 'From Mutiny to Calling upon the Author: Cave's Religion', in Karen Welberry and Tanya Dalziell (eds), *Cultural Seeds: Essays on the Work of Nick Cave*, Farnham: Ashgate, pp. 139–52.

Goethe, Johann Wolfgang von (1949), *Faust Part One*, trans. by Philip Wayne, Harmondsworth: Penguin.

—— (1959), *Faust Part Two*, trans. by Philip Wayne, Harmondsworth: Penguin.

'Hans' (2007), 'The Birthday Party (London 1st March 1980–August 1983) Bibliography (II)', http://www.fromthearchives.com/bp/bibliography2.html. Accessed 26 August 2011.

Jones, Amelia (1998), *Body Art: Performing the Subject*, Minneapolis: University of Minnesota Press.

Kafka, Franz (1981), *Franz Kafka: Stories 1904–1924*, trans. by J. A. Underwood, London: Macdonald.

Keidan, Lois and Stuart Morgan (2000), *Franko B*, London: Black Dog.

Lavery, Carl (2007), 'Genet's Sacred Theatre: Practice and Politics', in Ralph Yarrow (ed.), *Sacred Theatre*, Bristol: Intellect, pp. 127–43.

Lingis, Alphonso (2000), *Dangerous Emotions*, Berkeley, CA: University of California Press.

McCredden, Lyn (2009), 'Fleshed Sacred: The Carnal Theologies of Nick Cave', in Karen Welberry and Tanya Dalziell (eds), *Cultural Seeds: Essays on the Work of Nick Cave*, Farnham: Ashgate, pp. 167–86.

Pattie, David (1999), '4 Real: Authenticity, Performance, and Rock Music', *Enculturation, 2: 2*, http://enculturation.gmu.edu/2_2/pattie.html. Accessed 28 August 2011.

—— (2010), 'Saint Nick: A Parallax View of Nick Cave', in Karoline Gritzner (ed.), *Eroticism and Death in Theatre and Performance*, Hatfield: University of Hertfordshire Press, pp. 224–41.

Schneider, Rebecca (1997), *The Explicit Body in Performance*, London: Routledge.

Chapter 8

Welcome to Hell: Nick Cave and *Ghosts ... of the Civil Dead*

Rebecca Johinke

They dragged Jack and his shadow
From the hole
And the bulb that burned above him
Did shine both day and night
And his shadow learned to love his
Little darks and greater light
And the sun it shined [...]
A little stronger

(Cave 2007: 127)

Nick Cave loves films but not necessarily film-making. Cave's most significant contribution to the film industry is as a composer, musician and writer. He speaks enthusiastically about his passion for film and describes it as his favourite artistic medium. An avid watcher of movies, he relishes his periodic work behind the scenes contributing to scripts and soundtracks but he admits that he is less comfortable and convincing in front of the camera. His occasional forays into acting have not been hugely successful and have been confined to minor roles (often cameos) in 'art house' films. His performance as Maynard in John Hillcoat's *Ghosts ... of the Civil Dead* (1988 and hereafter cited as *Ghosts*) is generally recognized as his most convincing and memorable cinematic role. *Ghosts* was very positively reviewed but was not a commercial success and thus is often ignored, both in discussions about Cave's *oeuvre* and in more general discussions about Australian cinema. Its reformist agenda and on-screen violence (both explicit and implied) possibly deterred many people from seeing the film. In this chapter, I will argue that *Ghosts* is a film that deserves a larger audience and that Cave's contributions to the soundtrack and screenplay, as well as his bravura performance as the maniacal Maynard, warrant further critical attention. In addition to a comprehensive overview of the making of the film, I will make two main arguments about Cave's success as Maynard. The first builds on observations made by Adrian Danks (2009) about the theatrical power of Cave's voice. The second relates to Maynard's self-mutilation as a textual or rhetorical practice. (A note about attribution: the excellent 2003 DVD release of the film includes extensive interviews from 1988 and 2002 and a huge range of supplementary critical material. Unless otherwise stated, information about Cave and the making of the film comes from this source. In all other cases, additional sources are cited individually).

Given that Cave always surrounds himself with a group of musical and artistic collaborators, it is not surprising that film-makers (and friends) like John Hillcoat, Evan English and Paul Goldman have been an integral part of Cave's involvement in the film industry, starting with his early music videos for The Birthday Party. Although Cave's contribution to large-scale cinematic projects has been piecemeal, it is significant that it has been sustained over 30 years. (See Adrian Danks' 'Red Right Hand: Nick Cave and the Cinema' (2009) for an overview of Cave's forays into film-making and Amy Hanson's *Kicking Against the Pricks* (2005) for a complete rundown of Cave's film and television releases). He and long-term musical collaborators such as Warren Ellis, Mick Harvey and Blixa Bargeld have composed soundtracks for films such as Andrew Dominik's *The Assassination of Jesse James by the Coward Robert Ford* (2007) and Hillcoat's *To Have and to Hold* (1997), *The Proposition* (2005), *The Road* (2009) and, of course, *Ghosts*. Cave's cinematic *curriculum vitae* now looks impressive. Indeed, he even won a 2006 Gucci award for 'personalities outside the film industry who have made a remarkable artistic contribution to film over the past 18 months' (Dalziell and Welberry 2009: 2). This contribution looks set to continue given that, according to Internet sites like IMDB, Cave has two projects in development: *The Threepenny Opera* and *Death of a Ladies' Man* (an adaptation of Cave's recent novel *The Death of Bunny Munro*).

Australian Gothic and 'prison films'

Before I describe the making of *Ghosts*, I want to locate the film as Australian Gothic and as part of a genre of films called 'prison films'. The trope of Australia as a prison, the end of the earth, or as Hell, permeates Australian national literature, music and film. It is hardly surprising that Australia, as a penal colony, seeks to interrogate its colonial history in uncanny narratives about banishment, expulsion, purgatory and Hell. Ken Gelder (1998, 2007) and Gerry Turcotte (1998) have written extensively about representations of Australia as a Gothic (often uncanny) space and the liminal status of Aboriginal Australians in these texts. Rather than getting side-tracked about Gothic conventions here, I refer readers to their work (as sampled in my references). Suffice to say, the Gothic and grotesque gambol across Australian screens and canvases and these leitmotifs are, of course, familiar to consumers of Cave's work in all of its forms. As Roslynn Haynes argues, the Australian desert is often portrayed as a Gothic space in Australian film narratives (1998: 184–208). Both *Ghosts* and *The Proposition* are set in the desert. *The Proposition*, for example, positions Australia itself as Hell: a place that seems hotter than Hades and one that can only be tolerated by demons and 'savages' (always men). Most critics are quick to make the link between *The Proposition* and Cave's other work but *Ghosts* rarely rates a mention in these discussions. This is a disappointing oversight given that both films explore similar themes about crime, justice, imprisonment and mechanisms of power. While *The Proposition* mines the generic possibilities of the western, *Ghosts* revels in the conventions and clichés of the prison narrative. As Cave himself noted in a *Melody Maker* interview in 1988, he enjoys interrogating clichés (Reynolds 1988: 34). (Cave discusses this at some length on the 2003 *Ghosts* DVD). I will return to many of these points later in this chapter.

As one would expect, prison films are predominantly set inside prisons and deal with themes of justice, imprisonment, punishment, retribution and rehabilitation (Bennett 2006: 98; Nellis 1998: 2; O'Sullivan 2001: 319). Sadomasochism, homophobia and homoeroticism are also central to most prison narratives, as Sabine Büssing argues in *Of Captive Queens and Holy Panthers* (1990). More than merely a 'reflection' of prison life, prison narratives construct a reality about prisons and prisoners. As one recent study demonstrates, even prisoners watch prison films and their experience of incarceration is mediated through this viewing experience (Van den Bulck and Vandebosch 2003). However, as the film scholar and prison deputy governor Jamie Bennett contends, the audience for prison movies mostly comprises viewers who have no experience of prisons and rely on the media and narrative feature films for a mediated version of prison life, which in turn manufactures viewers' social constructions of (penal) reality (Bennett 2006: 97–9). One imagines that the same could be said for many film-makers, which suggests that the images of prisons traditionally seen on-screen are highly romanticized interpretations of prison life. As Nicole Rafter argues in *Shots in the Mirror: Crime Film and Society*, '[m]ovies of this type are essentially fantasies, films that purport to reveal the brutal realities of incarceration while actually offering viewers escape from the miseries of daily life through adventure and heroism' (2006: 163). As Rafter also explains, there is a long history of this escapist cinema, starting back in the silent-film era. In recent years, Frank Darabont has directed the two most commercially successful examples: *The Shawshank Redemption* (1994) and *The Green Mile* (1999). Stock features of classic prison films include the escape (often accompanied or preceded by a riot), and as in so many of these films the hero is an innocent man, this 'escape' (sometimes death) usually proves his innocence and exposes corruption and guilt in the system (2006: 166–7). Cut to the happy ending where we all feel good about good triumphing over evil.

Ghosts is not this kind of film. Instead, it can be located in a more recent subgenre of prison films with a harder political edge that attempt to give viewers a more realistic insight into the brutality of prison life and the broader political and economic conditions that perpetuate a system of locking up those who are already marginalized by race or socio-economic position. Often based on true stories and filmed in a documentary style (part of a rhetoric of authenticity), these reformist films provide a more challenging and elastic version of masculinity and there are few heroes or innocents on either side of the bars. These movies are much more honest about the sexual violence, brutality and the disproportionate number of minorities (especially black inmates) in the (western) prison population (2006: 174–85). They have a political agenda, not just an ambition to titillate or entertain. These films are far more subtle investigations about the power dynamics operating in western capitalist society and are often influenced by the work of Marx, Gramsci, Chomsky and Foucault. Having said that, even these reformist films engage with generic conventions in order to extend and explore many prison clichés. As Bennett explains, however, despite their earnest intentions these gritty polemics often inadvertently reinforce clichés about prison brutality and the character of prison inmates and usually fail in their goal to initiate progressive penal reform (Bennett 2006: 112). As Ina Bertand notes in relation to *Ghosts*, '[o]ne of the great mysteries of aesthetics is where to draw the line between exploitation and art', and all films based on prison memoirs are open to charges of exploitation, titillation or cliché (Bertand 2002: 1). The subject matter and how to approach it is extremely challenging but it is inappropriate to label a film a failure if it does not initiate widespread reform when, after all, the prison system is part of a much larger technology of control (what Foucault calls the 'carceral system') (Foucault 1991: 293–308).

Like *Ghosts*, most Australian prison films are based on prison memoirs written in an attempt to construct an alternative discourse about crime and punishment. In addition to a large number of films about Australian convicts and outlaws, like 'Mad Dog' Morgan and Ned Kelly, there are a small number of recent films about Australian prisons and a number of them are showcased on the 2003 *Ghosts* DVD. The first is Stephen Wallace's *Stir* (1980), starring Bryan Brown. The screenplay, written by Bob Jewson, recalls his experiences as a prisoner when he witnessed the 1974 prison riots at Bathurst that were subsequently the subject of a 1978 Royal Commission. The second is based on a play written by Ray Mooney, which was adapted for the screen by Alkinos Tsilimidos as *Everynight ... Everynight* (1994). It examines life inside Pentridge Prison's notorious H Division and stars David Field (who also stars as Wenzil in *Ghosts* and plays Keithy George in *Chopper*). The third is Andrew Dominik's *Chopper* (2000), about the notorious criminal, author and self-promoter Mark Brandon 'Chopper' Read (played superbly by Eric Bana). Although *Chopper* is Australia's best-known prison film, rather than being a film about prisons *per se*, its focus is the larger-than-life Read. Ned Kelly is evoked in most of these narratives and he remains an iconic figure for Australian artists and prison inmates, and even Cave's father (as many commentators have noted, Colin Cave was deeply interested in the Kelly myth (Cave 1980)).

When asked to locate *Ghosts* within the Australian prison film genre, Hillcoat cites *Chopper* and Rowan Wood's *The Boys* (1998) (a film about a group of violent misogynistic young men about to commit a crime that will put them in prison) as the two films that have the most in common with *Ghosts*. Better known internationally than any of these films, however, is the television series *Prisoner* (1979–86) (known outside of Australia as *Caged Women* or *Prisoner: Cell Block H)*, set in an Australian women's prison. Such narratives, sometimes described as 'babes-behind-bars' movies, are usually designed to titillate rather than provoke (Rafter 2006: 166–72). Very little has been written about any of these Australian prison narratives (apart from those texts listed in my bibliography) but I will not digress and discuss them any further here. It is, however, important to note that in all of these Australian prison narratives Aboriginal Australians are noticeably absent or marginal when in reality they form a disproportionately large percentage of the prison population.

Making *Ghosts ... of the Civil Dead*

Given that so little has been written about *Ghosts*, what follows is quite a lengthy history of the making of the film. Once again, unless indicated otherwise, this material was obtained from interviews and supplementary material on the 2003 DVD.

According to Evan English, it was back in 1984, when he was living with Cave and Paul Goldman in Los Angeles, that they all became interested in prison narratives. Hillcoat's enthusiasm for Jack Henry Abbott's *In the Belly of the Beast* (Abbott 1981 and republished in 1991) was the catalyst for the *Ghosts* project but certainly not the only generative factor. Abbott wrote to Norman Mailer from prison, as he wanted Mailer to know what jail was really like, not at all as it is portrayed in movies. At that time, Mailer was writing *The Executioner's Song* (1980) about Gary Gilmore. Abbott's thesis is that no one knows what it is like to be incarcerated until they have been locked up for at least a decade; it is only after that amount of time that prison life becomes part of your skin, bones, mind and soul (Mailer in Abbott 1991: iv). (The influence of Foucault is clearly central to Abbott's ideas about prisoners' bodies). A correspondence struck up between the men and the book resulted from that exchange. Through his correspondence with Mailer, the autodidact Abbott also acquired the literary tools to speak to an audience outside prison and share his story. Abbott was born in 1944 in a military base in Michigan. Abbott's father was in the military and his mother a sex worker. Almost immediately, he was placed in a series of unhappy foster homes and into juvenile detention at the age of nine. Apart from a few intermittent weeks and months, he spent his life in detention. Abbott describes himself as a 'state-raised convict' (1991: 3–22) and Foucault's prediction that such a system 'cannot fail to produce delinquents' is borne out in Abbott's history (Foucault 1991: 266). He was released from jail in the early 1980s (due, in part, to the publicity that his first book garnered) and he became quite a fashionable *cause célèbre* (McGivern 1982: 559–63). In Abbott's case, *In the Belly of the Beast* allowed him to construct a subjectivity that could be read by those outside the prison system, and his written words facilitated his temporary freedom. As he explains at some length in his second memoir entitled *My Return*, however, he found it almost impossible to interact with others in person when he was released (Abbott and Zack 1987). This led to a tragic incident only six weeks after his release in July 1981. During an altercation that arose after being asked to leave a café, he fatally stabbed a hospitality worker named Richard Adan. Abbott was convicted of manslaughter and returned to jail where he subsequently committed suicide in 2002 (Abbott 1991; Rosenwald 2002). *My Return* attempts to explain Abbott's (mis)reading of the exchange in the café and how, after a lifetime in jail, he was unable to communicate with those from a discourse community outside of the prison system. In one of the passages from *In the Belly of the Beast*, where Abbott details trying to obtain an autopsy for an inmate, he laments his inability to get justice for his friend and he writes '[a]s long as I am nothing but a ghost of the civil dead, I can do nothing' (1991: 115).

It is not surprising that after reading Abbott's book Hillcoat immediately wrote to him in prison and enquired about acquiring the film rights. Abbott corresponded with Hillcoat and the two men exchanged ideas about Michel Foucault's *Discipline and Punish*, René Girard's *Violence and the Sacred*, Dostoyevsky, Hegel, Genet and Kierkegaard. Despite being unsuccessful in obtaining the rights to the book, English and Hillcoat became consumed with the project and began reading widely, watching prison films and visiting prisons. They became particularly interested in the so-called New Generation or 'supermax' prisons such as the one in Marion, Illinois. Early on, English and Hillcoat entertained but ultimately rejected the idea of making a prison documentary or a hybrid combining elements of documentary and dramatic feature film (Hillcoat describes the style as 'faction'). Hillcoat, English and Gene Conkie travelled to America and a turning point occurred when they attended a high-level think tank in Colorado about correctional services and subsequently managed to engineer visits to notorious prisons like the above-mentioned Marion. Known as the 'New Alcatraz', it opened in 1963 to house high-risk prisoners formerly housed at institutions like Alcatraz (Richards 2008: 6–10). Accordingly, their interest expanded from telling Abbott's story exclusively; instead they hoped to broaden the focus to the status of correctional services in the 1980s. They found the perfect subject in David Hale, who became a consultant for the film and is portrayed as the character David Yale (played by Michael Bishop in the film). Hale became a guard at the age of 18; he grew up 'on the inside' and knew no other life than prison culture, which is typical of what Foucault calls a 'disciplinary career' (Foucault 1991: 300). Despite being accustomed to the endemic corruption and violence, he became increasingly dissatisfied with the decision-making and working conditions at Marion. At the time they made the movie in 1987, Marion had been in lockdown since 1983. Astonishingly, the lockdown remained in place for over 20 years until Marion was converted to a medium security facility in 2007 (Richards 2008: 6). Cave speaks passionately about conditions at Marion in a *Melody Maker* interview with Simon Reynolds and it is clear that Hale's story confirmed what English, Hillcoat and Cave had been reading about penal institutions (Reynolds 1988: 32). The group became increasingly fascinated by Foucault's theories about the carceral system, surveillance and the panoptic, the state and punishment, and the design of the new prisons. (They even employed Simon During as a Foucault specialist). In particular, it became an obsession to get the architecture just right in order to give voice to Abbott's and Hale's stories and articulate Foucault's theories. English, Hillcoat and Cave make it clear that they believe the state oversees the institutionalization of the least powerful people in society, particularly the poor. As Bertrand observes, *Ghosts* highlights the Foucauldian premise that the prison system (as an agent of the state) creates rather than rehabilitates criminals and the system is designed to legitimate violence against the populace (2002: 2). Thus it serves itself, rather than citizens, by endlessly justifying the *status quo* and ever increasing spending on police, surveillance and correctional services. This carceral system is now an industry and one reliant on the poor young black men who are vastly overrepresented as inmates in the Australian and American prison population. At the time that Cave and the others were preparing to shoot the film, Indigenous deaths in custody were finally garnering serious attention and in 1987 a Royal Commission was launched to investigate the issue. (For an excellent overview of the situation in the United States, see

144

The Gender of Racial Politics and Violence in America (Pinar 2001). Jacqueline Z. Wilson devotes a chapter to racism in *Prison: Cultural Memory and Dark Tourism* (2008) and Chloe Hooper's *The Tall Man* (2008) provides a disturbing insight into Indigenous deaths in custody in Australia.)

Race, however, is not addressed explicitly in the film, although Abbott devotes a whole chapter to this issue in *In the Belly of the Beast* (1991: 135–54). This omission may be because *Ghosts* centres on two white men's experiences or because the film never explicitly locates itself as Australian or American. We know that the prison is located in a desert but nothing more and so the narrative is not located as part of a national discourse about imprisonment. Naturally, even though *Ghosts* is an adaptation, there is no requirement for the film-makers to adhere exactly to the source text and I do not want to make an argument for fidelity to the original.

Given the film-makers' political agenda, it is somewhat ironic that *Ghosts* attracted finance via the Australian government's 10BA tax breaks and the film-makers freely admit that such a political polemic would not have been made without such assistance. (The 10BA tax breaks offered investors a 100 per cent tax deduction for investment in the film industry in the 1970s and 1980s in Australia.) Although based on Cave's original script, the screenplay changed considerably during the shoot and Cave, English, Hillcoat, Gene Conkie and Hugo Race shared the final writing credits. In late 1987, the film was shot in Port Melbourne in a disused factory. For most of the key people involved, *Ghosts* was their first experience of making a full-length feature film and the combination of this inexperience and a low budget made the shoot especially hard work. Chris Kennedy, the production designer for the film, recounts what a tough shoot it was making a low-budget film with such a diverse, challenging and explosive cast. Although based on real prison designs, the sets were made chiefly of cardboard and many were assembled, dismantled and then reassembled many times over as the makeshift materials gradually disintegrated: a fitting end for a Gothic prison that is anthropomorphized as an embodiment of the technology of imprisonment. Despite these budgeting impediments, Kennedy won an Australian Film Award (AFI) for best production design for the film and the film was nominated in eight other categories.

Casting was extremely challenging. As I have already noted, Abbott writes that over time prisoners develop a particular physiognomy, what he calls the 'lumpen proletarian cast of the criminal' (1991: 85). Deeply affected by Abbott's description of the imprint that prison life leaves on the skin and bodies of prisoners, Hillcoat, English and the casting director Lucy MacLaren took meticulous care to ensure the cast looked authentic. Accordingly, the majority of the 90-strong cast were not professional actors but former prisoners, prison guards, police and security guards (with the odd rock star like Cave or Dave Mason thrown in for good measure). Prison activists like Brett Collins were employed to help cast the film and to help with rehearsals. Several of the actors have reported how challenging the shoot was; in particular, the immersion week of rehearsals. Michael Bishop (who played the character based on David Hale) speaks approvingly of the depth of research behind the film and the level of verisimilitude expected from actors resulting from the immersion week. He also wryly notes that they watched endless footage of Chopper Read. Vincent Gil (who plays Ruben, the character based most closely on Abbott) was clearly deeply affected by the shoot. Gil reports that a number of ex-felons appeared on set affected by drugs and returned to jail soon after. Most commentators report that the shoot was tense, with Cave under considerable pressure to capture the psychotic temperament of Maynard. According to Cave, Hillcoat sought to maintain the tension between the 'inmates' and 'guards' and separated the groups during breaks. All the while, Cave would stalk the set sizing up his next on-screen antagonist (Johnston 1995: 226). The wrap party is now the stuff of legend. Ian Johnston also tells another version of this story (1995: 227).

The film opens with the warning that the film is based on true events, before the camera sweeps across an empty expanse of desert and distant purple ranges. The setting is eerily reminiscent of an Albert Namatjira painting. The camera, which operates as the mobilized gaze, then settles on a prison and we see a naked man being processed for admission. Computer graphics scroll across the screen and a disembodied female voice intones: 'Welcome to Central Industrial, part of Correctional Services' rapidly expanding network of new generation facilities, dedicated to the goal of humane containment. We are the future in containment'. A group of new prisoners shuffles in under heavy guard. (It is difficult to watch this set up and not be reminded of the rise of Immigration Detention Centres in the Australian desert and what that may say about the death of civil rights in Australia). *Ghosts* has an ensemble cast and is stitched together with a very loose narrative thread; we chiefly follow the character of Wenzil (David Field), who is seen fresh faced and naked in the above-mentioned shot. Although we never find out the circumstances that led to his imprisonment, it is clear that he is a relative innocent (a young punk rather than a dangerous felon). His wavy hair, boyish face, tattoo-free body and lack of overt musculature signal that he has not done serious time before: according to genre conventions, he is coded as a 'fish'. We read his character through his physique (as in many prison films, the camera fetishizes the nude male body). The ritual of the new arrival's body gradually transforming into a prisoner's body embodying a narrative of incarceration is a familiar trope in the genre. His arrival coincides with the arrival of a high-risk killer, Grezner (Chris de Rose), who has killed a prison guard at another facility and so is under 24-hour police protection. We are then introduced to a number of inmates who have short cameos, from the lifers, many of whom have very little experience of life outside a prison, to the drug barons, drug addicts and transvestites. Presumably, many of the older prisoners in these scenes are the real life ex-cons who played many of the minor roles in the film. We hear snippets of some characters' stories but there is little character development; the narrative is deliberately suggestive and fragmented.

The film documents the gradual rise in tension as conditions begin to disintegrate. An increasing number of external crackdowns take place, in which discrete units strip search the prisoners, confiscating drugs, weapons and personal effects. An increasing number of high-risk prisoners and 'psychos' are also introduced into the general prison population. This signals Cave's entry as Maynard. Soon after, an inevitable riot is triggered by the murder of Grezner by a prison guard (who disguises it as a suicide and scrawls 'Welcome to Hell' on the cell wall in what appears to be blood). A prisoner then manages to kill one guard and wounds two others. The story ends with a female news journalist (the only female cast member) reporting about the riot from outside the prison walls. We then learn that a number of prisoners have inexplicably been returned to the community (presumably as a mechanism to frighten the public and legitimize social control). The film ends with the chilling vision of Wenzil (now a killer with 'CUNT' tattooed on his forehead) following a woman at a train station. The station looks and sounds very much like the prison; the same female voiceover intones from the train station public address system. Ruben's apocalyptic theology that society will reap what it sows warns viewers about what to expect.

Cave's contribution

Having located the film generically and provided a short history of the shoot and an overview of the plot, I want to focus here on Cave's contribution more explicitly. As an artist perhaps best known for his murder ballads, it is no surprise that Cave found his imagination fired by Abbott's sad tale. In 1986, Cave wrestled with Abbott's story and while busy working on the *Ghosts* script wrote the songs 'Your Funeral, My Trial' and 'Jack's Shadow' (Dax 1999: 111). 'Jack's Shadow' provides a particularly harrowing commentary on Abbott's experiences in solitary confinement and his disorientation when he is released. In an interview with Simon Reynolds in *Melody Maker* in 1988, Cave confesses that in researching and filming *Ghosts* he developed a less romantic view of imprisonment than the one expressed in many of his earlier songs (1988: 32–4). It was also during this time that Cave wrote one of his most powerful songs about capital punishment and the electric chair: 'The Mercy Seat'. Reynolds and Press take issue with comments that Cave has made about the song and the supposed 'nobility' of crimes of violence (1995: 30). Cave discusses the genesis of the song at length in the 1998 interview with Reynolds:

> [i]t's the Throne of God, in the Bible. Where he sits and throws his lightning bolts and so forth. But it's also about this guy sitting on Death Row, waiting to be electrocuted or whatever. It's juxtaposing those two things. A person in his final days, thinking about Good and Evil and all the usual fare.
>
> (Reynolds 1988: 32)

When Reynolds then asks Cave whether he has 'a kind of ethics of violence' and asks whether 'the *crime passionel* – [has] a kind of aesthetic integrity', Reynolds is putting words in Cave's mouth (1988: 34). Cave responds by saying '[t]hat's one way of putting it, I suppose. There's something more noble in revenge, than in … sadism, or violence through greed. Maybe there's something more aesthetically pleasing about it, I don't know' (1988: 34). Once again, it is evident that the line between exploitation and art is a difficult one to negotiate, and Cave has never been content to take the safe path. In the same interview, Cave expresses his outrage that the penal system is focused on punishment rather than rehabilitation. He admits:

> [m]y social conscience is limited in a lot of ways; there's not much I feel angry about that doesn't affect myself quite directly. But the prison system – not particularly capital punishment – but the penal system as it is, and the whole apparatus of judgement, people deciding on other people's fates … that does irritate and upset me quite a lot … I did a lot of homework when I started work on the script. The initial plan was to use the prison world to create a certain kind of readymade atmosphere. But over the eight drafts, what emerged was a particular vision of the whole penal system as almost a plot by the higher powers to perpetuate the whole system of crime, keep it rolling, keep criminals on the streets.
>
> (Reynolds 1988: 32)

During the interview, Cave expresses sympathy for both the prisoners and the prison guards and discusses the political motivations of the film-makers.

Cave's initial draft of the screenplay set the narrative in a Victorian Gothic institution. As he explains to Melanie Brellis in an interview conducted for *Tension* during filming, his original script was rewritten many times and the final version bears very little relation to it (Brellis 1987: 13). Maynard's dialogue and physiognomy remain Cave's most obvious contribution to the screenplay, but this does not trivialize or downplay its significance. Cave makes a significant impact on the screen given that he does not appear until 55 minutes into the 90-minute film. Even in that 35-minute window, he gets little screen time; Maynard is not able to mingle with other prisoners and does not carry out any of the attacks or murders that occur at the end of the film. As Adrian Danks notes, given the collective menace of the cast, it is remarkable that Maynard makes such an impression with so little screen time. He suggests that Cave's performance 'draws heavily upon the connotations of violence, discordance and dark elemental morality associated with Cave's image at the time' (Danks 2009: 116). Indeed, the young Cave, a post-punk musician best known for his snarling stage persona and his heroin addiction, certainly had an intimidating reputation and it is clear that both Cave and Hillcoat exploited his anti-hero status.

It is more than mere reputation, however, that makes Cave's embodiment of Maynard so convincing. Cave's performance as Maynard screams for attention. Steven Connor's work on the power of the voice suggests that the voice can impose itself over space and voice also 'procures space for itself' (2000: 12). (Angela Jones makes a similar observation about Connor's work on the voice and rage in a footnote in her essay about Cave and Grinderman (2009: 127)). This is exactly what Maynard does when he enters the prison and immediately imposes his presence. Connor's arguments resonate if one considers that, as a musician and entertainer, Cave is accustomed to dominating performance spaces with his voice. Connor suggests that the power of a voice can signify or conjure up an embodied voice, what he calls the 'vocalic body' (2000: 35). Danks proposes that Maynard has a 'sonic' or 'aural' presence and this appears to be an example of what Connor is arguing (2009: 166). Even behind bars,

Maynard projects himself beyond the bars and exudes menace, and in doing so illustrates the power of the voice when most other means of performing agency are denied. As an aside, Abbott suffered from a stutter when addressing guards and the only time he did not stutter was when screaming abuse at them. He compares his situation with stutterers who can sing without stuttering (Abbott 1991: 15). Abbott also writes about prisoners who use incessant taunts and insults as a means to wear other prisoners (and guards) down. It becomes a form of violence or acoustic assault that cannot be escaped and so must be adroitly managed and turned into a reluctant 'conversation' or simply endured (1991: 65). As Connor notes, we cannot choose not to hear something (2000: 16). Thus, even when absent from the screen, Maynard is not absent from the film as we cannot avoid his cries. Maynard heralds his own entrance with '[t]here goes the neighborhood' and then follows it up with lines like '[h]ere I am motherfuckers', '[b]eat me down and kill me' and '[o]fficer, come here. I wanna spit in your fucking eye!'. At every turn, he screams racist, misogynistic and homophobic abuse at 'niggers', 'greaseballs', 'pussies' and 'faggots'. Famously, there was no script for any of Cave's scenes and he was encouraged to improvise. As Cave recounts on the 2003 version of the DVD, he based Maynard on a fellow inmate he encountered in one of his many brief interludes in police station lock-ups. According to Cave, while he was detained in a New York police station, a detainee in the next cell screamed abuse constantly over a 24-hour period and his hyperbolic rants were at times amusing but always deeply offensive and tiresome. It appears that Cave took notes.

Maynard's sonic impact is amplified by the fact that there is very little dialogue in the film and the soundtrack – itself composed by Cave, Blixa Bargeld and Mick Harvey – is haunting but unobtrusive. His screams reverberate and resonate and, like the eerie sound of Anita Lane's voice on the soundtrack, they are difficult to dislodge from one's head. In his interview with Brellis, Cave admits that given his script changed so dramatically during the production process, he worried that atmospherics were being sacrificed for politics (Brellis 1987: 13). His worries were groundless as the soundtrack is extremely powerful and amplifies the sparse dialogue. As Bertrand notes, 'sound is a significant aspect of the argument' and it increases the sense of discordance and alienation established on-screen (2002: 3). The stark soundtrack, with Bargeld's tin whistle, ratchets the tension: the diegetic sound mainly comprises the public address system, cheesy music and groans from pornographic films viewed on inmates' televisions, along with the sound of muffled assaults. This is not a film in which characters engage in prolonged dialogue: they scream or use their bodies to speak for them.

Maynard's blood

Finally, I want to discuss Cave's performance as Maynard in terms of the abject and self-mutilation as a textual or rhetorical practice narrating his subjectivity. Apart from his voice, one of the most disturbing facets of Maynard's persona is his self-mutilation. Cave recounts that he cut himself to add realism to the performance and that at least some of the blood on-screen is his own (Brellis 1987: 13). He also contributed details like double 'HATE' tattoos on his fists to exaggerate the menace and physicality of Maynard's character (1987: 13). Thus we witness Cave as Maynard carving up his body (being written on) and writing in his own blood on a cell wall. Graffiti has long been a part of prison culture; a way for prisoners to leave a mark, tell their story or communicate with fellow inmates (Wilson 2008: 67–130). What makes Maynard's graffiti so disturbing is not just the text (scatological) and drawings (disembodied women's torsos and genitals) but the fact that we witness him using his bloodied arm like an artist's palette. According to prison studies, it is relatively common for prisoners under severe stress to use blood and body wastes as writing tools or missiles (Rhodes 2007: 559). These are deliberately transgressive acts of abjection: they disturb order and do not 'respect borders, positions, rules' (Kristeva 1982: 4). It is when audiences witness such acts on-screen that they require decoding, as viewers often react with shock and incomprehension: nothing is familiar. For example, this is illustrated very powerfully in *Hunger* (2008), Steve McQueen's film about Robert 'Bobby' Gerard Sands and the 'dirty protests' conducted by Irish Republican prisoners in the late 1970s (McQueen 2008). Sands employs masticated food, urine and faeces as weapons against the guards and starves himself as an act of resistance. Similarly, Abbott speaks of writing with his own blood because he has 'nothing else – and because these things are excessively painful to recall. It drains me' (1991: 37). It is impossible to know if Abbott is being sarcastic, poetic or merely pragmatic but we learn from *In the Belly of the Beast* that he spent months at a time in solitary confinement, sensory deprived, with little food, and inadequate toilet facilities. In a high security prison cell, perhaps Maynard is just using one of the only writing implements at hand and Cave may be rehearsing an idea and a lyric soon to appear in several of his songs. As most critics note, in addition to dead women, Cave's songs are suffused with religious images of suffering, carnality, blood, violence and murder, all of which suggest abjection. (As John Baker reminded me in correspondence about this point, Christ himself allows his tormentors to 'inscribe' their savagery onto his body, making of him a canvas). 'Red Right Hand', of course, references Milton's 'red right hand' and the song first appears on the 1994 album *Let Love In*. It is now one of Cave's best-known songs and has subsequently been referenced in several television shows and films (Hanson 2005: 98). The image of the bloodied right hand appears again in 1996 in 'Song of Joy' on *Murder Ballads* (Cave 2007: 243–5). Perhaps his role as Maynard provides him with an opportunity to make what is usually a literary metaphor, literal. Lyn McCredden notes that given these persistent tropes in Cave's work, Julia Kristeva's work on purification, catharses and religion provides a lens with which to view Cave's *oeuvre* (McCredden 2009: 167–85). She argues that 'Cave's work amounts to an idiosyncratic but also embracingly contemporary theology of the fleshed or carnal sacred' (2009: 168). McCredden examines many of Cave's lyrics and *The Proposition* in relation to religion and abjection but, disappointingly, she does not discuss *Ghosts*. Zoe Alderton suggests that his often violent and religious writing is a 'linguistic elevation of mundane and sordid life to the realm of the sacred, rather than a celebration of brutality' (McCredden 2009: 169). Thus, writing in blood becomes simultaneously sacred and carnal.

In this instance, Maynard's body is a site of protest and one that Cave may have based on an infamous Australian prisoner. As Jacqueline Zoe Wilson explains, prison studies report that rates of self-harm (para-suicide) and suicide are extremely high in the prison population, especially so in 'supermax' institutions (2004: 12). She notes that '[a]part from deliberate drug-overdoses, the most common form of inmate para-suicide is self-mutilation, usually with edged weapons – what prison parlance terms "slashing up"' (2004: 12). The bodies of the prisoners become texts, but ones that are part of what Amanda Crawley locates as 'a vocabulary of transgression' recognized and read by those within the prison discourse community (2001: 305). As the film-makers were aware, unless their cast embodied their roles, they would be rendered illegible and inauthentic to many of the viewers they hoped to engage. Cave clearly read widely about prison writing and prison culture and understands that Maynard's body is a metaliterary text, which must be read along with Cave's script. Johnston suggests that the notorious prisoner and self-mutilator Garry David (also known as Garry Webb) was one of the inspirations for Maynard (1999: 225). I can find no other reference to David in the commentary about *Ghosts* but this thesis certainly makes sense. In many ways, his story mirrors both Chopper's and Abbott's (both Chopper and David were born in 1954). His mother was an alcoholic, his father sexually abused him and he spent most of his childhood in institutions before graduating to prison. It is estimated that he spent 33 of his 38 years institutionalized before he died in prison from self-inflicted wounds. David was a favourite of the tabloids given his extreme self-mutilation and auto-amputation (like Chopper, he hacked off his own ears but he also cut off and ate his own nipples, carved off pieces of his scrotum, swallowed razor blades and slashed his abdomen). His self-mutilation was front-page news in Australia for many years and so it is likely that Cave did know about this case. Like Chopper and Abbott, David was an avid reader and writer and he actively constructed his own celebrity. At the time of his death, he had been commissioned to write his autobiography (Attwood 1993; Conroy 1993; Kearns and Conroy 1993). In *Ghosts*, perhaps Cave helped to write part of it for him.

As a means of concluding, I want to suggest that in writing about Jack Henry Abbott, like his father before him, Nick Cave has written himself into the Australian prison genre. Norman Mailer recounts that 'Abbott had his own voice [and that he] had heard no other like it' (Mailer in Abbott 1991: x). Perhaps he is right, but Abbott's story is sadly not unique. In Australia, it is echoed by Mark Brandon 'Chopper' Read, Garry David, Bob Jewson, and many others right back to the iconic outlaw Ned Kelly. All are remembered chiefly because of the rhetorical impact of the texts written about their incarceration. Their accounts gave them a voice that other incarcerated men did not and do not possess. Black voices are inevitably silenced, and indeed are liminal even in this chapter. Cave helps make Abbott's, Hale's and David's voices heard by screaming out their stories and writing them in bloodied script. *Ghosts … of the Civil Dead* is a dark tale about shadows but it deserves more light.

References

Abbott, Jack (1991), *In the Belly of the Beast*, intro. by Norman Mailer, New York: Vintage. First published 1981.

Abbott, Jack and Naomi Zack (1987), *My Return*, Buffalo, NY: Prometheus.

Alderton, Zoe (2009), 'Nick Cave: A Journey from an Anglican God to the Creative Christ', *Literature and Aesthetics*, 19:2, pp. 169–86.

Anon (2010), 'Nick Cave', http://www.imdb.com/name/nm0147022/. Accessed 9 September 2010.

Attwood, A. (1993), 'Garry David, and the Deeper Darkness Within', *The Age*, 14 June (obtained online via Factiva).

Bartlett, Thomas (2004), 'The Resurrection of Nick Cave', http://dir.salon.com/story/ent/feature/2004/11/18/cave/index.html. Accessed 11 February 2011.

Bennett, Jamie (2006), 'The Good, the Bad and the Ugly: The Media in Prison Films', *The Howard Journal*, 45:2, pp. 97–115.

Bertrand, Ina (2002), 'Bordering Fiction and Documentary: *Ghosts … of the Civil Dead*', *Senses of Cinema* [Online] 19, March–April, http://archive.sensesofcinema.com/contents/01/19/contents.html. Accessed 10 June 2010.

Brellis, Melanie (1987), 'Nick Cave: Up and Out in Melbourne and Berlin', *Tension* 12, pp. 13–15.

Büssing, Sabine (1990), *Of Captive Queens and Holy Panthers: Prison Fiction and Male Homoerotic Experience*, Frankfurt am Main, Bern, New York, Paris: Peter Lang.

Cave, Colin (1980), *Ned Kelly: Man and Myth,* North Ryde, NSW: Cassell Australia.

Cave, Nick (2007), *The Complete Lyrics 1978–2007*, London: Penguin.

—— (2009), *The Death of Bunny Munro*, Melbourne: Text.

Chomsky, Noam (1997), *Media Control: The Spectacular Achievements of Propaganda*, New York: Seven Stories.

Connor, Steven (2000), *Dumbstruck: A Cultural History of Ventriloquism*, Oxford: Oxford University Press.

Conroy, P. (1993), 'I Am Not Afraid of Death but I Am Afraid of Life', *The Age*, 12 June (obtained online via Factiva).

Crawley, Amanda (2001), 'Grammatical Fictions: Reading and Writing the Self in Prison', *French Cultural Studies*, 12, pp. 303–18.

Creed, Barbara (2005), *Phallic Panic: Film, Horror and the Primal Uncanny*, Melbourne: Melbourne University Press.

Dalziell, Tanya and Karen Welberry (2009), 'Introduction', in Karen Welberry and Tanya Dalziell (eds), *Cultural Seeds: Essays on the Work of Nick Cave*, Burlington: Ashgate, pp. 1–9.

Danks, Adrian (2009), 'Red Right Hand: Nick Cave and Cinema', in Karen Welberry and Tanya Dalziell (eds), *Cultural Seeds: Essays on the Work of Nick Cave*, Burlington: Ashgate, pp. 109–21.

Darabont, Frank (1999), *The Green Mile*, United States: Warner Bros.

—— (1994), *The Shawshank Redemption*, United States: Columbia Pictures and Warner Bros.

Dax, Maximilian (1999), *The Life and Music of Nick Cave: An Illustrated Biography*, trans. by I. Minock, Berlin: Die-Gestalten-Verlag.

Dominik, Andrew (2000), *Chopper*, Australia: Mushroom Pictures & Twentieth Century Fox.

English, Evan (2005), 'Ghosts … of the Civil Dead: The Official Site', http://ghostsofthecivildead. com/index.html. Accessed 1 June 2010.

Foucault, Michel (1991), *Discipline and Punish*, trans. by Alan Sheridan, London: Penguin. First published 1977.

Forster, R. (1997), 'The Bad Seed from the Bad Seed: A Cultural Perspective on the Work on Nick Cave', *Overland*, 149, pp. 60–3.

Gelder, Ken (2007), 'Australian Gothic', in Catherine Spooner and Emma McEvoy (eds), *The Routledge Companion to Gothic*, London, New York: Routledge, pp. 115–24.

Gelder, Ken and Jane Jacobs (1998), *Uncanny Australia*. Melbourne: Melbourne University Press.

Hanson, Amy (2005), *Kicking Against the Pricks: An Armchair Guide to Nick Cave*, London: Helter Skelter.

Hayles, Roslynn D. (1998), *Seeking the Centre: The Australian Desert in Literature and Art*, Cambridge: Cambridge University Press.

Hillcoat, John (2003), *Ghosts … of the Civil Dead*, Australia: Umbrella Entertainment. DVD. First released 1988.

——— (2005) *The Proposition*, Australia: First Look Pictures.

Hooper, Chloe (2008), *The Tall Man*, Camberwell, VIC: Hamish Hamilton.

Israel, Michael (1983), 'Jack Henry Abbott, American Prison Writing, and the Experience of Punishment', *Criminal Justice and Behavior*, 10, pp. 441–60.

Jayasinghe, Laknath (2009), 'Nick Cave, Dance Performance and the Production and Consumption of Masculinity', in Karen Welberry and Tanya Dalziell (eds), *Cultural Seeds: Essays on the Work of Nick Cave*, Burlington: Ashgate, pp. 65–80.

Johnston, Ian (1995), *Bad Seed: The Biography of Nick Cave*, London: Abacus.

Jones, Angela (2009), 'Grinderman: All Stripped Down', in Karen Welberry and Tanya Dalziell (eds), *Cultural Seeds: Essays on the Work of Nick Cave*, Burlington: Ashgate, pp. 123–36.

Kearns, L. and P. Conroy (1993), 'Garry David Dies', *The Age*, 12 June (obtained online via Factiva).

Kristeva, Julia (1982), *Powers of Horror: An Essay on Abjection*, New York: Columbia University Press.

McCredden, Lyn (2009), 'Fleshed Sacred: The Carnal Theologies of Nick Cave', in Karen Welberry and Tanya Dalziell (eds), *Cultural Seeds: Essays on the Work of Nick Cave*, Burlington: Ashgate, pp. 167–85.

McEvoy, Emma (2007), '"Now, who will be the witness/When you're all too healed to see?' The Sad Demise of Nick Cave', *Gothic Studies*, 9:1, pp. 79–88.

McGivern, Gary (1982), 'Honor Among Thieves', *Crime Delinquency*, 28, pp. 559–63.

McInnis, David (2006), '"All Beauty Must Die": The Aesthetics of Murder, from Thomas De Quincey to Nick Cave', *Traffic*, 8, pp. 117–38.

Murphie, Andrew (1996), 'Sound at the End of the World as We Know It', *Perfect Beat*, 2:4, pp. 18–42.

Nellis, Mike (1988), 'British Prison Movies: The Case of *Now Barabbas*', *The Howard Journal*, 27:1, pp. 2–31.

O'Sullivan, Sean (2001), 'Representations of Prison in Nineties Hollywood Cinema: From *Con Air* to *The Shawshank Redemption*', *The Howard Journal*, 40:4, pp. 317–34.

Pinar, William (2001), *The Gender of Racial Politics and Violence in America*, New York: Peter Lang.

Rafter, Nicole (2006), *Shots in the Mirror: Crime Films and Society*, second edn, Oxford: Oxford University Press.

Reynolds, Simon (1988), 'Knight of the Living Dead', *Melody Maker*, June 18, pp. 32–4.

Reynolds, Simon and Joy Press (1995), *The Sex Revolts: Gender, Rebellion, and Rock'n'Roll*, Cambridge, MA: Harvard University Press.

Rhodes, Lorna (2007), 'Supermax as a Technology of Punishment', *Social Research*, 74:2, pp. 547–66.

Richards, Stephen C. (2008), 'USP Marion: The First Federal Supermax', *The Prison Journal*, 88:6, pp. 6–22.

Rosenwald, Michael (2002), 'Jack Henry Abbott, Longtime Inmate, Brief Literary Star', *The Boston Globe*. 11 February.

Simon, Jonathan (2000), 'The "Society of Captives" in the Era of Hyper-incarceration', *Theoretical Criminology*, 4:3, pp. 285–308.

Tsilimidos, Alkinos (1994), *Everynight … Everynight*, Australia: Siren Visual Entertainment.

Turcotte, Gerry (1998), 'Australian Gothic', in Marie Mulvey-Roberts (ed.), *The Handbook to Gothic Literature*, Houndsmill, Basingstoke, Hampshire, London: Macmillan, pp. 10–19.

Van den Bulck, Jan and Heidi Vandebosch (2003), 'When the Viewer Goes to Prison: Learning Fact from Watching Fiction', *Poetics*, 31, pp. 103–16.

Wallace, Stephen (1980), *Stir*, Australia: Smiley Films.

Welberry, Karen (2009), 'Nick Cave and the Australian Language of Laughter', in Karen Welberry and Tanya Dalziell (eds), *Cultural Seeds: Essays on the Work of Nick Cave*, Burlington: Ashgate, pp. 47–64.

Welberry, Karen and Tanya Dalziell (eds) (2009), *Cultural Seeds: Essays on the Work of Nick Cave*, Burlington: Ashgate.

Wilson, Jaqueline Z. (2004), 'Dark Tourism and the Celebrity Prisoner: Front and Back Regions in Representations of an Australian Historical Prison', *JAS* 82 (June), pp. 1–13.

—— (2008) *Prison: Cultural Memory and Dark Tourism*, New York, Peter Lang.

Woods, Rowan (1998), *The Boys*, Australia: Roadshow Entertainment.

Chapter 9

'People Just Ain't No Good': Nick Cave's Noir Western, *The Proposition*

William Verrone

Nick Cave's lyrics and music may be described as 'cinematic' because they conjure such profoundly visual imagery, stimulating listeners to picture places and people with relative ease. Cave's first foray into screenwriting has produced an inimitable film that addresses major issues that permeate his musical work, primarily betrayal, violence, questing and redemption. *The Proposition* (2006) is a noir western, mainly because it combines thematic traits similar to film noir, while firmly rooting itself within the western genre. Because of its sensationally dark subject matter and its treatment of characters that are duplicitous, unfaithful and violent, *The Proposition* reminds us of the inherent ability of people to transgress while seeking transcendence – essentially, it shows us the brutal nature of individuals who perform bad deeds in the name of 'individualism' and redemption. However, Cave is not simply interested in portraying a kind of stylized violence on-screen; rather, the film is concerned with the difficult task of maintaining individual integrity and forging identity amidst the overwhelming sense of oppression and societal constraints that inhibit such growth. Many of Cave's lyrics deal with transgressive behaviour and the attempt at redemption. *The Proposition* focuses on the somewhat feeble attempts of a handful of characters to strive for personal salvation, even though their journeys are predominately self-defeating. The film carefully balances the antithetical ideas of faith and treachery, offering both an ambiguous moral tale and a rather unambiguously literal depiction of violence and cruelty.

I would like to address how *The Proposition* deals with themes of violence and redemption, and also how it offers a nuanced and complex take on the struggle between good and evil, especially in terms of viewer sympathy and empathy. Additionally, I would like to address *The Proposition* as a genre film, but more in terms of how it simultaneously addresses and undermines typical tropes of the western: death and salvation, transgression and transcendence, frontier expansion, civility and discontent, and redemption through destruction. The film also contains quest narrative and religious parable, two issues that appear as themes in some westerns, but are more precise concerns or themes in Cave's musical work (e.g., 'The Mercy Seat', 'The Good Son', 'Red Right Hand'). The film's tenuous delineation of good and evil negates the social categories that determine its content and form through the way it makes its own contradictions visible. *The Proposition* articulates a conflict of identification that challenges any simple alignment with the status quo (the 'good guys') or any simple opposition to law such as the Burns brothers themselves, the main characters in the film, and the supposed 'bad guys'. The film thus presents a kind of ideological statement about society, law and order, and the need for escape through its use of quest and parable. Thematically, the film is more in the line of *Murder Ballads* and *Henry's Dream* than, say, *The Boatman's Call*, but while 'there is an undeniable gothic gloom haunting the film, [the director] and Cave are hardly mere sadistic stylists' (Barsanti 2007).

Introduction

The Proposition is a western, which is a genre rich in the kinds of themes that Cave wants to explore, but it is unique because it transposes the setting to the Australian outback of the 1880s. *The Proposition* is about the attempt to civilize an untamed land, where untamed 'bushrangers' (Australian outlaws) and lawmen dictate the rules that govern themselves and others. The plot revolves around Captain Stanley (Ray Winstone), a British lawman/soldier, who is sent to 'govern' the land, but who ultimately becomes overly obsessed with destroying the Burns brothers; outlaws who have terrorized others and defied the law. After the opening titles of the film, we are immediately thrust into a bloody shoot-out between Stanley and his men and the Burns gang, after which Stanley catches Charlie (Guy Pearce) and Mikey Burns (Richard Wilson). The aftermath of the shootings sets up the titular proposition that Stanley offers to the middle Burns brother, Charlie: he, Charlie, must hunt down and kill his older, psychotic and renegade brother Arthur (Danny Huston), and in return Stanley will let Charlie's younger brother, Mikey, free.

This proposition gives Cave ample room for investigating the brutality of men. For example, while we eventually see that Arthur is the embodiment of evil, Charlie is also uncivilized and will kill for gain. Likewise, even Stanley appears somewhat sadistic in his cruel punishment(s) of Mikey. The setting is always fundamentally important to westerns, and Cave makes the outback a physical and emotional presence. The Australian outback of the 1880s looks and feels overwhelmingly oppressive – the wide-open spaces seem confining, cruel and sullen. The world of *The Proposition* is hot, lurid, hostile, unforgiving, and it breeds heartless men. The overpowering sense of futility and loss hovers in the air and fills the characters with a sense of doom. The cinematography captures the beauty and oppression of the outback. According to John Hillcoat, the film's director, the dichotomy between the beauty and brutality of the outback mirrors the same dichotomy in the characters. He suggests that 'these were brutal times, but the land also had a great beauty to it. I think it's a metaphor for the whole thing. In the middle of the day it's so harsh and oppressive yet when the sunsets come it's stunningly beautiful. It goes from one extreme to another' (Roddick 2006). The outback is horizontal, orange and red and brown – earthy. One of the reasons *The Proposition* is a noir western is because the characters are thrust into uncompromising situations that force them to behave with bloodlust and greed. Even though these characteristics might describe a depressing film, they instead point towards the need for deliverance or redemption. This redemption may be found in numerous ways (through love, personal contemplation or restored order), but it comes only with sacrifice. Salvation is difficult to achieve, as it should be in this type of brutal western.

Part of the appeal of *The Proposition* is its daring: it is a smart film, intelligently written, brilliantly filmed, and insightfully constructed to create tension and appreciation. It is vicious, but it needs to be. The characters are all somehow trapped in cyclical patterns of violence, predicated on a severe masculinity that is appropriate for westerns, but also predetermined as a catalyst for doom, which is typical of many films noirs. As Steve Neale notes of the evolution of the western, '[variants] in which the hero's relationship to civilized society undergoes considerable modification and in which images of a troubled or untrammeled masculinity are especially prominent' in revisionist westerns, determining their narrative structure (2000: 140). *The Proposition* is not just a revisionist western in that it rethinks and reconfigures generic tropes that categorize westerns; it also subverts these tropes so that we see how the western simultaneously provides a particular backdrop and demonstrates how that very backdrop can be manipulated. *The Proposition* is a re-imagining of bushranger life in which ruthlessness abides and men act out of fear and individualism, a kind of naturalistic battleground for contrary ideologies. The film offers a good example of a particular type of western in which noir sensibilities shape theme and content, mostly, as Thomas Schatz suggests, because noirs are 'considerably more pessimistic and brutal' (1981: 112).

Westerns, film noir and *The Proposition*

Westerns were once the most popular genre in Hollywood. The iconography of the western is immediately recognizable, and its general simplicity, in terms of a clear delineation between good and evil, gave the western its popularity among moviegoers for several generations. Westerns were produced steadily between the 1930s and 1950s before the popularity of European art cinema changed the film-making landscape in Hollywood, giving rise to the 'revisionist Westerns' of the 1960s and 1970s. *The Proposition* can be called a western, but it is a unique hybrid film that simultaneously addresses and undermines the specificities or limits of genre categorization. According to Barry Keith Grant, 'in genre films, iconography refers to particular objects, archetypal characters and even specific actions. In the western, the cowboy who dresses all in black and wears two guns, holster tied to either thigh, is invariably a villainous gunfighter' (2007: 12). *The Proposition* does not make these traits overtly noticeable and instead makes them greyer, like the worlds of film noir.

Westerns are typified by a handful of recognizable traits. According to Steve Neale, the classic western plot articulates

[s]ettling on or near a frontier [...] with advancing law and order [...] where savagery and lawlessness pose a local and momentarily significant challenge [...] with three central roles, the townspeople as agents of civilization, the savages or outlaws who threaten this

group, and the heroes who are above all 'them in the middle' [...] and it entails narratives in which violent confrontations of various kinds are central [...] such as the 'chase and pursuit'.

(2000: 140)

This basic outline can be applied to *The Proposition*'s narrative structure. The film is set in the Australian outback, where Stanley sets up his law-enforcing camp; the Burns brothers pose a threat to the town by becoming well-known outlaws; Stanley presumably is the hero (though the film clouds this significantly); and there are indeed many violent confrontations that hinge upon a 'chase and pursuit'. Westerns, however, provide endless variations on these generic tropes, making Cave's ripe for re-interpretation. The concise heroic story of the western is turned on its head; the elemental visual appeal of the wide-open spaces of the landscape becomes a menacing and confining threat; and there really is no clear marker of good and evil, except only the identification of Stanley as the law. According to Joseph Reed, '[Westerns] show us at our best (Pioneer Woman) and our worst (Gunfighter) and so provide an ideal at the same time that they give us the perverse mythicization of the sociopath' (1989: 255). Many westerns follow this idea, which is important to consider because the combination of *severe* markers of good and evil allows spectators to inherently and instinctively know right from wrong. *The Proposition* does not make things so easy. The characters are driven by instinct – even naturalistic impulses – and this makes them morally ambiguous. Thomas Schatz correctly notes that 'when we step back to get a broader picture, we notice that the Western depicts a world of precarious balance in which the forces of civilization and savagery are locked in a struggle for supremacy' (1981: 47). This is true of *The Proposition*: Stanley and his men are in Australia to 'tame the land', but his supremacy is constantly thwarted and overridden by nature and by the savagery of the Burns brothers.

Westerns are almost always historical by nature, if only because they draw upon historical references and material, usually depicting an ostensibly real past that shapes the present in terms of personal and national identity and interpersonal relationships. History may serve the western as a backdrop, but, as Janet Walker suggests, '[h]istory is argumentative and discursive, [so] westerns give narrative form to ideological beliefs and values' (2001: 5). More importantly, westerns 'privilege the individual and individualism over society and social responsibility', which gives rise to the larger thematic concerns of outlaws and their behaviour (McGee 2007: 33). Because westerns foreground individuals, they can be said to be archetypal, depicting ideological beliefs or values or tapping into myths that present common shared experiences. And while myths can be interpreted in multiple ways or even subvert historical narratives, they still can outline the universality of individuality and violence that occurs in many westerns. For example, Sam Peckinpah's 'revisionist' westerns like *The Wild Bunch* (1969) or *Pat Garrett and Billy the Kid* (1973) subvert the hero/villain dichotomy, as do Cave and John Hillcoat. Even so, Cave and Hillcoat make this territory their own. In Cave's words, 'I think John's heavily influenced by the anti-westerns and revisionist westerns of the 70s – *McCabe and Mrs. Miller* and

Peckinpah's stuff. But I think we felt that the average Australian had a different view of their history than the average American' (Balfour 2006). In westerns, the experience one gains or encounters comes not just from violent behaviour, but rather from the desire for extreme forms of individualism that leads to violent behaviour, reiterating the myths of frontier expansion and individual drive that mark many westerns. Most apparently individualistic creative expression is ideologically determined, and Cave approaches this realm of discourse in *The Proposition* by creating characters whose philosophical positions speak to larger issues of community, wealth, ownership and love. Cave's film focuses on the individual stories of several characters, providing a narrative that encompasses a wide range of stories and meanings that converge into one.

The western-as-myth typifies a certain narrative construct in which 'the idea that frontier existence and frontier encounters were characteristically marked by opportunity and danger, hardship and bounty, adventure and violence' features extensively (Neale 2000: 134). And while Cave has these thematic concerns at the forefront of his film, they are complicated by the ambiguous make-up of the characters, all of whom are questionable in terms of personal motivation and moral expression. For example, while we may understand Stanley's mission of civilizing the land (and by extension the people of the land, which includes the native aborigines), we also want to see Charlie succeed, suggesting that we favour the 'villain' and his savage duty. Charlie's brother Arthur is charismatic and menacing, charming and ruthless, fascinating and repugnant. Perhaps these mixed feelings towards him align him (and Charlie and Stanley) as noir protagonists. Noir 'protagonists are often caught in a web of circumstances beyond their control', making them act in often violent ways in order to seek retribution for the wrongs imposed upon or created by them (Grant 2007: 25). As Jim Hillier and Alastair Phillips note, '[f]ilm noir is populated by characters who have lost direction and very often have no real place left to go' (2009: 7–8). The characters in *The Proposition* certainly feel as if they are at dead-ends, unable to carry on unless they engage in one final act of violence. While they have all come to this certain place (the outback), they are essentially trapped in circumstances that dictate their fates.

Film noir has been called a genre, a historical moment of thematic conflation, and a recurrent style (Grant 2007: 24–8). These films are marked by shady characters performing shady deals who engage in acts of violence. They are laden with corrupt officials or populated with criminals; they present morally ambiguous narratives; and they are generally pessimistic, dark, fatalistic and charged with sexual innuendo (often in the form of an ever-present femme fatale), causing anxiety to dictate action. The language is terse and direct. Film noir is defined by style and tone, which, along with its characters, allows us to define *The Proposition* as a noir western. The spaces and places of film noir are full of shadows and darkness; by contrast, *The Proposition* subverts this, positioning itself in the wide-open spaces of the outback, but the spaces are nonetheless dark in tone. The spaces of film noir sometimes serve as allegorical places where a sense of loss is played out through the increasing desperation of the (male) protagonist. Noir was (and still is) a psychological battleground;

it deals almost exclusively with the inner world of the protagonists manifested through outward action. Perhaps Paul Schrader has articulated the tropes and characteristics of film noir better than others; his seminal essay 'Notes on Film Noir' outlines the thematic ideas and stylistic tendencies that, generally speaking, can be seen in *The Proposition*. Schrader suggests there were four influences that shaped or 'brought about' the film noir: 'War and Postwar disillusionment; Postwar Realism; The German Expatriates; and The Hard-Boiled Tradition' (1986: 170–5). While these might explain the historical noirs of the United States, they do not necessarily translate so easily to other films from other countries. However, the corresponding ideas of disillusionment as theme and realism as style mark *The Proposition*. Also, what Schrader calls the 'overriding noir theme: a passion for the past and present, but also a fear of the future', corresponds both to the moral ambiguity of the characters in *The Proposition*, and the larger idea of Australia itself forging its own identity amidst cruelty, injustice and outside influence (1986: 177). Schrader also argues that '[n]oir heroes dread to look ahead, but instead try to survive by the day, and if unsuccessful at that, they retreat to the past. Thus film noir's techniques emphasize loss, nostalgia, lack of clear priorities, and insecurity, then submerge these self-doubts in mannerism and style' (1986: 177). The main characters in *The Proposition* exhibit such behaviour. Stanley is haunted by an idyllic past, which he tries to recreate with his wife through their meticulously decorated house with its white-picket fence and gardens; Charlie is also haunted by his past (and present) but is forced to look ahead; and Arthur survives through daily ritualistic violence, and when confronted about it, retreats to the past, telling Charlie at one point 'they are family'. These traits make *The Proposition* compositionally tense, its characters morally ambiguous, and its tone dark. The transgressions of outlaws provide the most telling stories in westerns. The lawmen try to restore order, and while this may be characteristic of many western films, *The Proposition* serves as a reminder of just how difficult it is to achieve a sense of stability in an environment that is rife with chaos and destruction. Refining the land means taming the Burns brothers and repressing brutish, cruel and inhumane impulses. Setting a fictional film in this time frame points to the film's gritty realism: men driven by impulsive need for land, wealth and personal identity; aboriginal peoples displaced by encroaching civilization (and indeed the aborigines in the film have much to offer about the cruelty of man); and the futile attempt at community, whether small, as with the Burns brothers, or larger, as with Stanley's desire to build a stronger, safer community for everyone. The outback provides an inhospitable cover for the outlaws, who are driven by the desire for redemption only to discover that redemption is found in death. Accordingly, '*The Proposition*'s aim is not to place its characters against a beautiful backdrop but to link them directly to the land's Darwinian indifference' (Roddick 2006). Noirs usually take place in large urban centres, but the transitory, criminal spaces of the city environment can be transferred to the expanses of the outback, where there are equally dangerous demarcations between dark and darker. According to Neale, '[the] modern West and the old frontier alike [are] spaces in which social tensions of various kinds are played out, rather than [...] sites in which the nature of these tensions are initially defined' (2000: 139).

The Proposition as noir western

In essence, *The Proposition* investigates the associations between law, violence and the formation of the ordinary self. These ideas of self-identity and violence, coupled with the need for stability, are central to Cave's music, from *Tender Prey* to *The Lyre of Orpheus*. Searching for something – a quest – provides abundant room to explore the interrelations of order and disorder, or stability and violence and law and outlaw behaviour. According to Patrick McGee, the 'dichotomy of absolute systems of value vs. individualism dominates western narratives' (2007: 36). This kind of narrative also occurs in film noir. *The Proposition* is structured as a split narrative: the need for order, with Stanley and his wife, and the chaos of disorder, with the Burns brothers. These two clashing narratives – and themes – create the sense of fatalism in the film, which is more a characteristic of noir than westerns. Because westerns deal with extreme forms of masculinity, the characters often suffer unhappy fates, the only 'heroes' being the ones who sacrifice themselves for the better cause of the community. Rob Nelson points out that what the characters in *The Proposition* have in common is 'the desire for community amid the well-founded expectation of imminent, violent death' (2006). But as the film shows, achieving this goal of community is not easy. The sense of community is constantly thwarted, displaced, rearranged and also subverted. Westerns often address issues of maintaining community, whether it is a social community or a family. According to McGee, many westerns display a triptych-style plot that hinges upon the way people accept or deny the role of community, focusing on the people in charge (lawmen), and those opposed (the outlaws). He suggests that

> three positions are identified: the law as the expression of social dominance; the outlaw as the refusal of social dominance but without any effective concept of an alternative community; and the 'normal' subject of the community that identifies with the law but without the conscious knowledge of the community's subjection and implication in the violence of social domination.
>
> (McGee 2007: 159)

The Proposition examines similar issues, pitting the British administration against a family of Irish outlaws (inherent nationalities pit them against one another), with the native aborigines aligned with and against both. Stanley decrees himself the 'authority' of the town, the purveyor of social justice; Charlie and Arthur both deny this and therefore seek alternative ways to exist by transgressing social and moral boundaries; and the people who follow Stanley do so without really understanding or knowing about his own brutish tactics in maintaining or establishing 'order' and dominance. But Cave also uses this territory to explore fundamental questions about power struggles and the need for capitulation. These are men who forge ahead despite their shortcomings or self-doubts, whether or not they decide to stay in society (Stanley), leave it (Arthur), or struggle to appease both inclinations (Charlie).

According to John Saunders, when discussing the format for westerns,

[w]hether the complexities derive from historical contingency or more 'universal' moral questions, we need to feel that the action calls them into play, not as problems to be resolved by any final gun-down, but as gains and losses to be cast up in any adequate account of the human condition.

(2001: 34)

Charlie's quest puts him in a moral dilemma, but we get the sense that he wants to do what is best for himself. Once he meets up with his brother, he is faced with the reality of the moment, and finds it far too difficult to fix both himself and save his younger brother as Stanley commanded. Arthur waxes philosophical about the need for love and community, for shared commonalities and responsibilities, but Charlie is too tired, too unforgiving, and too morally ambiguous to heed everything his brother suggests. (Ironically, they decide to leave together to save Mikey – which shows Arthur's power over his brother). If Hillcoat 'has a sense from Cave of the brothers' relationships to one another, he isn't telling: a low-angle shot of stringy-haired Charlie atop his horse, swigging a bottle under a dark-blue sky while Cave's music score swirls and howls, makes plain that *The Proposition* has more to do with mood than meaning' (Nelson 2006). If this is the case, then the film ultimately lets us know that in this time frame and in this setting, anything goes – as it should. And in this sense too it shares with noirs the importance of foreboding.

Cave's take on the western borrows familiar tropes of the genre as a whole, but, as Szaloky asks, 'if indeed the western genre is based on the emptying out of history, what is there to be revised and rewritten into a new western history?' (2001: 49). For starters, Cave 'revises' the optimism found in western expansion (an American theme) and transplants it to the outback, where growth and development become entirely fatalistic. The storyline itself – a man needing to kill his brother under direction of the law – is contrary to the simple moral dichotomy that outlines many typical westerns. *The Proposition* is a dark film, but its philosophical underpinnings make it a tragedy of both individual and universal proportions. For instance, Charlie's quest raises challenging questions about survival and the ironic need to kill in order to survive (something that occurs in noirs as well). The proposition Charlie accepts has tragic proportions; it is a game in which no one wins and multiple people die. More appropriately, in westerns 'the outlaw hero is poised between the wilderness and civilization, self-interest and social responsibility' (Saunders 2001: 64). These juxtapositions are found within the 'good bad man', Charlie. Moreover, as mentioned, westerns are arguably mythological in structure, which makes them less historical than a playground for archetypes and symbolic references. In essence, despite the 'real' setting of the film, Cave explores universal issues that have less to do with history (though it is historical) than with themes. According to Janet Walker, 'through the lens of history, we come to realize that westerns incorporate, elide, embellish, mythologize, allegorize, erase, duplicate, and rethink past events that are themselves – as history – fragmented, fuzzy, and striated with fantasy constructions' (2001: 13). If this is true for most westerns, then *The Proposition* possibly points to a revisionist way of understanding the past, especially because Cave's interest lies in the characters – the very people who create and destroy generic tropes of the western. Ironically, it is the very people who claim to 'save' the territory, like Captain Stanley, who ultimately cause more harm to others (particularly the indigenous peoples) than good. In interview, Hillcoat discusses the relationship between the bushrangers (Irish), the lawmen (British) and the natives (aborigines):

[t]he bushrangers were outlaws who went into the remote areas: outback Australia was a final frontier full of people trying to escape their past, very extreme and harsh and brutal. The clash was between the outlaw Irish-convict generation, represented by the brothers, and the British, with the aboriginals in conflict with both of them – three ways, like a triangle. The bushrangers either utilized the aboriginals' knowledge to help them escape from the law or were tracked down and caught by the same trackers. There was a symbiotic relationship, either antagonistic or for mutual gain.

(Roddick 2006)

We see the trackers help Captain Stanley, Arthur and themselves. This 'triangle' also helps explain why the film exists in a morally grey realm, where allegiances are unclear. Brutal tactics to 'cure' brutal men seem excessive, but in Cave's outback they are the norm. As Cave suggests, when discussing Australia's history and the idea of having three separate types of people vying for space and place, 'I don't think we see things in black and white, or good guys and bad guys, or villains and heroes. We have a much more conflicting, ambiguous shame-faced view of our history. I think we basically see it as a history of failure and incompetence' (Balfour 2006). In one horrific scene, Stanley flogs Mikey with 40 lashes. The brutality of the scene makes his wife, Martha, faint, makes the once-applauding townspeople disgusted, and even causes Stanley to see that the excessive punishment was too cruel. The struggle with what to do – with moral decisions – underscores many of the scenes in the film, but we get the sense that the characters will always struggle to discover what is right.

It almost seems paradoxical to call the film morally complex, simply because the lines of right and wrong are laid out from the start. We know who is supposedly good, Stanley, and we know who is supposedly bad, the Burns brothers. But because the issues of power, land rights and fraternity are called into question, we quickly realize the difficulty of hashing out perfect lines of discrimination and separation. When describing the characters of the film, and the difficulty for spectators in latching onto one particular sympathetic character, Cave says,

[o]ur heroes are murky characters. So, we wanted to write a story where you go to a film and expect your radar to focus on who's the one to sympathize with and who's the one you want to see get their comeuppance in the end. This radar is confused throughout and sometimes you feel aligned to one character and then you shift your allegiance to

somebody else, and that in the end they are a group of people in a place that they should never be and they're being slowly dismantled by their own folly.

(Balfour 2006)

There are no heroes in *The Proposition* in the traditional sense; instead, in their attempts at transcending boundaries, the characters in *The Proposition* are ultimately 'dismantled by their own folly'. Spectator sympathy is thwarted throughout. The Burns brothers and Captain Stanley engage in a permanent struggle that ultimately seals their fates. It seems to be a no-win situation for all characters, like in many noirs, where the protagonist meets his fate through his ill-conceived plans and actions.

Westerns feature highly individualistic and strong-willed men, who live by their own codes of behaviour. Rarely do they yield to anyone. In *The Proposition*, the three main characters, Charlie, Arthur and Stanley, all are inclined to do what they deem necessary in order to survive. Their transgressions immediately make them unlikely to ever fit into a societal group – they are loners. Even Stanley, who is married to Martha (Emily Watson) and has men who are his inferiors and therefore listen to his commands, seems quite unnatural in the role of community 'saviour'. According to Patrick McGee, 'the Western has repeatedly formulated the question of who has the right to wealth, the right to power that wealth seems to bestow, and the right to freedom' (2007: xiv). All three of these categories – wealth, power and freedom – help identify and define the characters in *The Proposition*. Stanley's home displays wealth, he is the one with (seemingly) the most power, and he too is in search of freedom, from dealing with the uncivilized peoples of the outback. Like many of Cave's protagonists, the men in *The Proposition* are constantly searching for something, whether it is solace, love, power, insight or freedom. The ragged characters of the film all display triumphs of masculinity, but only at a price: 'by recognizing its limits and the moral uncertainty it tries to disavow' (McGee 2007: 110). While the characters in the film really have no moral compass, except perhaps for Stanley, they all renounce any attempts to stabilize their transgressive behaviour.

Cave's transposition of the western genre to the Australian outback has resulted in a distinctive film that depicts the violent ways of the morally ambiguous 'good' and 'bad' men of Australia in the 1880s. The violence in the film is brutally realistic and unflinching, and lends the film its authenticity, equating violence with suffering and loss. The film received criticism over its extreme violence, but Cave was quick to point out the lighter side of the film. He says,

a lot of weight has been put on the violence in this film as if that's all it's about and there is violence in the film and it's graphic and brutal. But there's a lot of levity, from my point of view, in the dialogue that counterbalances the violence. It's that sort of stuff I really enjoy writing, the dialogue and the humour and some of the tenderness that goes with that.

(Carnevale 2006)

Hillcoat has also stressed the historical accuracy of the violence. As Cave suggests, 'when John deals with violence, I think he deals with it in a realistic way and that it's a fundamental part of the story. It was a violent time and a violent so-called "civilizing of the country"' (Balfour 2006).

In keeping with the authenticity of the film, Cave and Hillcoat treat the aborigines with respect and aplomb. 'The challenge for [Cave] was to avoid making an American western yet at the same time avoiding an overt parochialism. Cave sees the film as being both Australian yet intrinsically universal' (Fischer 2006). One thing that makes the film distinctly Australian is the presence of the aborigines. Archival photographs of aborigines and white settlers accompany the credit sequence; many of the aborigines are shown in chains. The film addresses this 'slavery' to some extent; in one scene, aborigines in shackles are led to Stanley and his men so they can be questioned about the whereabouts of Arthur. They call Arthur the 'dog man' and begin to howl, undermining Stanley's authority and giving them a sense of power both by humiliating him, and through their suggestion that Arthur has more control over them. Traditional American westerns often pit the 'cowboys' against the 'Indians'. According to Saunders, '[w]hether we take the simple collocation of cowboys and Indians or the more sophisticated binary opposition between civilization and the wilderness, [the Indians'] role is central to [the western]' (2001: 93). By contrast, Hillcoat treats the aborigines with respect. As he mentions in an interview, 'the main thing for [the aborigines in the cast] was getting to see things that have never been portrayed before, like on all the different levels of how their community is integrated. [We] wanted to get it as truthful as possible' (Carnevale 2006). If the wilderness of the outback corresponds to the aborigines and their community, then Cave very adeptly portrays them as not merely keepers of the outback – the true 'owners' of the land and its wealth – but also as having the right to defend their land. Many of the aborigines in the film commit acts of violence; some have, for example, banded together to be part of Arthur's posse, and therefore kill for and with him. But the aborigines are not treated as pawns in a political agenda (unlike Native Americans in many American westerns). In Cave's words:

[the film] has also to treat Aboriginals without an agenda. Aboriginals are usually portrayed in films as people who exist to show white people what the Aboriginal situation is, rather than as being an integral part of the film itself. There's always an agenda. They were extremely excited about being part of a film without politics. At the same time, it showed things that pretty much aren't shown in Australian films, particularly black on black violence. Especially black on black violence. And that there was a resistance, to be in a film where there was an opportunity to fight back, to kill a few whites, those things are rarely portrayed in Australian films.

(Carnevale 2006)

In one graphic scene, an aborigine spears Charlie as he treks across the blazing outback in search of his brother. In another, an aborigine named Two Bob, a member of the Burns gang, slits the throat of another aborigine who has helped Stanley. The aborigines protect themselves just as the white bushrangers do, and use violence if necessary.

The Proposition strips away the romanticism of place and hero-worship often associated with American westerns. According to Carol Hart, 'Stanley's civilizing mission is what gives rise to his proposition. Stanley can no longer abide such policing rules, because these rules resist abidance in the place of unruliness that he and his young English wife, Martha, have sought to tame' (2006). Stanley's mission is solely to civilize the land, and in order to do so he must first get rid of the outlaws who make the land inhospitable and dangerous. Upon offering his proposition, Stanley informs Charlie that he will 'civilize' Australia – quite an ironic comment given the rest of the film. It is ironic, of course, that these claims are made in the name of 'democracy', but here again Cave seems to suggest that any attempts at stability and transformation are futile, that violence will always win in the end. According to Hart,

> [t]he landscape in *The Proposition* is the transcendent image that not so much allows the film to reveal itself, but rather serves to redeem it. [The] end result is a masterful representation of the Australian Outback, which is invariably as vast and majestic as it is claustrophobic and unforgiving. Ideas of land are never far from notions of home and family, and the film thoughtfully recognizes these links.
>
> (2006)

The outback provides a complementary setting for the themes Cave explores. It is a place of unrelenting discomfort for the characters in the film, and so it creates tension. But it also offers moments of tranquillity, especially when we see Martha's attempts at creating a *home*. Settings in westerns are so vital to the iconography and demographics of the genre that it seems impossible to imagine them separate from thematic concerns or atmosphere and mood, which can also be said of film noir. Barry Keith Grant suggests, 'in noirs such as *The Naked City* (1948), the city is a palpable presence, taking on a menacing quality that threatens to overwhelm the individuals who dwell in it' (2007: 24). Likewise, Cave's outback conditions characters, creates mood, and stifles ambitions.

The film also reflects many of Cave's concerns including love, affection and compassion. The love depicted in *The Proposition* stems from not just the brothers (though a warped relationship indeed), but also from the presence of Captain Stanley's wife, Martha, who represents sophisticated, domesticated English propriety struggling with Australian primitivism. She expresses her femininity through domestic chores and maintaining a white-picket fence house with homely accoutrements to match. Her role is in stark contrast to that of her husband. Representations of masculinity abound in westerns, and a specific generic trope of westerns is the *necessity* of masculine brutality as opposed to the femininity that is often the foundation of social and stable relationships. Martha is not just a representation of femininity, but also the embodiment of class, private property and community. She also represents desire, for she is the only figure who exudes any kind of sexual presence for the men in the film. The attention given to the relationship between Stanley and Martha belies any suspicion that the film is strictly concerned with the violent world of men.

Conclusion

In an interview regarding the interrelations between music and film, Cave says,

> you can go deeper with film, and really run with something for an extended period of time. With a song, you are constantly back at the start again; you write one song, you are back at having to work out what your theme is again and what you want the next song to be about. But to tell an extended story like a film is something that feels quite natural for me.
>
> (Fischer 2006)

Cave's ability to tell a magnificent and engrossing story is the foundation for *The Proposition*. Like his music, the film has finely drawn characters, whose stories are central to our enjoyment (and understanding) of it. The score for the film, which Cave composed with Bad Seed Warren Ellis, works wonderfully with the images on-screen. It is at once sparse and haunting, boisterous and loud, intimate and mournful. The music ties into the film's narrative in such a way as to complement it and to suggest a theme. According to Nelson, 'Cave's intermittently abrasive music, with its quasi-industrial clang, suggests that the future will offer no reprieve, and that maybe it doesn't matter' (2006). I do not think that Cave set out to write a completely western genre movie; rather, he seems far more interested in nuanced characters and their interpersonal relationships. The characters are all on personal quests to redeem themselves; 'any transformation of social consciousness necessarily involves some turning inward and alienation from the socius as it currently exists' (McGee 2007: 33). Stanley's quest is in the name of 'society', but he clearly has a personal agenda. His attempts at redeeming society are ultimately doomed, but the journey he undertakes is as revelatory (and melancholy) as Charlie's uninvited mission. According to Paul Seydor, when discussing the themes of Peckinpah's revisionist westerns, '[the] theme is a trek into the wilderness where, away from society, a person may be reborn or in some sense reconstituted, often through an ordeal of physical crisis or a trial of violence' (1980: 21). *The Proposition* explores the darker sides of men's souls, their capacities for inflicting pain and their frail stabs at happiness and redemption, which follows a similar pattern of trekking into the wilderness to find the self through physical and psychic endeavour.

All of the characters transgress during the course of the film. They all want redemption somehow, and Arthur in particular has a rather skewed version of it. He continually stresses the importance of 'family' over all else, but in his sadistic behaviour, he demonstrates something contrary: he kills people at will, randomly and for fun.

When Charlie finds him, Arthur lectures him on the meaning of fraternity and familial behaviour. The opening of the film, which sets the film's tone, shows the brutal killing of the Hopkins family by the Burns brothers, the destruction of a family that makes Stanley, who captures Mikey and Charlie after a shootout, offer his proposition. In another scene, one of Arthur's young gang members asks Arthur for the definition of 'misanthrope'. Arthur replies, '[s]omeone who hates every other bastard'. The young man then asks, '[i]s that us?', to which Arthur answers, '[g]ood lord no, we are a family' (Hillcoat 2005). As Hart astutely notes, '[the] bonds of family are not inextricably tied to blood, but [...] the formations of family arise out of the "idea" of family. And so it is here that we see the manifestation, the personification perhaps, of the penal colony and its being based on an idea rather than blood neatly articulated' (Hart 2006). The striving for community is a goal that Arthur hopes to maintain and achieve, but his ruthless actions ultimately prove that he is incapable of having a 'true' family, especially with his own brothers. Family strife and/or union is a common theme in westerns. According to McGee, '[the] family as a structure reproduces not only the social relations of production, in the form of the class system, but also the contradiction between individual desire and social conformity, to which the Western frequently offers an imaginary solution' (2007: xv). The Proposition certainly adheres to this idea because Arthur yearns for family but he is an individualist, ruthless enough to destroy his family in order to create an imaginary family. Again, Cave makes an interesting turn when Charlie and Arthur decide to band together to rescue Mikey and capture Stanley and his wife, which results in more bloodshed and death. All of the characters also seek transcendence, a moment of overcoming their boundaries or personal limitations. The lone bounty hunter – played by John Hurt – Charlie meets while he is trekking through the outback, who is also searching for Arthur, presents a philosophical spin on Charlie's goal. The bounty hunter spouts crazy poetry, but is articulate and seemingly well educated. But he also appears racist, and after agreeing to help Charlie, turns on him. According to McGee, the type of lone wanderer that Hurt plays is 'the drifter [of] the spirit of divine authority and the instrument of transcendent morality' (2007: 194). If this is so in the case of the bounty hunter, Cave makes the character much more ruthless and morally ambiguous, but he does ultimately cause Charlie to realize at the end of the film that his life of carnage has been empty of meaning. Seeing the 'real' family of Stanley and his wife, whose relationship is delicately portrayed and carefully nuanced, causes Charlie to momentarily discover redemption.

Cave gives us a truly mesmerizing portrait of how good and evil mix to create morally ambiguous men. The themes of revenge and retribution are played out as in traditional westerns, but Cave intuitively knows that such lines are often blurred, so he subverts them. While seeking redemption, the characters of The Proposition become blinded by power, embrace violence and finally seek vengeance. The accuracy of the setting, narrative and characterization also make the film inspired in its triangular structure. As Hillcoat notes, 'there are certain aspects to [Australian] history that we wanted to include, but without getting bogged down. Nick brought those alive through the conflict between the environment and the European immigrants, and between the Irish and the British, and the British and the Aboriginal community. Basically, it's a panorama of life from that time' (Roddick 2006). The vista created is indisputably ruthless, callous and cold-blooded. The struggle to create a civilized country is difficult – or at least paved with blood: 'civilization emerges from a gun barrel, and its discontents are everywhere' (Baumgarten 2006). Ultimately, the film offers a complex study of the fine distinctions between community and individuality, good and evil, and the constant need for some form of solace.

References

Balfour, Brad (2006), 'Nick Cave Offers His Proposition', http://www.popentertainment.com/nickcave2.htm. Accessed 4 May 2010.

Barsanti, Chris (2007), 'The Proposition', http://www.filmjournal.com/filmjournal/reviews/article-display.jsp?vnu_content_id=1002463034. Accessed 4 May 2010.

Baumgarten, Marjorie (2006), 'The Proposition', http://www.austinchronicle.com/gyroscope/Calendar/film?Film=oid%30372689. Accessed 10 February 2010.

Carnevale, Rob (2006), 'The Proposition – John Hillcoat/Nick Cave Interview', http://www.indielondon.co.uk/Film-Review/theproposition-john-hillcoat-and-nick-cave-interview. Accessed 4 May 2010.

Fischer, Paul (2006), 'Nick Cave – The Proposition Celebrity Interview', http://www.girl.com/nick-cave-the-proposition.htm. Accessed 2 February 2010.

Grant, Barry Keith (2007), *Film Genre: From Iconography to Ideology*, London: Wallflower.

Hart, Carol (2006), 'Portraits of Settler History in *The Proposition*', http://www.sensesofcinema.com/2006/38/proposition/. Accessed 14 October 2010.

Hillcoat, John (2005), *The Proposition*. Australia: First Look.

Hillier, Jim and Alastair Phillips (2009), *100* Film Noirs, London: Palgrave Macmillan.

McGee, Patrick (2007), *From Shane to Kill Bill: Rethinking the Western*, Malden and Oxford: Blackwell.

Neale, Steve (2000), *Genre and Hollywood*, London: Routledge.

Nelson, Rob (2006), 'The Bad Seeds: Nick Cave's Western "Proposition" Plays Like a Threat', http://www.citypages.com/2006-05-24/movies/the-bad-seeds/. Accessed 10 February 2010.

Reed, Joseph W. (1989), *American Scenarios: The Uses of Film Genre*, Middletown, CT: Wesleyan University Press.

Roddick, Nick (2006), 'Ballad of the Wild Boys', http://www.bfi.org.uk/sightandsound/feature/49267. Accessed 4 May 2010.

Saunders, John (2001), *The Western Genre: From Lordsburg to Big Whiskey*, London: Wallflower.

Schatz, Thomas (1981), *Hollywood Genres: Formulas, Filmmaking, and the Studio System*, Philadelphia: Temple University Press.

Schrader, Paul (1986), 'Notes on Film Noir', in Barry Keith Grant (ed.), *Film Genre Reader*, Austin: University of Texas Press, pp. 169–82.

Seydor, Paul (1980), *Peckinpah: The Western Films*, Urbana, IL: University of Illinois Press.

Szaloky, Melinda (2001), 'A Tale N/nobody can tell: The Return of a Repressed Western History in Jim Jarmusch's *Dead Man*', in Janet Walker (ed.), *Westerns: Films through History*, London: Routledge, pp. 47–70.

Walker, Janet (2001), 'Introduction: Westerns through History', in Janet Walker (ed.), *Westerns: Films through History*, London: Routledge, pp. 1–26.

PART IV

Influences

Chapter 10

Nick Cave and Gothic: Ghost Stories, Fucked Organs, Spectral Liturgy

Isabella van Elferen

Around his neck hung a thoroughly fucked guitar. His skin cleared to his bones, his skull was an utter disaster, scabbed and hacked, and his eyes bulged out of their orbits like a blind man's. And yet, the eyes stared at us as if to herald some divine visitation. Here stood a man on the trashold of greatness; here stood [...] a Christ akimbo on Calvary. Blixa Bargeld.

(Cave 1988: 128)

Ghostly presences and fucked instruments

On 28 April 2008 Nick Cave played the Heineken Music Hall in Amsterdam. On stage appeared a pale, skinny figure, with dyed black hair and a rather sleazy moustache, fighting with the electronic instrument in front of him. Expostulating. 'Dutch people from Amsterdam, [...] my organ is fucked. [...] It's a fucked organ. Without it [...] you'll be going "what is it?"' After a series of frustrated fiddlings, impatient interjections and amused photography, the band could start playing the song about Lazarus' return from death. An amateur clip of this incident, of course, can now be found on YouTube, in bad audiovisual quality ('GustavZomerschoe' 2008). It is almost like a Nick Cave video. I was in the audience that day, and remember thinking how interesting it was that Cave's media would work against him. This chapter explores Cave's relation to Gothic, and the way media work (or do not work) is a vital aspect of that relation.

Nick Cave's work is often associated with both literary and subcultural Gothic. His citation-laden lyrics and his novels (*And the Ass saw the Angel* (1989) and *The Death of Bunny Munro* (2009)) blend high- and low-brow references ranging from the Bible, Milton, Yeats and Eliot to horror, road movies and pornography, into dark pastiches revealing an entwined fascination for romanticism and perversion. Cave's music shows a similar abundance of historical and contemporary references, and a similar penchant for dark romance, as nostalgic folk tunes are combined with industrial noise, (post-) punk racket with bluesy melancholy, and spooky echoes with rock bravura. His videos present classic performance footage mixed with film noir-ish mises-en-scènes, steampunk media assemblages with theatrical settings and explicit horror. These characteristics have made Nick Cave very popular in Goth scenes, and have simultaneously led literary criticism to assert that he represents strands of Gothic described as postmodern, Australian and/or Southern (Friedman 2007; Hart 2009).

Catherine Spooner even goes so far as to describe him as an 'icon' of contemporary Gothic, and Emma McEvoy maintains that his work with the Bad Seeds 'creates a new dimension to the Gothic aesthetic' (Spooner 2006: 9; McEvoy 2007: 79). The eerie universes of Cave's works certainly do have many parallels with Gothic literature and film, but is that enough to qualify him as Gothic? How do these literary and cinematic traditions translate into a musical Gothic idiom? How Gothic, in short, is Cave's musical universe?

Style and tropes

Whether in literature, film or popular music, Gothic narratives are first and foremost ghost stories. They are typically set in eerie empty spaces like deserted ruins, desolate landscapes, urban labyrinths or the endless void of cyberspace, and these spooky spaces are haunted by all sorts of spectral appearances. The absent presence of a ghost signifies undeath, its persistently haunting nature unyieldingly foregrounding unprocessed traumas or obsessions lurking in the unconsciousness of certain persons, historical periods or cultures; hence Cathy's return to Heathcliff as the ghost of all-consuming love, or the ghost of Frankenstein haunting technological discourses. Moreover, as Jacques Derrida has pointed out, 'a spectre is always a *revenant*', a coming back: the logic of haunting necessarily engenders a collapse of linear time (2006: 10–11). The pervasive spectrality of Gothic stories points out that time in this genre is always out of joint, that every present is haunted by ghosts of various pasts and every self haunted by their own repressed fears and desires. And since fear and desire are twin drives, Gothic ghosts are simultaneously dreadful and appealing – Dracula being the prime example.

The Gothic genre does not just narrate ghost stories, it wallows in them. It paints landscapes that are bleaker than bleak, its ghosts are not just attractive but lasciviously sensual, and Gothic haunting turns nostalgia into a perverse overwriting of the past. Blood drips off the pages of a Gothic novel. Bats fly out of the Gothic film screen. Gothic style, in short, is over the top in all ways. This was noticed at least as early as 1797, when an anonymous critic in *Spirit of the Public Journals* identified a whole list of stock ingredients (castles, secrets, skeletons, found manuscripts) with which anyone could compose a Gothic novel. But the genre is also very self-aware of that, so self-aware, in fact, that a self-conscious, ironic artificiality is one of its indispensable characteristics. This becomes most evident in the omnipresent intertextualities within Gothic productions, ranging from the self-referentiality of early Gothic novels to the cartoonesque stage designs in Tim Burton's films.

Nick Cave's lyrical style shares many characteristics with the Gothic, but also veers off from it in some ways. Zooming in directly on spectrality and haunting, trauma and obsession, it contains less elaborate descriptions of deserted spaces than traditional Gothic texts do. Some of his songs quite straightforwardly give a voice to the (un)dead, such as Jack's Shadow, Lucy or Elisa Day in 'Where the Wild Roses Grow'; these ghosts make the past reappear in the present and unveil hidden secrets or truths. Other songs chart the internal rumblings of the haunted self, observing carefully and mercilessly the confrontation with one's own spectres; examples are poor old Henry, Lottie in 'The Curse of Millhaven', and even Orpheus and Eurydice in 'The Lyre of Orpheus'. Other songs, such as 'The Mercy Seat', 'Stagger Lee' and 'Red Right Hand', do not describe spectrality so much as haunt listeners themselves, speaking from the point of view of lustful evildoers, perverts and murderers. These songs are uncomfortably powerful explorations of the Gothic simultaneity of fear and desire.

Like any Gothic writer Cave exults in stylistic excess. If castles and skeletons are the stock features in Gothic novels, death and romance are those of Cave's lyrics. How many murderer POVs, how many cunts can one *take*? Just like Gothic fictions, Cave's texts are ironically artificial. 'The Weeping Song' is so over the top the tearful affects it relates seem to veer towards a parody of sadness; this parodic overturning of emotion is confirmed by the video to this song, in which Cave and Bargeld row a boat sailing on what is evidently black plastic. The irony is heightened by the pervasive intertextuality of the whole oeuvre. The Birthday Party's early lines 'Horror bat/Bite!/Cool machine/Bite!/Sex vampire/Bite!' invoke and – perhaps unintentionally – comment on the overtly Gothic tone of Bauhaus' work, and the Gothicized references to the Bible, John Milton and other texts illustrate Cave's self-aware positioning within established literary traditions (Cave 2007: 32–3).

Cave does not only reshape the Gothic in his lyrics; his music, too, is imbued with spectrality and overstylization. His lyrical ghosts acquire an audible voice, a voice that is as threatening or seductive as the singer decides to make it. Musical ghosts are much more effectively uncanny than literary ones, not only because auditive perception has a more direct effect than textual, but more importantly because tempo and rhythm, melody and harmony, vocal and instrumental timbre underline and intensify what is being expressed. 'Song of Joy' from *Murder Ballads* (1995) is an interesting example. The song is a Gothic frame story: a lonely wanderer tells us the story of his wife and three children, who were killed in ghastly fashion one night when he was away on a visit. As the story unfolds the listener cannot shake off the uncomfortable feeling that the husband might have been involved in the killings – typically Cavean Gothic, in short. The narrator speak-sings his story in an unpleasantly low and out-of-tone voice, revealing detail after gruesome detail in a tantalizingly slow tempo, lustfully tasting the rhythms of the words on his tongue ('Aahr you – BBekkenennMMeInn?'). His tale is accompanied by slender organ chords overlaid with the dry sounds of a bar piano that almost sounds like it is played in a cold church or ruin through the heavy reverb added in postproduction, an effect that is enhanced by the echoing backing vocals going 'La la lalala' in endlessly rising and descending scales. A repetitive electronic bleep gives the suggestion of intensive care monitors, as if the victims are somewhere still, barely clinging onto life. And to confirm explicitly that the song is supposed to sound like an old spooky film, 'the wolves howl, the serpents hiss' in the background (Cave 2007: 245). This song, with its ridiculously ironic title, is Gothicized-over-the-top, a musical language in excess of its own limits, musical expenditure through the cracks of tonality engendered by Cave's self-celebratory vocal inadequacy.

Besides such literal ghostly vocalizations, Cave's work also indirectly invokes musical ghosts through the spectral dimensions of pop music itself. His pastiches of (post-)punk, blues, gospel, rock, industrial, folk and Goth styles are collections of musical revenants that invite past narratives to overlay the present. Lyrical intertextuality thus meets musical intertextuality, which enables a conflation of multiple times and spaces. In the case of 'Song of Joy', the here and now of the song's narration is simultaneously haunted by at least the times and spaces of the narrator's horrific past, the Milton quotes in the text, old horror movie soundtracks, the suggestive bleep-bleep of the electronic instruments, the bar room amateur style of the piano part, the 1960s organ timbre, and the Bad Seeds' sing-along backing vocals.

Nick Cave's Gothic, thus, is spectral, excessive and exhibitionist, its style one of its most important characteristics. Yet stylistics alone is a somewhat fragile basis for the definition of a whole genre or an artist's investment in it. If Gothic 'signifies a writing of excess', the nature of the excess must be studied alongside the style of writing (Botting 1996: 1).

Transgressive themes

The theme of Gothic ghost stories is the anxiety that sets in when familiar values are transgressed and exchanged for the borderland of the unknown, the unseen and the unheard. Set in evacuated spaces, Gothic narratives revolve around the exploration of the borders of the knowable. Wandering around in the liminality between such opposites as past and present, life and death, love and hate, good and evil, the characters in Gothic tales confront their own and their audience's latent fears and desires regarding such dichotomies. Here Chris Baldick's definition of Gothic comes to mind: Gothic revolves around spectral transgressions of time and space, endorsing 'a sickening descent into disintegration' (1992: xiii).

Gothic twilight zones are classic examples of what Freud has termed *das Unheimliche*: the home, the safe area of the familiar, is made unhomely, uncanny, when repressed fear or desire acquires an absent presence within it. Gothic ostentatiously pushes the uncanny into its audience's willing or unwilling face, demanding that every reader, viewer or listener confront their own spectres. It enforces the mirror image that one would rather not see, exposing the inevitable presence of pasts, others, fears within the here, the now, the self. In this way Gothic offers a social and cultural critique that unveils the Freudian repressed in various audiences and eras (even though, as Martin Heidegger has noted, the known should always-already be uncanny because of the presence of the unknowable; from a Heideggerian point of view, therefore, Gothic critique should not even be necessary (Heidegger 1993: 101–104)).

Nick Cave's work quite precisely matches this critical aspect of Gothic. The themes of his lyrics consistently transgress the borders of life and death, good and evil, past and present, sacred and secular. Playing with the boundaries of consciousness, morality and reason, the 'sickening descent into disintegration' is indeed his chief theme. He himself motivates his thematic choice in the best Gothic tradition:

[t]he writer who refuses to explore the darker regions of the heart will never be able to write convincingly about the wonder, the magic and the joy of love, for just as goodness cannot

be trusted unless it has breathed the same air as evil – the enduring metaphor of Christ crucified between two criminals comes to mind here – so within the fabric of the Love Song, within its melody, its lyric, one must sense an acknowledgement for suffering.

(Cave 2007: 8)

Cave's songs consequently are simultaneously discomforting and appealing – what if 'the valley of the shadow of death' proves a lovely walk? What if love and death are linked more closely together than we might like to think, as in 'Where the Wild Roses Grow'? What if the evil ghosts of the past would roam the present? Asking such questions in his lyrics and intensifying their effective and spectral qualities through his musical settings, Cave creates in his works a typically Gothic version of the uncanny. Spooner writes with regards to Gothic ghosts that '[t]he past chokes the present, prevents progress and the march towards personal or social enlightenment' (2006: 18–19). This rings very true for the ghosts in Nick Cave's works – Henry, the Red Right Hand, John Finn's wife, Sorrow's child. Awoken by a song, they reappear from their hidden corners and haunt the here and now, choke the self.

The music video to 'Where the Wild Roses Grow', a duet with Kylie Minogue from *Murder Ballads*, can illustrate the way in which Cave's usage of Gothic tropes and style expresses the themes of transgression and uncanniness. The video lays out a thoroughly deceptive atmosphere through a careful use of the lyrical, musical and visual media involved. The text of the song starts as a love poem, but turns out to be the story of a murder told in dialogue by killer and victim. Two ghosts, then, causing various overlapping temporalities – a dead girl speaking, the evil voice of a murderer, but also a very female singer and a grumpy dark male singer – while they tell the transgressive tale of love spilling over into death. The dialogue is shaped musically as a melancholy duet for male and female voice in a slow 6/8 measure and G minor key. A musical element of unease is created by the singers' use of their voices: whereas Cave's voice is eerie and excessive on its own, Minogue exceeds her usual vocal range as the female part is set much too low for her voice (as is clearly noticeable in live performances). The story is set visually in the romantic atmosphere of a river bank against a late afternoon sun – a desolate space and literal twilight zone, an intertextual reference to Charles Laughton's *Night of the Hunter* (1955), which adds yet another spectral layer. The deceptive tranquillity of the mise-en-scène is countered by the viewer's gradual realization that the lovely girl in the video is the murder victim in this story, and that the conventional male gaze of the camera is nothing less than the murderer's gaze. The visual fragmentation of the story against the chronology of the text, and the over-aesthetic and over-intertextual iconography of the white dress, the snake, the gloves and the weeping willow complete the ambivalent stylization of this video. The video stops time in the romantic/fatal moment right before the murder, and thereby emphasizes the uncanniness of that moment: does the audience perceive a hidden identification with this love's spilling over in death? This music video is Gothic in the transhistorical, critical sense: the twilight zone created through a careful use of traditional tropes unveils the fluid borders between good and evil, past and present, violence and jouissance. Cave's Gothicizing of the love duet and the romantic music video exposes 'The Secret Life of the Love Song'.

It becomes clear from this example that media play a vital role in Gothic criticism, as they do in Nick Cave's Gothic version of rock music. They are the channels between excessive style and transgressive thematic.

Uncanny media

'To tell a story is always to invoke ghosts' (Wolfreys 2002: 3). The act of narration invites spectres of past, present and future, and is haunted by long-hidden anxieties or desires. The uncanny is therefore an indispensable part of storytelling; it is the unrepresented lurking behind presentation, the unknown saliently present in the known. And it is not only literature that is uncannily destabilized by its own technology: every act of mediation, be it textual, visual or auditory, evokes a Gothic conflation of overlapping temporalities and realities. Moreover, a medium itself can function as a 'third space' between the mediated phenomenon and its audience. The effects of hypermediacy, the emphatic foregrounding of the media involved in mediation – and yes, the excessive, self-aware style of Gothic is hypermedial – can highlight this medial space as a 'hauntic' twilight zone between performance and spectator. Gothic *narratives* are thus encapsulated in the Gothic *narrative act* of mediation (Van Elferen 2010: 286–8). Media can house Gothic narratives and simultaneously underline their narrative performativity: if a castle is built with the sole purpose of being inhabited by a haunting ghost, architecture becomes an agent. The Gothic medium is not just the message; it is an indispensable constructing instrument without which the message would not come through. The fact that Gothic style is so excessive, ironic and hypermedial supports its workings: it is the act of mediation itself that enables Gothic to expose the repressed.

In his essay on the love song, Nick Cave proves himself a Gothic narrator by all standards. When he notes that 'the Love Song holds within it an eerie intelligence all of its own – to reinvent the past and to lay it at the feet of the present', he reflects on the spectral dimension of intertextuality that he so abundantly employs (2007: 3). Cave also comments on the independent medial agency of the Love Letter and the Love Song; his personifying capitalization of these words is telling. These genres, he argues, 'hold within them a power that the spoken word does not have'. They 'reinvent [...] one's beloved', and even have the power to 'imprison them [...], for words become the defining parameter that keeps the image of the loved one, imprisoned in a bondage of poetry' (2007: 15). From a media theoretical perspective what Cave points out is that these media can establish a space of their own, in between writer and written matter. His pervasive irony, which is nothing but a hypermedial comment on the act of writing, underlines the distances between style, theme and mediation in his work and thereby increases his message of entwined romance and perversion. Will Self points exactly to this principle when he praises Cave's ability to repeatedly ironize received values (Cave 2007: xii).

'Loverman' from *Let Love In* (1994) can illustrate the way Gothic stylistics, transgression and uncanny mediation meet in Nick Cave's media use. The lyrics of the song paint a familiar Cavean picture: the lover is a monster – '[t]here's a devil waiting outside your door/How much longer?' (2007: 218) – ready to devour his loved one in a rage of love-lust-violence. The musical settings of the couplets are subdued and repetitive, Cave's low, descending melodies alternated in endless call-and-response with slow, almost whispered phrases in the raspy timbre of Harvey's and Bargeld's backing vocals. Cave voices the devil, the backing vocals express the unease it causes; together they evoke musical reminiscences of the hidden, the forbidden, the perverse. The instrumentation is scarce but scary, consisting of faint guitar screeches and electronic noises, slow sidestick snare drums and a single tubular bell at the first beat of each second bar. Like in other Cave songs, the connotations are both music historical and cinematic, evoking Einstürzende Neubauten's bleak industrial soundscapes as well as technodystopian movies. Each chorus, by contrast, is an explosion of rock violence as melodies, volumes, screaming vocals and instrumental intensity all rise up: 'I am what I am what I am what I am' (Cave 2007: 218–19). Lyrics and music are thus once again spectral, excessive and hypermediatized through repetition – an effect that is strengthened by the reference to Gertrude Stein's rose.

The video to this song is centred even more explicitly around media and mediation. A scenic set-up shows a hypnotic circle, which aligns perfectly with the repetitive melodies and structure of the song. The band relate in a short interview on the DVD that actual hypnosis occurred during the shootings; while hypnosis brings the unconscious to the surface and blurs the borders between known and unknown, the artwork of the video expresses this theme through a focus on the artificial nature of mediation. Media are consistently placed in the foreground. There are countless shots of the hypnotist, musical instruments, audio recorders, and ears and eyes; the letters 'LOVERMAN' are painted on papers and bodies and then destroyed; and the consistent use of 'old media' such as crumbly black and white footage for the hypnotic scenes (couplets) alternated with handheld colour recordings and extreme close-ups in the performance sections (choruses) is suggestive of the medial abyss between spectators' and recorded realities. An extended section with a tape recorder, outmoded head phones and microphones lets the focus of attention zoom in on auditive media and their uncanny agency. The camera style is dominated by over-editing and tilts, but not in the rhythmical style of an MTV video – this video is meant to undermine the song's content, not to underline it. If the lyrical theme of this song is the dark side of love, then its artistic expression takes the guise of Gothic hypermediacy and irony: there is more than what your ears and eyes tell you. It is the reliability of human perception that is at stake here, and it is solely the uncanny aspect of mediation that achieves that effect.

The contrast to the 'Wild Roses' video seems enormous, conceived as it is like a closed cinematographic world without performance interludes, suggesting a difference between two realities. But its narratological principles are very similar to those of 'Loverman'. Exactly because of the cinematographic consistency in 'Wild Roses' the spectator is taken back by the story being told there: the media involved narrate a ghost story and subsequently, through their own medial agency, deconstruct narration by foregrounding the gap between form – romantic love duet – and content – murder story. The video's highly staged quality functions as another type of hypermediacy, an overstatement of the narratological artificiality of the song, which in turn makes the spectator realize with a shudder that evil can wear an enticing guise. Just like in 'Loverman', it is the act of mediation, which is nothing other than the guidance of perception, which highlights the unreliability of perception itself.

Music video endorses multimedial perception, and in it the Gothic instrument of uncanny mediation is intermedially doubled and highlighted. But it is a music-dominated form of mediation (as a video is essentially a film clip accompanying a song), and the strong Gothic performativity of these both clips, I want to argue, is most poignantly caused by music's tremendous uncanny agency. It is surprising that the impressive body of Gothicist research as good as ignores music, as the musical medium pushes both the medial self-awareness and the transgression that characterize Gothic to their utmost limits; indeed, it does this to such an extent that it necessitates a re-evaluation of the balance between 'writing' and 'excess', which is so important for the scholarly understanding of the genre (more on this below). If every mediation has a spectral dimension, this holds especially true for musical mediation, since musical spectrality is much more profound and disturbing even than the voicing of ghosts and the evocation of past times described above. It allows ghosts and revenants to actively interfere with the lived and embodied presence of the listener – it transgresses the distance between medium, message and audience and thus quite literally makes the home unhomely. How? Through our personal investments in music.

Lawrence Grossberg has argued that audiences' interactions with cultural texts, and especially rock music, operate according to ideological and affective 'mattering maps', intricate charts of partly personal, partly collective cultural capital that may contain specific sensibilities, identifications, inscriptions, practices, memories and desires (1992: 56–60). These collections of investments are not medially restricted, as music can matter visually, and film can have sonic associations. Each time a text is read or a piece of music is heard, one's mattering maps will be activated, get jumbled up and be reconsolidated; so when Cave combines industrial noise with a blues piano, listeners are not only reminded of the mattering maps surrounding these isolated elements but will also build new sections in their charts that may contain diverse ingredients like Nick Cave's face, Einstürzende Neubauten, blues history, the Goth subcultural capital of Gothic literature and film, and a vivid picture of the undoubtedly dark lyrics the singer has draped over his music.

This has important repercussions for the understanding of Gothic mediation. Musical *mémoire involontaire*, the unwilled evocation of memories and the inadvertent jumbling of mattering maps conflate past and present in exactly the way that Derrida envisioned when he described spectrality and hauntology (2006). Musical citations and references function as very direct spectral voices; in musical experience time is always out of joint. Every new listening experience, moreover, re-inscribes former ones with new connotations and readjusts the listener's mattering maps, even in the case of songs that one has heard countless times before: 'both audiences and texts are continuously remade – their identity and effectiveness reconstructed – by relocating their place within different contexts' (Grossberg 1992: 54). This means that time is not only out of joint but also subject to continual rewriting. Musical experience, I want to argue, turns repetition into difference, and spectrality into transgression, and this is why music offers a more excessively Gothic and more profoundly uncanny mediation than other media. It should be noted that this also holds true for the experience of new music or background music – Muzak has become rich through the exploitation of the involuntary workings of inattentive listening.

'A writing of excess'?

Fred Botting's definition of Gothic signifying 'a writing of excess' has long been an obligatory starting point for Gothicist research (1996). While a large part of such studies focuses either on the writing – that is, varieties in the supernatural, spectral and stylistic aspects – or on the excess – that is, the various transgressions of consciousness, temporality and normativity – Botting insistently deals with the relations between style and theme that characterize the genre. Gothic, in his reasoning, signifies a self-aware writing of transgression, a writing so conscious of its own function as a screen for fears and desires that this mediation itself becomes the message; the narrative theme of transgression is no more and no less than one aspect of this writing of excess. In his more recent work Botting goes a step further: he no longer discusses individual media but the hyperreal (the accumulation of media upon media creating reality by proxy as described by Baudrillard (1994)) and discusses Gothic excess in terms of the Freudian death drive. He argues that the omnipresence of medial simulation and of consumable monstrosity have conflated 'writing' and 'excess' in a permanent 'horreality' (Botting 2008: 160–76). Gothic under these circumstances is nothing but the pointless transgression of the no longer existing paternal principle, an endless death drive game: 'Go-o-o-othic' (2008: 194–205). Compelling as Botting's analyses are, they reveal a lack of differentiation between media theory and psychoanalysis – and therefore between outside and inside or style and theme of Gothic – that was already noticeable in his earlier work. Although the Lacanian-Baudrillardian continuum from fear/desire to screen to media provides a convenient model for many aspects of media culture, I would argue that Gothic discloses the fissures in the model *exactly because* it operates both on psychological and medial levels. Gothic's complex relation to media, and especially music, invites a re-opening of academic cold cases. Is there really no difference (any more) between medium and message?

'In the dark mirror Gothic holds up to psychoanalysis repetition reduces the image to sameness, an inertial reflection occluding difference', says Botting (2008: 187). I asserted in the previous paragraph that the Gothic medium is an important instrument that helps the construction of, but is not synonymous to, the message. Even if hyperreality and hyperconsumption have rendered in- and outside indistinct and difference extinct, Gothic's emphatic distancing of style, theme and mediation allows a clear view of its transgressive

185

content – a psychological content to which mediation has enabled a gateway. Thus, in paraphrase of Botting, in the dark mirror Goth holds up to psychoanalysis, repetition becomes difference again, and spectrality re-enables transgression. The Gothic mirror does not signify the dissolution of the difference between psychology and media, as Botting suggests; rather it establishes an uncannily reflecting but simultaneously permeable border between them. Precisely because of its hypermedial distancing of stylization from theme, it safeguards the possibility of transgression. Gothic is therefore a writing of access as well as excess (cf. Van Elferen 2010: 288).

It is here that the role of music in Gothic is of critical interest. The analyses in this chapter have shown that 'Gothic music' is operative on (at least) four levels. Firstly, music can give audible voices to Gothic ghosts and thus meets the trope of spectrality. Secondly, it engenders an overlap of various musical times and realities and thus establishes the transgression that is the theme of Gothic. Thirdly, it can be excessively stylized, self-aware and hypermedial just like other media. Finally, music allows listeners to actively participate in Gothic transgression through its intricate entanglement with personal mattering maps, thus allowing the access of Gothic audiences *into* the fissure between medium and message. Gothic music, therefore, shows the importance of mediation and 'writing of excess' in the genre but it simultaneously enables an active participation in its transgressive practices. This becomes tangibly evident in Goth subculture, where such participation is live and embodied. (My book *Gothic Music: The Sounds of the Uncanny* (University of Wales Press, 2011) deals more extensively with the relations between Goth and Gothic (sub-) cultural capital, practices and music). At Goth parties clothing, absinthe bars and clove cigarettes function as hyper-explicit but very visceral media that evoke the ghosts of other eras. Dancing to Goth music, however, endorses a physical – and drug free! – entry into the borderlands that party organizers envision. Goth music is at once a statement of self-aware spectral stylization ('Bela Lugosi's dead …') and a transgressive move beyond that medial level via memories, mattering maps and motion. Music's capacity to engender and accompany such transgressive processes, of course, has long been known and used in churchly and profane ritual: that is why it is so important in liturgy. In the case of Gothic, music functions as a spectral liturgy that makes the 'dark mirror' of Gothic become three-dimensional, inhabitable, spatio-temporally infinite. Gothic music therefore demonstrates that the distance between medium and message has far from collapsed, as it allows Goth/ic audiences to creep into the cracks between them.

Cave's Gothic

Not traditionally Gothic but heavily leaning on the genre's tropes and themes, Nick Cave's exploitation of the uncanny potential of mediation does justify popular perceptions of him as a Gothic narrator. Because of their over-the-top ghostliness, their obsession with (sexual) transgression, their self-aware stylistic flamboyance and pervasive irony, Cave's songs are haunted and haunting: the listener perceives in them the ghosts of other texts and times and is simultaneously made aware of the uncanny presence of her own repressed fears and desires. He has thus created his own, Gothic-ish musical subgenre that could best be described as rock gone spectral.

As a very important by-product, the case study of Nick Cave has moreover demonstrated that a more thorough involvement of music in academic debates surrounding Gothic can lead to important new insights into the genre's relation to media. Gothic music enables a liturgical move from ghost story to experienced transgression, from Gothic style to theme; and in terms of scholarly approaches Gothic music exposes the remaining gaps between medium and message, and between media theory and psychoanalysis in the era of horreality. While Cave's lyrics certainly signify a writing of excess, his music is therefore also a writing of access, a spectral liturgy of which he is the high priest.

It could be argued that Cave's Gothic streak is diminishing as he ages, and this is largely due to his changed – read: less uncanny – usage of his lyrical and musical media (cf. McEvoy 2007). Cave's references to the Bible and religious poetry, identified above as part of his specific brand of Gothic, have changed rather drastically in recent years. While in his earlier work with The Birthday Party and the Bad Seeds the theological references show a kinship with Gothic's overdrive of Catholic bombast and irrationalities, his solo work seems more invested in the author's personal relationship with religion (cf. Eaglestone 2009). In the way he describes the development of his poetic and religious interests from the Old to the New Testament, the change from Gothic stylistic jouissance to a less stylized, less ironic, more personally invested stance is clearly noticeable:

> I soon found in the tough prose of the Old Testament a perfect language, at once mysterious and familiar, that not only reflected the state of mind I was in at the time but actively informed my artistic endeavours. [...] The God of the Old Testament seemed a cruel and rancorous God and I loved the way He would wipe out entire nations at a whim. [...] God was talking not just to me but *through* me, and His breath stank.
>
> [In the New Testament] I slowly reacquainted myself with a Jesus of my childhood, that eerie figure that moves through the Gospels, the Man of Sorrows, and it was through Him that I was given a chance to redefine my relationship with the world. The voice that spoke through me now was softer, sadder, more introspective.
>
> (Cave 1997: 138–9)

Even though Jesus' ghostliness and the sadness of Cave's voice still tie in with Gothic tastes, the sting of irony and self-aware artificiality is gone. Similarly, romance becomes less and less dark, and more and more everyday in Cave's later work. From *The Boatman's Call* (1997) on, he increasingly sounds so sincere that Gothic stylization and hypermediacy seem to have disappeared: this is less of an ironic juggler with tropes and style, and more of an authentic author. And for all the things that Gothic is, authentic it is not.

So yes, Nick Cave's organ is fucked. Fucked organs challenge the Gothic narrator-priest. They are the thoroughly uncanny media that may convey his spectral liturgy.

References

Baldick, Chris (ed.) (1992), *The Oxford Book of Gothic Tales*, Oxford: Oxford University Press.

Baudrillard, Jean (1994), *Simulacra and Simulation*, Ann Arbor: University of Michigan Press.

Botting, Fred (1996), *Gothic*, London: Routledge.

——— (2008), *Limits of Horror: Technology, Bodies, Gothic*, Manchester: Manchester University Press.

Cave, Nick (1988), *King Ink*, London: Black Spring.

——— (1997), *King Ink II*, London: Black Spring.

——— (2007), *Nick Cave: The Complete Lyrics 1978–2007*, London: Penguin.

Derrida, Jacques (2006), *Specters of Marx: The State of the Debt, the Work of Mourning and the New International*, New York/London: Routledge.

Eaglestone, Robert (2009), 'From Mutiny to Calling upon the Author: Cave's Religion', in Karen Welberry and Tanya Dalziell (eds), *Cultural Seeds: Essays on the Work of Nick Cave*, Farnham: Ashgate, pp. 139–66.

Friedman, Jason K. (2007), 'Ah Am Witness to Its Authenticity', in Lauren M. E. Goodlad and Michael Bibby (eds), *Goth: Undead Subculture*, Durham/London: Duke University Press, pp. 207–14.

Grossberg, Lawrence (1992), 'Is There a Fan in the House?: The Affective Sensibility of Fandom', in Lisa Lewis (ed.), *The Adoring Audience: Fan Culture and Popular Media*, London: Routledge, pp. 50–65.

'GustavZomerschoe' (2008), 'Nick Cave Live HMH Amsterdam 2008 Dig Lazarus, Dig!!!', http://www.youtube.com/watch?v=CzmRasQgG2k. Accessed 28 August 2011.

Hart, Carol (2009), '*And the Ass Saw the Angel*: A Novel of Fragment and Excess', in Karen Welberry and Tanya Dalziell (eds), *Cultural Seeds: Essays on the Work of Nick Cave*, Farnham: Ashgate, pp. 97–122.

Heidegger, Martin (1993), 'What is Metaphysics?', in David F. Krell (ed.), *Martin Heidegger: Basic Writings*, London: Routledge, pp. 89–110.

McEvoy, Emma (2007), '"Now, who will be the witness/When you're all too healed to see?": The Sad Demise of Nick Cave', *Gothic Studies*, 9: 1, pp. 79–88.

Spooner, Catherine (2006), *Contemporary Gothic*, London: Reaktion.

Van Elferen, Isabella (2010), 'Haunted by a Melody: Ghosts, Transgression, and Music in *Twin Peaks*', in María del Pilar Blanco and Esther Peeren (eds), *Popular Ghosts: The Haunted Spaces of Everyday Culture*, New York: Continuum, pp. 282–95.

Wolfreys, Julian (2002), *Victorian Hauntings: Spectrality, Gothic, the Uncanny and Literature*, Houndmills: Palgrave Macmillan.

Chapter 11

The Singer and the Song: Nick Cave and the Archetypal Function of the Cover Version

Nathan Wiseman-Trowse

A small proscenium arch of red light bulbs framing draped crimson curtains fills the screen. It is hard to tell whether the ramshackle stage is inside or outside but it appears to be set up against a wall made of corrugated metal. All else is black. The camera cuts to a close-up of the curtains, which are parted to reveal a pale young man with crow's nest hair wearing a sequined tuxedo and a skewed bow tie. The man holds a lit cigarette and behind him, overseeing proceedings, is a large statue of the Virgin Mary. As the man with the crow's nest hair walks fully through the arch he opens his mouth and sings the words '[a]s the snow flies, on a cold and grey Chicago morn, another little baby child is born'. The song continues with the singer alternately shuffling as if embarrassed by the attention of the camera and then holding his arms aloft in declamation or fixing the viewer with a steely gaze. His miming is less than perfect, but something about his performance suggests that this is not entirely without deliberation. Half way through the song the man removes his jacket, revealing a waistcoat. As he completes his performance the man moves backwards, drawing the curtains before him, and the song ends.

The pale young man with the crow's nest hair is Nick Cave and the song is 'In the Ghetto', written by Mac David and released by Elvis Presley in 1969. Presley's version of David's song is notable for a number of reasons. It was the first Presley release to make it on to the Billboard Top Ten in four years, boosted by Presley's public resurrection via his televised 'Comeback Special' *Elvis* the year before (Binder 1968). It also stands out in Presley's canon as the closest he gets to overt social commentary, chronicling as it does the brief and violent life of a disenfranchised young man growing up in the projects, culminating in his death and the birth of another child who is bound to follow the same path.

Cave's version of 'In the Ghetto' is similarly notable but for different reasons. Released in 1984 on Mute Records, it was the debut single by Cave's new band Nick Cave and the Bad Seeds, and it marks a radical departure from Cave's previous band The Birthday Party. Where The Birthday Party trod a line between violent post-punk alienation and bluesy swagger, Cave's first release with the Bad Seeds is a remarkably faithful rendition of the Presley version, albeit with some minor changes. The strings remain, giving a mournful but soft backing to the martial drumbeat, but the backing chorus of 'in the ghetto' from Presley's release is replaced by a heavily affected upwards glissando played with what sounds like a slide on electric guitar. Similarly, Cave's vocal performance is far less polished than Presley's and betrays a slight snarl in places. The video also seems to hark back to the showmanship associated with Presley, yet its amateurish look suggests something much more related to the DIY aesthetic of punk, shot as it is in the garage of the video director Evan English. One might be reminded of Sid Vicious' demolition of 'My Way' (1978), which culminates in Vicious pulling a revolver on the unwitting audience from a Vegas-style stage. However, where Vicious' performance is deliberately ironic and confrontational, challenging not only how one might read the song and its previous incarnations but also the relationship between performer (most notably Frank Sinatra) and audience, Cave's performance is more difficult to decode. It is at once both subtly ironic and reverential, interpretive yet faithful. Cave's reading of 'In the Ghetto' challenges the Presley version with the aesthetics of post-punk practice, yet it succeeds also in incorporating an older, more problematic tradition, that of the 'crooner', into post-punk's own lexicon. It seems to be the first visible incarnation of Cave as an artist who has subsequently positioned himself in a dialectical relationship between the traditions of (primarily) American popular song and avant rock.

Why cover?

That Cave's first release with the Bad Seeds should be a cover version seems prophetic. Not only does it mark out a break in what was expected of Cave based upon his previous career with The Birthday Party, but it also heralds a continuing fascination with other people's songs that has been visible throughout his subsequent output. In 1986 Nick Cave and the Bad Seeds released *Kicking Against the Pricks*, an album of cover versions that included songs by Johnny Cash, John Lee Hooker, Roy Orbison and The Alex Harvey Band, amongst others. While *Kicking Against the Pricks* and 'In the Ghetto' stand out as notable engagements with the cover version for Cave, his entire career illustrates an ongoing connection to the cover with over 60 songs by other artists recorded and released by Cave in various incarnations since 1977 and countless live performances not committed to tape, perhaps the most intriguing of which is a cover of Destiny's Child's 'Bootylicious' (2001) performed at a charity auction in London in 2007 (Maes 2010).

Most of these cover versions seem to illustrate Cave's own musical influences. Amongst the list of artists covered by Cave are a sizable proportion of blues and country artists and notable singer songwriters such as Leonard Cohen, Bob Dylan, Neil Young and Johnny Cash. While these songs might go some way to flesh out Cave's own musical inspiration, they also serve another purpose. Cave's covers help to place him within certain musical and cultural traditions, often traditions that compete with each other, that grant his own music legitimacy and authenticity. Cave's covers act as a framework by which to understand his complete output within certain discourses. It is not the intention of this chapter to suggest that Cave is self-consciously aligning himself with certain musical traditions to bolster his own critical reception, but it does seem clear that his choice of cover versions provides a way of understanding Cave as an artist and his own compositions within a historical and aesthetic context for the audience.

Dai Griffiths illustrates how the performance of cover versions can have significant ramifications for the articulation of gender, race, place and other aspects of identity formation. Griffiths suggests that 'covers illustrate identity in motion' and this is certainly the case with Cave's choice of songs (2002: 51). However, while Griffiths is illustrating the fluidity of identity formation across covers as the performer or performance shifts across gender, race or class lines, Cave's covers often maintain an uneasy allegiance with the originals. If the significance of the cover version is manifest in its difference or similarity to an original then Cave's choices say much about how we might perceive his canon as a whole, offering the opportunity to shape interpretive strategies that extend beyond the individual cover version in question.

Griffiths identifies two types of cover version, the 'rendition' and the 'transformation'. The rendition is a 'straightforwardly faithful version of the original, carrying with it some of the connotation of performance in classical music' (2002: 52). A prime example of this is Ride's cover of 'The Model' (1992), which almost perfectly replicates the instrumentation of the Kraftwerk original, with only the noticeable difference in vocal timbre marking it out as another performance. A transformation, however, suggests a more radical interpretation of the source material, often involving changes to instrumentation, arrangement and even lyrics. The lines between these two categories are often far from clear. Cave's reading of 'By the Time I Get to Phoenix', which features on the Bad Seeds' 1986 album *Kicking Against the Pricks*, shows how both strategies manifest themselves within a single performance. Immediately we are challenged by the problem of what constitutes the 'original' by which Cave's performance might be judged. Jimmy Webb originally wrote the song and its first release was by Johnny Rivers in 1965. However, the most famous version of the song is Glenn Campbell's release two years later. Furthermore, the song has been recorded by Isaac Hayes, Harry Belafonte (the source for another Cave cover, 'Did You Hear about Jerry?', performed at a few dates in Melbourne in November 1985 and considered for inclusion on *Kicking Against the Pricks*), Pat Boone, John Denver, Frank Sinatra, Roger Whittaker, Andy Williams, Liberace and Thelma Houston amongst others. Cave's performance bears the closest similarity to the Campbell version and in many ways is a faithful rendition; however, it is slower (and therefore almost a minute longer), lacks the string arrangement of Campbell's version and Cave's vocal performance elaborates on the lyrics in a number of ways. However, compared to Cave's version of Pulp's 'Disco 2000', 'By the Time I Get to Phoenix' seems a relatively faithful rendition rather than a transformation. 'Disco 2000', recorded as a B-side for Pulp's 1992 single 'Bad Cover Version', turns an upbeat chart hit (originally released by Pulp in 1995) into a lilting waltz with arpeggiated guitars and ethereal backing vocals. Cave's performance explicitly transforms Pulp's original into something that fits within his own recognizable aesthetic in an overt manner.

These two examples, and there are many others throughout Cave's career so far, point towards the motivations for covering songs in the first instance. Many bands in their early years will participate in song-getting, gathering songs to cover both as a means to build on performance and songwriting skills and as a strategy of identity formation

(Shehan Campbell 1995). This might work through covering songs that are direct stylistic inspirations for the band – which would tend to be done relatively faithfully as renditions – or they might be transformations of songs that would sit incongruously within the band's own repertoire without significant stylistic revision. A band that I have long since left performed a cover version of Danielle Dax's 'Cat House' (1988) as a faithful rendition, signalling our own position within a certain discourse of alternative rock music, yet we also covered Atomic Kitten's 'Whole Again' (2001) as a metal song. Here the transformation acts as a means of articulating power and difference over the original and, by implication, the pop genre from whence it comes. It therefore becomes an act of 'authentication'. It is clear to see how Cave's renditions, however faithful, connect him to past discourses of popular music, not just as inspiration, but as a way of reading him as an artist. The influence of the blues, for example, might be evident in his own work but the covers of John Lee Hooker and Leadbelly songs mark him out as part of that tradition (albeit problematically in terms of ethnicity and nationality), often legitimizing his other songs and himself as an artist. 'Disco 2000', however, works to transform the original away from a pop discourse towards something less immediately commercial and more 'grounded'. That is not to say that this particular example is not dripping with irony, but Cave's straight-faced performance provides the space to read the song in new ways that connect with other facets of popular music history than simply indie pop. Where Cave has arguably succeeded in his use of cover versions is in incorporating competing discourses, primarily post-punk rock music, American roots music and the Tin Pan Alley tradition, to define a space for his own work that exists between the different positions. As such Cave marks out both similarity and difference in a network of affiliations that listeners have the opportunity to interpret.

Locating an 'original'

At this point the issue of exactly what Cave is connecting to through his cover versions needs to be addressed. When I hear 'By the Time I Get to Phoenix' I compare it to the Glenn Campbell version, the version that I heard before all others, as suggested above, the most commercially successful and widely consumed, which becomes my 'original'. That it is not the first recording of that particular song is of no relevance to me, although upon coming across Johnny Rivers' version I might choose to change my mind. Anteriority and precedence are an issue to an extent – I knew the Campbell version before I knew the Cave version – but I also know that Campbell did not write the song, and that in this case it was written by Jimmy Webb, not an anonymous Brill Building hack but a much fêted American songwriter responsible for a range of what are usually referred to as 'standards' such as 'Wichita Lineman' (1968) and 'MacArthur Park' (1968). Therefore my interpretation of Cave's cover is shaped by its relationship to a soft country sound and a more commercial yet critically appreciated form of songwriting craft. The fact that it is a song that is almost entirely performed by people other than the man who wrote it does provide a space for any artist to transform it to their own ends, but the shadow of Campbell's version hangs over every other version that I have ever come across. Of course such a valuation is highly subjective, but if Cave has proven anything over the long course of his career it is that he is a consummate scholar of popular music, and it seems unlikely that he is totally unaware of the connections that he is making to other artists and genres. Therefore the archetypes of the genius songwriter and the commercial country crossover artist are evoked.

A more clearly defined example can be seen through Cave's connection to the pantheon of elder statesmen singer-songwriters such as Leonard Cohen, Bob Dylan, Neil Young and Johnny Cash. Of the covers that Cave has recorded or performed throughout his career, Cohen looms larger than most with at least nine recordings or performances by Cave: 'Avalanche' (From Her to Eternity, 1984), 'Tower of Song' (*I'm Your Fan*, 1991), 'I'm Your Man', 'Suzanne' (Lunson 2005), 'There is a War', 'Diamonds in the Mine', 'Don't Go Home with Your Hard-on', 'Memories' and 'Dress Rehearsal Rag' (all performed as part of the *Came So Far For Beauty* Cohen tribute concerts between 2004 and 2006). While Cave's interpretations of Cohen's work might be wildly transformative (see 'Tower of Song' as an example), the connections that they make to an artist who is widely understood to have produced a strong body of work that has maintained its artistic integrity through the commercial pressures of the popular music industry have ramifications for Cave's own work. Similarly Dylan, Young and Cash function not only as touchstones for Cave's influences but also as aesthetic or artistic archetypes. Here the quantity of covers performed by Cave and his various musicians helps to delineate how we might perceive Cave. The wealth of cover versions coalesces to provide a network of meaning that gives context to Cave. The singer-songwriter connections allow him to occupy a position within contemporary popular music that shows Cave to be a new manifestation of artists whose careers, whilst still ongoing in most cases, have secured them a place within the critical pantheon (and I use the word deliberately) of popular music history.

Whilst it might seem obvious to say that Cave's work is inspired by artists such as Cohen, Cash, Dylan or others and that therefore it makes sense that he should cover their work, such a claim fails to account for the remarkable ways in which such covers are used to define Cave as an artist himself. Returning to 'In the Ghetto', it becomes obvious that Cave is pushing against his own status in the early 1980s as a post-punk firebrand 'who plays with madness' (Reynolds and Press 1995: 269). As Ian Johnston puts it in his biography of Cave, 'In the Ghetto' was

> the beginning of Cave's long retreat from the kinetic style of stage performance that he had presented in The Birthday Party, which he felt was all too often dictated by the audience. He told Richard Guillart: 'You'd be looking at the audience, they're all leering back at you, and you know they want you to do a back-flip. So you do one and feel like an idiot … All the great works of art, it seems to me, are the ones that have a total disregard for anything else; just a total egotistical self-indulgence'.
>
> (Johnston 1995: 146)

Similarly, Amy Hanson describes Cave's first single with the Bad Seeds as

> less a cover song, than a plea – for retribution, for justice, for humanity. And it certainly couldn't have been farther from Cave's in-your-face spit and bite that fans were surely expecting. It was a brilliant choice for a break in sound.

> (2005: 55)

That 'break in sound' has been vital to Cave's subsequent career, providing a space for him to redefine not only what his records sound like, or his performance style, but the very aesthetic of what he represents. Elvis Presley surely represented everything that British post-punk railed against, and as such it made some sense that Cave covering The King would provide an escape route from a scene from which Cave felt increasingly alienated in the latter years of The Birthday Party. But Cave's performance of the song seems to transcend mere irony, and while it fits easily into his own usage of the Presley mythos through the 1980s (see Wiseman-Trowse 2009), perhaps Mac David's status as a songwriter and craftsman redefines Cave more radically than any Elvis connotations. It is from this point on that Cave ceases merely to be a perceived psychotic Aussie Jim Morrison wannabe, garnering acclaim instead for his status as a songwriter of worth – however that might be defined – a transformation that would continue through the 1980s and reach its culmination with *The Good Son* in 1990.

The cover as archetypal image

How might such engagements between Cave and his source material be understood? My suggestion above that Cave's link to David might be more significant than the Presley connection is further validated by Cave's choice to cover the work of other significant songwriters (Jimmy Webb, Jacques Brel and a plethora of singer-songwriters such as those mentioned above). Yet it also requires an appreciation of those songwriters as significant on the part of the audience, something that might be problematic if the listener does not know David or Webb's work, or if they might understand their significance in other ways. The punk audience who first engaged with Cave's work might well have found such associations with certain aspects of popular music history troubling. What is perhaps more important is Cave's positioning, through the use of cover versions, as a significant songwriter himself. Such aesthetic reflection can be seen in other aspects of his choice of covers. American roots music (encompassing blues, country and folk) has always been an important resource for Cave from his earliest recordings and a cursory glance at his choice of covers shows a wealth of American traditional compositions ('Stagger Lee', 'Oh Happy Day', 'Jesus Met the Woman at the Well', 'Black Betty' and others). Again, and this seems particularly important for an Australian performer who has lived in a variety of countries at various times, Cave's interpretations make links both to his own compositions and his other work in the fields of literature and film-making. They act as authenticating devices that, through Cave's own interpretations, reflect back upon himself as an artist. This is not to suggest that Cave is an authentic bluesman, but his work becomes placed within specific lineages, an effect illustrated by the release of the two *Original Seeds* compilations in 1998 and 2004 (Rubber Records), which collected prior versions of songs covered by Cave, and *Mojo* magazine's *Bad Seeds Nick Cave: Roots and Collaborations* CD, issued free with the magazine in the United Kingdom in 2009, which charted a similar course. The very act of these releases shows how Cave's work connects with a history of popular music that shapes our perceptions of him in the present, as a significant singer songwriter, as a contemporary manifestation of folk idioms, as a connection between punk and more archaic forms.

I suggested above that if one is not aware of Cave's sources it might be difficult to extrapolate such effects from the musical and cultural connections that he makes. However, what stands out when looking back to take a holistic view of Cave's covers is the articulation of what might be understood as popular music archetypes. Popular music is one of the few cultural forms where one artist might take another artist's work and re-perform it. Writers rarely rewrite other authors' work, although there are examples, and visual artists rarely 'cover' other artists, although again there are exceptions. Cinema might come closer, with reworkings of older films being particularly prevalent. However, what might be considered as an actual cover version, at least in terms of rendition, is still relatively rare, with Gus Van Sant's shot-for-shot recreation of Hitchcock's *Psycho* (1998) or John Badham's remake of Besson's *Nikita* (1990) as *Point of No Return* (1993) being notable exceptions. Griffiths' exploration of cover versions shows how popular musicians use the cover to engage with changing contexts of the same source material, both invoking a past text and creating something else out of its new context. Cave's position as a musician, performer and songwriter over the past three decades has been overshadowed by his connections to punk and post-punk, and whether he would find this desirable or not (countless interviews with him have suggested that he finds such connections increasingly irksome; for example, see Barron 1988), it has reshaped the covers that he performs, whether that be through the resurrection of folk forms such as the murder ballad or the recontextualization of the crooner tradition that his covers of Presley, Campbell and Pitney have achieved. In most cases Cave is connecting with recognizable archetypes of popular music history that are re-presented through his own archetypal imagery.

In a 1989 interview with Simon Reynolds in *New Musical Express* magazine Cave, in conversation with Mark E. Smith of The Fall and Shane MacGowan of The Pogues, expressed concern at the mythologization of his music:

NME: You must be aware that, consciously or otherwise, you've each created a particular myth that has arisen, in part, from your songs.

SM: Nobody created my mythology, I certainly didn't.

NC: No, you (the press) created it.

SM: The media has a lot to answer for, you're all a bunch of bastards however friendly you are.

NC: Let's not talk about the media. Why the hell are you talking about mythologies? That tends to suggest it's somehow unreal.

SM: It seems to me that in your songs, Nick, you're doing a Jung-style trip of examining your shadow, all the dark things you don't want to be. A lot of your songs are like trips into the subconscious and are therefore nightmarish.

NC: Possibly.

(Reynolds 1989)

Cave's reticent response points to the connection to the real, to the 'authentic' that he wants his music to have, and while 'mythologization' might be an appropriate way to understand his work and his place within discourses of popular music archetypes, the very function of archetypes transcends the cursory role of myth and reconnects his work (and, by implication, his covers within that body of work) through the social and the cultural back to the body. Carl Jung understood archetypes as aspects of the collective unconscious that shape or give form to one's engagement with the external world (Jung 2002). Archetypes themselves are unknowable, yet their manifestations as archetypal images in the conscious realm point to the connection between the interior psyche and the body, manifesting instinctual modes of behaviour and response. For Jung, archetypes are latent in the collective unconscious, awaiting actualization within the personal unconscious in the individual. The element that initiates and articulates actualization can be understood as the archetypal image.

Using this understanding of the cover version, the song transcends its materiality and acts as a fulcrum between the collective and personal unconscious to articulate discourses that give shape and meaning to Cave's actions in the real world. Archetypal images (and here I mean not only the songs themselves but the performers, performances, writers and even genres associated with them) instigate connections for the audience, and one would suspect Cave himself, that shape how we read his performances. The bluesman, the country singer, the Tin Pan Alley songwriter, the French *chanteur* and the rock 'n' roller all assume significance as archetypes that stretch beyond their incarnations as popular musicians. They instead connect with unconscious responses to the world through the body in performance. Hence Cave's uncomfortable response to the mythification of his own work. He is right that in many ways the media plays a significant role in slanting what he does as a musician, but it is difficult to approach Cave's work without exploring the role that myth has to play. Here the myths, not only about his own work but the sources that he gets from elsewhere, are real, telling stories about the individual within the world. As such, unconscious archetypes are connected to the body through performance and materiality in a way that grants Cave's work authenticity. David Pattie explores similar territory when he deconstructs the self-mutilation of Richey James, from the Welsh band Manic Street Preachers, as he cuts '4 REAL' into his arm after a gig in front of the *New Musical Express* journalist Steve Lamacq:

> James's gesture conforms to accepted rock iconography: but it also exceeds it, moves beyond it into rather more troubling territory [...] James's act, it would seem, is directed first of all at himself. It takes a public concern – the authenticity or otherwise of the Manics as a group – and turns it into a private, desperate act of self confirmation, as though the only way that James has to convince himself that he is not, ultimately, a charade, is to inscribe his authenticity, slowly and painfully, on his own skin.
>
> (Pattie 1999)

While an extreme example, the body here acts as the last bastion of authenticity, the site of a perceived reality beyond which it might be difficult to move. Cave's early, visceral onstage persona is largely abandoned in the mid-1980s but the figure in the sequinned tuxedo who steps through the curtains is no less physical and the connections that he makes to the body become articulated, not through the extremities of his own physicality, but through, in the case of 'In the Ghetto', Presley in 'an advanced state of disintegration, finally present[ing] the truth about himself [...] with such passion that his performance was totally uncontrived' (Johnston 1996: 146). As such, Cave's pseudo-shambolic performance in the video rearticulates the archetype inherent in Presley's own rendition in a manner that reminds us of the physicality of the function of the archetype itself.

The cover as assemblage

There is, however, a problem with such a reading of Cave's covers. While archetypal imagery engages with the collective unconscious, the cover version does suggest a certain amount of cultural competence from the listener. As David Brackett puts it:

> [i]f musical meaning is conveyed through a code that is sent or produced by somebody then it also must be received or consumed by somebody. This raises the question of 'competence': what is the relationship between sender and receiver, and how does this affect the interpretation of musical messages?
>
> (Brackett 2000: 12)

In the case of the cover version, responses will vary wildly dependent upon one's knowledge of previous incarnations of the song. Leonard Cohen's 'Hallelujah' provides an appropriate example here. Originally released on the *Various Positions* album in 1984, Cohen's composition has had a tortuous route through the interpretations of other artists. The song was first covered by John Cale on *I'm Your Fan* in 1991, then, most famously, by

Jeff Buckley on *Grace* in 1994. Buckley based his own version primarily around Cale's interpretation rather than the Cohen original (Browne 2001: 166). Alexandra Burke reached the UK number one spot with her cover of 'Hallelujah' in 2008, a song chosen for her as winner of the British television talent show *The X Factor* (Buckley's version went in at number two behind Burke's, following renewed interest in his interpretation). This version was in turn inspired by a performance of the song on another talent show, *American Idol*, by Jason Castro in 2008, which directly links back to Buckley's version. In this sense Cohen's version becomes increasingly irrelevant as each successive version effectively covers the last. Wherever one might choose to place the original, the point here is that the original is not necessarily the archetypal image that is specifically engaged with to create meaning in relation to the cover version.

How then are we to judge the cover and its articulation of archetypes that shape the way in which we see Cave? As the case of 'By the Time I Get to Phoenix' shows, it is not always the significance of the original recording that has the most bearing on the cover version. Rather one might best understand Cave's use of covers as a way of constructing meaning through various engagements (with the variety of versions of the song, some more culturally significant than others, and his own semiology at any given time) that he might direct but has little ultimate control over once the song reaches the ear of the listener. In this sense the cover acts, as Gilles Deleuze might put it, as an assemblage, as a conjunction of aesthetic ideas and experiences that gives form to Cave as we experience him. While Deleuze's radical epistemology might seem at odds with the analytical psychology of Jung, the cover version (like certain other cultural forms) illustrates how experiences assemble to provide new forms of manifestation and interpretation. As Semetsky puts it,

> [t]he Deleuzian level of analysis is 'not a question of intellectual understanding [...] but of intensity, resonance and musical harmony' (Deleuze 1995: 86). It is guided by the 'logic of affects' (Guattari 1995: 9) and as such is different from a rational consensus or solely intellectual reasoning. Its rationale is pragmatic and the thinking it produces, over the background of affects – Jung would've said, feeling tones – is experimental and experiential.
>
> (2003: 4)

In this way Cave's covers are constantly unfolding new possibilities, read via the experiences of listeners around the loci of previous song-versions, writers, life experiences. The connection to archetypal images evoked by the cover version is multiple and often contradictory, proposing a self (combining Cave as artist, the listening subject and previous performers and writers) that manifests new connections to the archetype that might give Cave some form of power or meaning. Semetsky points to the multiplicity of our perception of an artist like Cave when she suggests that 'the Self, defined by Jung as a collective noun, expresses itself via enunciation, which is always already, as Deleuze says, collective, that is plurivocal' (Semetsky 2003: 7). In listening to Cave's covers we focus on one assemblage of collective experiences that connect via the psyche back to the body.

The argument above might immediately suggest that there is no inherent truth or baseline to judge Cave's covers against, yet the cover version has clearly proved an invaluable tool for audiences looking to gain meaning from his career and his place within a canon of popular musicians. Each song marks a point (or multiple points) of becoming, a leap into new perspectives on Cave that have little to ground them on close inspection other than archetypal connections that he is choosing to make by each song that he picks to perform or record. Cave reinvents himself through each performance: 'there is no return to the subject, to the old self, but invention and creation of new possibilities of life by means of going beyond the play of forces' (Semetsky 2003: 9). This is as true of his choice of cover versions as it is of each song written by himself or the Bad Seeds. The cover merely shows the extent to which Cave as performer transforms with each new engagement, each new assemblage into something both new and something deeply recognizable. As such, we are left with a position where the man in the sequinned tuxedo and the crow's nest hair is not only ironic but sincere, himself and someone else, transient yet deeply authentic.

References

Badham, John (1993), *Point of No Return*, Burbank, CA: Warner Brothers.

Barron, Jack (1988), 'Nick Cave: The Needle and the Damage Done', in *New Musical Express*, 13 August 1988, London: IPC Media.

Besson, Luc (1990), *Nikita*, Neuilly-sue-Seine: Gaumont.

Binder, Steve (1968), *Elvis*, RCA: New York.

Brackett, David (2000), *Interpreting Popular Music*, Berkley and Los Angeles: University of California Press.

Browne, David (2001), *Dream Brother: The Lives and Music of Jeff and Tim Buckley*, London: Fourth Estate.

Deleuze, Gilles (1995), *Negotiations 1972–1990*, trans. by Martin Joughin, New York: Columbia University Press.

Griffiths, Dai (2002), 'Cover Versions and the Sound of Identity in Motion', in David Hesmondhalgh and Keith Negus (eds), *Popular Music Studies*, London: Arnold, pp. 51–64.

Guattari, Felix (1995), *Chaosmosis: An Ethico-aesthetic Paradigm*, trans. by Paul Bains and Julian Pefanis, Bloomington and Indianapolis: Indiana University Press.

Hanson, Amy (2005), *Kicking Against the Pricks: An Armchair Guide to Nick Cave*, London: Helter Skelter.

Johnston, Ian (1996), *Bad Seed: The Biography of Nick Cave*, London: Abacus.

Jung, Carl (2002), *The Archetypes and the Collective Unconscious*, trans. by R. F. C. Hull, London: Routledge.

Lunson, Liam (2005), *Leonard Cohen: I'm Your Man*, Santa Monica, CA: Lions Gate.

Maes, Maurice (2010) *Nick Cave Collector's Hell 1977–2009*, http://home.iae.nl/users/maes/cave//songs/songscov.html. Accessed 3 May 2010.

Pattie, David (1999), '4 Real: Authenticity, Performance and Rock Music', *Enculturation*, 2:2, http://enculturation.gmu.edu/2_2/pattie.html. Accessed 12 May 2010.

Reynolds, Simon (1989), 'The Three Horsemen of the Apocalypse', in *New Musical Express*, 25 February 1989, London: IPC Media.

Reynolds, Simon and Joy Press (1995), *The Sex Revolts: Gender, Rebellion and Rock 'n' Roll*, London: Serpent's Tail.

Semetsky, Inna (2003), *The Unconscious Subject of Deleuze and Guattari*, http://arts. monash.edu.au/cclcs/research/papers/unconscious-subject.pdf. Accessed 16 May 2010.

Shehan Campbell, Patricia (1995), 'Of Garage Bands and Song-getting: The Musical Development of Young Rock Musicians', *Research Studies in Music Education*, 4:1, pp.12–20.

Van Sant, Gus (1998), *Psycho*, Los Angeles, CA: Universal.

Wiseman-Trowse, Nathan (2009), 'Oedipus Wrecks: Cave and the Presley Myth', in Karen Welberry and Tanya Dalziell (eds), *Cultural Seeds: Essays on the Work of Nick Cave*, Farnham: Ashgate, pp. 153–66.

Chapter 12

Nick Cave: The Spirit of the Duende and the Sound of the Rent Heart

Sarah Wishart

In 1998 Nick Cave, invited to hold a class on songwriting at the Vienna Poetry Academy, was asked to write an accompanying piece on his practice. The resulting essay, 'The Secret Life of the Love Song', was a meditation on the mixture of rapture and pain at the heart of the love song. Cave used the Portuguese term *saudade* to describe this dialectic of agony and joy that is, for him, the absolute essence of the love song. He even goes so far as to say that if the song did not contain this dialectic, it would not be a love song: 'those songs that speak of love, without having within their lines an ache or a sigh, are not Love Songs at all, [...] and are not to be trusted' (Cave 2007: 8).

Cave refers to a piece of work written by the Andalusian poet and playwright Federico Garcia Lorca to open up his own thoughts on the love song. In *Play and Theory of the Duende*, written in the early part of the twentieth century, Lorca worked through the quality he calls *duende* in relation to a variety of art forms, as well as to how this art was experienced by its audiences. Cave saluted Lorca's attempts to explain something unexplainable and in particular focused on one specific quote: '"[a]ll that has dark sound has duende", he says, "that mysterious power that everyone feels but no philosopher can explain"' (Cave 2007: 7). This quote, though central to Lorca's deliberating on duende, is actually not from Lorca at all but is credited to the 1930s Flamenco singer Manuel Torres (Lorca 1998: 49). This quote is not only central to Lorca's consideration of duende but also to that of most writers who attempt to struggle with the concept.

Cave, like Lorca before him (and perhaps all the philosophers Torres references), attempts repeatedly to explain what Lorca calls duende and what Cave identifies as the 'inexplicable sadness' at the heart of the love song, a loss that is literally unspeakable (Cave 2007: 7). Laura Barton, responding to Cave's essay, suggests that his description of duende becomes, for her, the moment when she is finally able to conceive of the previously indescribable aspect of the love song:

[n]ot so very long ago I received an email upon the subject of duende, a topic about which I knew little, but which I have since learned is what Nick Cave has described as 'the eerie and inexplicable sadness that lives at the heart of certain works of art'. It was nice, I felt, to put a name to a face.

(Barton 2008)

Yet it is a subjective term and one that people struggle in defining. Amanda Michaels suggests that it is an 'ahistorical feeling that is difficult to put into words, that causes even the most eloquent speaker to talk in circles, and yet is arguably the aim at the heart of every artistic venture' (2009: 3). The difficulty of defining this crucial ingredient of the artistic endeavour might equally explain the consistent return to try to do so. In one of Cave's attempts, he describes it as being 'a howl in the void, for Love and for comfort' (Cave 2007: 7). Using this imagery in relation to a love song evokes a terrible existential truth at the core of the human relationship: pain and love are intertwined. Cave shows that duende can be present in all the forms the love song takes – whether it be within the keening sound of an Andalusian lament or hidden within a well-known pop ballad. If a love song is really a love song, then it must contain duende and if it does not, then it is not a love song. Cave calls upon the writer to take responsibility for delving into the dark side of the opposing forces at work within the love song when he acknowledges that

[t]he writer who refuses to explore the darker regions of the heart will never be able to write convincingly about the wonder, the magic and the joy of love, for just as goodness cannot be trusted unless it has breathed the same air as evil [...] so within the fabric of the Love Song, within its melody, its lyric, one must sense an acknowledgment of its capacity for suffering.
(2007: 8)

In order to further understand the role of duende across the breadth of Cave's work, I will examine the background to duende in Lorca's work and touch upon its cultural presence in Spain. I will investigate the relationship of duende with love's opposing forces of pain and joy. I will also consider Lorca's concept of duende as an effect on the audience, in relation to the work of Nick Cave.

'The Play and Theory of the Duende'

On 20 October 1933, financially enabled to visit Argentina due to the success of his play *Blood Wedding*, Lorca had been booked to speak at the first of a series of lectures. Addressing the members of The Friends of the Art Club, his topic was 'The Play and Theory of the Duende'. Lorca's biographer Ian Gibson described the moment when 'Lorca conquered in one evening the heart of Buenos Aires' (1989: 366). Christopher Maurer continues to emphasize the significance of that one night for Lorca as he suggests in his introduction to his translation of Lorca's essays that, on the same evening, the concept of the duende became 'a cornerstone of his poetics' (Lorca 1998: viii). This lecture had evolved from an earlier piece Lorca had written in order to attempt to promote the Andalusian *cante jondo* – which translates as 'deep song' (Lorca 1998: vii). These writings and lectures sprang from Lorca's desire to promote this form of music, from his own region of southern Spain, to a much larger international and intellectual community.

Frustrated with the reputation of this music as amateurish and unworthy of much note, Lorca wanted to shine a new light on the art form. By the time he wrote the piece that specifically concentrated on duende, Lorca's perspective had arguably been further affected by his exposure to American music that reflected some of the attributes of the *cante jondo*, such as the spirituals, blues and jazz he had been exposed to during his time in New York. This, alongside his involvement with professional *cantaores* and dancers such as Manuel Torres, extended his attempt to expose the fascinating concept of duende he felt lay at the heart of the difference between the *cante jondo* and other more accepted and 'professional' variations on the flamenco style (Lorca 1998: viii).

The definitions of duende stretch between a supernatural figure and an essence of inspiration. The Oxford English Dictionary (OED) defines the term as both 'a ghost, an evil spirit' and as a creative/destructive force: 'magic and fire' (OED 2010). In her article on the work of translating Lorca and the understanding of duende, Maria Chesiniuk acknowledges this issue when she suggests one path to better understanding duende might be via the word *juego* in Lorca's essay: 'it is the most appropriate way to describe the complex qualities of the duende as suggested by its multiple definitions' (2006). She cites 11 in the 1956 edition of the Spanish dictionary, including 'the ability or art with which one attains or disturbs something', or a deception or even 'between and among certain elements' (2006). This moving away from the word duende to try and explain it is symptomatic of the difficulty not just of translating an untranslatable word, but also of the myriad uses of the term. In Amanda G. Michaels' article on digital poetry, she defines duende as 'a ghost, an evil spirit, a goblin-like creature. In the context of the arts, it is a delicately nuanced term, suggesting "the obscure power and penetrating inspiration of art", and is most closely associated with the music of flamenco' (Michaels 2009: 1). That the supernatural aspect of duende is experienced in a duality both as a sprite or fairy as well as a magical power or spirit that possesses an artist can certainly be linked to the duality that Cave associates with the term. The word might be used to suggest that a dancer or singer might lack technical brilliance, but that their 'fire' is something akin to a 'demoniacal intensity', which sweeps audiences off their feet' (OED 2010). They are possessed by their duende, and, crucially, it is something that belongs in essence to them. Lorca suggests that an artist's muse comes from outside of them, but that duende is within and the struggle is due to this:

> [b]ut there are neither maps nor exercises to help us find the duende. We only know that he burns the blood like a poultice of broken glass, that he exhausts, that he rejects all the sweet geometry we have learned, that he smashes styles, that he leans on human pain with no consolation.
>
> (1998: 51)

Lorca agrees with the seemingly crucial thought from Manuel Torres that 'all that has black sound has duende' and sees an inherently tortured experience at the heart of the process; he considers it to be 'a power not a work. It is a struggle, not a thought' (1998: 49). The artist must struggle to bring the work into creation. This is echoed in Jason Webster's autobiographical work, *Search for the Duende*, when the leader of the flamenco group he is playing with explains his own perspective on the line walked in life as in music that takes one to duende; he tells him that

> [t]his is flamenco, *churumbel* [...] This. This life [...] You want to experience real flamenco? You want to know what *duende* is really about? It's about this. It's about living on the edge – *a tope*. It's about singing so hard you can't speak anymore. Or playing until your fingers bleed. It's about taking yourself as far as you can go, and then going one step further.
>
> (Webster 2003: 178)

Webster's experiences focus on a particularly masculine community, seen here in an arguably traditional macho concept of art making – this description has some value in attempting to understand the struggle that duende appears to represent to both Lorca and Cave. Lorca describes duende as being from the blood, a distinctly physical relationship, in contrast to the relationship a poet has with his muse. This physical struggle calls to mind the Biblical story of Jacob and the Angel, a man and an impossibly strong invisible entity struggling on a mountaintop (Genesis 32: 22). This imagery sits with Cave's take on the love song as something that brings him closer to God. Describing the love song as similar to the Christian Psalm, Cave suggests that 'both are messages to God that cry out into the yawning void, in anguish and self-loathing, for deliverance' (Cave 2007: 12). However, this is not a benevolent religious effect. It is a tortured experience seen in the way that Lorca explains the effect of the Gypsy *siguiriya*, which is a form of flamenco within *cante jondo*. He describes how it 'begins with a terrible scream that divides the landscape into two ideal hemispheres. It is the scream of dead generations, a poignant elegy for lost centuries, the pathetic evocation of love under other moons and other winds' (Lorca 1998: 4). Lorca takes this dark/light dialectic even further when he says that 'duende does not come at all unless he sees that death is possible' (1998: 58). In *Morphology of the Duende*, a study on the presence of modernity and death in Lorca's work, Eric Reinholtz draws the conclusion that duende is 'analogous to Freud's idea of "unconscious loss" in the dichotomy between mourning and melancholia' and therefore 'demands constant artistic revitalization as it "smashes styles" and established aesthetic paradigms with the same inexorable reality of "human pain with no consolation"' (Reinholz 2007: 139). Moving away from other art forms, Reinholtz shows that Lorca felt duende was most present within song. 'He found this still unnamed duende to be at its most powerful in the genre's "perfect prototype" the Gypsy siguiriya' (2007: 141). It is in music that duende is most present for Lorca, and also for Cave.

Lorca returns repeatedly to the fact that many artists and thinkers had struggled to know duende. Perhaps the most significant for Lorca, as he draws parallels with other writers, is his suggestion that Frederick Nietzsche's work *The Birth of Tragedy* is such an attempt. This significance is due to two issues; firstly, Nietzsche's attempt to work through the dialectic at the heart of art is an attempt, Lorca feels, to discover duende by another name: 'is in sum, the spirit of the earth, the same duende that scorched the heart of Nietzsche, who searched in vain for its external forms [...] without knowing that the duende he was pursuing had leaped straight from the Greek mysteries to the dancers of Cadiz or the beheaded Dionysian scream of Silverio's siguiriya' (Lorca 1998: 49). Secondly, Nietzsche's establishment of the duality at the heart of this mystery supports both Lorca's metaphor of the landscape split into two, and Cave's idea of the dark/light dialectic discovered at the point that a song becomes a love song.

The Birth of Tragedy

In *The Birth of Tragedy*, Nietzsche makes use of the physical representation of two Hellenic gods to define his theories on tragedy, and his theories on modern culture:

> [a]rt derives its continuous development from the duality of the Apolline and Dionysiac [...] between the Apolline art of the sculptor and the non-visual Dionysiac art of music. These two very different tendencies walk side by side, usually in violent opposition to each other.
>
> (Nietzsche 1993: 14)

Nietzsche goes on to further define this dialectic as 'the separate art worlds of dream and intoxication' (1993: 14). This idea of the split between the two forces being reflected in dream and intoxication lends some perspective upon Cave's dialectic of the necessary presence of both joy and pain in the love song. In their study of *The Birth of Tragedy* Burnham and Jesinghausen consider that Nietzsche felt that 'the opposing drives are interdependent. Moreover they complete each other, bringing both to their highest realization' (2010: 33–4). For Cave also the split is essential, the two parts equally interdependent if the love song is to attempt to address the full darkness and light involved with matters of the human heart. I do not have the space to do justice to a considered study of the links between Cave, Nietzsche and Lorca's work in this area, but as I move away from Nietzsche's work, I would like to consider his question, 'what would music be like if it were no longer romantic in its origins, as German music is, but Dionysiac?' (Nietzsche 1993: 10). I would argue that the Dionysiac music might sound a lot like The Birthday Party. There is the howl there, the scream; Dionysius might be present on stage. As Burnham and Jesinghausen suggest, '*The Birth of Tragedy*, Nietzsche wants us to believe, is a covert hymn devoted to Dionysius; there is a wild, disembodied, dithyrambic voice in the background singing the god's praises' (2010: 9). This description of Nietzsche's text referencing a performance also echoes Cave's musings upon the love song, when he describes it as 'the raving of the lunatic supplicant petitioning his god' (Cave 2007: 7). If agonized performance was central to the concept of duende then the early shows of The Birthday Party certainly compare to the idea of a Dionysiac performance. In these shows, Cave howls into the microphone and throws his skeletal frame around onstage as if possessed. As Burnham and Jesinghausen suggest, the intoxication of the Dionysiac performance creates a moment where 'one loses identity', leading to a situation where 'the Dionysiac renews the natural "bond" between human beings, who no longer see themselves as separate individuals, constrained and isolated by artificial laws' (2010: 43). This moment of losing one's identity in the immersion in the art is, then, the moment when the great distance between Lorca's concept of duende and Nietzsche's concept of the Dionysiac is visible. Although Lorca's duende suggests that there is a moment of losing one's self in the song, which resonates with the punk performance that draws its audience into feeling the same excitement as the lead singer writhing on stage, this loss-of-self also has to occur within the essence of the indescribable sadness that Cave and Lorca describe as the essence at the heart of the love song. This is supported by Cave: 'in contemporary rock music, the area in which I operate, music seems less inclined to have at its soul, restless and quivering, the sadness that Lorca talks about. Excitement, often; anger, sometimes, but true sadness, rarely' (2007: 8). In light of this perspective on the kind of performance that Cave undertook as the frontman with The Birthday Party, I would suggest that he might be channelling Nietzsche's idea of Dionysius. However, the agonized figure struggling with his fate and petitioning his god that Cave evokes in *The Secret Life of the Love Song* comes through more in his fictional characters such as Euchrid Eucrow rather than in Cave's performances on stage.

And the Ass Saw the Angel

Euchrid Eucrow is the central character in Cave's first novel, *And the Ass Saw the Angel*. The novel tells the story of Euchrid, delivered into the world via an episiotomy performed with the broken neck of the bottle his vile mother has been drinking from when she passes out, mid-delivery, in an alcoholic fugue (1989: 7–8). Euchrid is the main narrator, lying in the swamp, awaiting his own death as he sinks slowly into a mud pit. He is awaiting his slow death, as he is pursued by a mob following his murder of the symbol of light and joy to a town devastated by three years of rain, a child called Beth Swift. Euchrid regularly delivers monologues of deep sadness and tragic situations that he has had to face throughout his life. He describes himself in the prologue as 'the loneliest baby boy in the history of the whole world. And that's no idle speculation. It's a fact. God told me so' (1989: 18). Euchrid, mute and driven to the margins by the inhabitants of the local township along with his dysfunctional parents, describes a miserable half-life, subject to random acts of extreme violence. Yet, unlike the villagers, Euchrid is one of the few who can appreciate the beauty of the world in the figure of the local prostitute, who the villagers beat to death, and the presence of God. 'Something that had been rooted deep in the hearts of these pious souls, that had shone through their eyes, had now vanished. […] Gone was the God in them' (1989: 123). Beth Swift, child of the murdered prostitute, Cosey Mo, held responsible for the end of the three-year downpour, sees Euchrid as the Angel of the title of the book. There is great tenderness in the exposition of their oddly innocent and yet deeply disturbing relationship, which eventually results in Euchrid attacking Beth with a sickle, Euchrid's awful slow suicide and the subsequent birth of their son. When Euchrid visits Beth and has sex with her, although it is deeply questionable as to whether this is a consensual union, the description is not of a violent nature: 'the breath of her words against the skin of mah face. […] A brush of lavender across mah cheek. Your little doll … Little doll is prepared. Blushing blackness. Blushing blackness. Deadtime' (1989: 275). Their relationship echoes Lorca's assertion when he says, 'duende does not come at all unless he sees that death is possible' (1998: 58). *And the Ass Saw the Angel* is a slow, awful journey into the heartland of a tragic town and a man doomed to be denied love and tenderness before he was even born. It is a tragic story, pocked with a deep sadness throughout.

Despite the actions of Euchrid, I as a reader, was drawn into his world, and into his motivation. I was not the only one. As L. J. Lindhurst, reviewing the book, agrees,

> Cave delivers his colorful story with such brilliance, with such compelling conviction, that its internal logic grows disturbingly appealing: Why, *of course* it makes sense to have the exhumed skeleton of your infant twin brother for company in your swamp grotto. And *of course* you need to dig a snake pit in the floor of your house. *And the Ass Saw the Angel* presents an image of the world so distorted it seems to operate on a different moral plane; but like a reflection in a funhouse mirror, the illusion only subverts what's already there. Whether or not one accepts the moral in Cave's haunting tale of microscopic cogs and catastrophic plans, it's hard not to be carried away by the terrible beauty of its telling.
>
> (Lindhurst 2003)

Cave's capacity in *The Ass Saw the Angel* to draw the reader into the emotional life of its strange narrator leads me onto the third aspect of duende for Lorca. It is something that Maurer, in his introduction to Lorca, describes as 'an inexplicable power of attraction, the ability, on rare occasions, to send waves of emotion through those watching and listening' (Lorca 1998: ix). Even though Euchrid is a violently troubled man, with a problematic history, Cave still manages to pull his audience in. There is imagery that stays with you long after you have finished reading. The image of Euchrid lying on a bed of mud, slowly sinking, looking upwards to the heavens as the skies blacken and the crows circle stayed vividly in my memory, even after I had forgotten the general plot (Cave 1989: 3). Equally, I remembered the intensity of the description of the connection Euchrid experiences with Cosey Mo, after she is beaten and virtually scalped by the local mob led by the preacher Abie Poe (1989: 109).

This capacity to affect a reader is echoed in Lorca's description of the power of a poem to affect its audience in ways other than just to stay in their minds, it goes beyond this in fact: 'the magical property of a poem is to remain possessed by duende that can baptize in dark water, all who look at it' (Lorca 1998: 58). This, like many renditions of what duende is, inherently conceives of it as a live moment, it affects the audience in the way it possesses them, makes them act. Could duende then be seen as a moment of performance? Performance is notoriously ephemeral and hard to capture: much like the concept of duende. Duende can only be achieved in a rare, fierce moment of performance, and you have to be there to experience it.

Like performance, duende has a complex relationship with audience. Without response, can a performance be said to contain duende if there was no one there to be caught up and appreciate it? It perhaps is useful to consider duende in this exchange between performer and spectator. Ian Gibson describes it as 'that mysterious communicative power known as duende' (1989: 113). He suggests that Lorca's duende 'came to denote a form of Dionysian inspiration always related to anguish, mystery and death, and which animates particularly the artist who performs in public – the musician, the dancer or the poet who recites his work to a live audience' (1989: 114). The idea that this moment of artistic creation can affect an audience in this way returns us again to the Nietzschean dialectic. The intoxicating potential between performer and audience is echoed in Maria Delgado's suggestion that 'duende's potency as a referent for the metaphor of artistic creation goes beyond the registers of the rational or the explainable – it is an invisible link that binds artist and audience through the thrill of the live' (Delgado 2008: 191–2). In contrast, Cave's lecture, commissioned as it was to run in parallel to his teaching on songwriting, rarely considers the listener. Instead 'The Secret Life of the Love Song' concentrates on the experience of the writer of the song. Yet, in order to have potency, the love song must affect its listener.

'The Secret Life of the Love Song'

Although Cave's lecture was focused on the aspects of the love song important to him as the writer, some are equally important to the listener. Here, Cave could be seen to be summing up the effect on the audience as he declares that

> the peculiar magic of the Love Song, if it has the heart to do it, is that it endures where the object of the song does not. It attaches itself to you and together you move through time. But it does more than that, for just as it is our task to move forward, to cast off our past, to change and to grow, in short to forgive ourselves and each other, the Love Song holds within it an eerie intelligence all of its own – to reinvent the past and to lay it at the feet of the present.
>
> (2007: 3)

Cave is describing the experience of the writer here, but it could equally be seen to be the experience of an affected audience. In Jason Webster's account of his youthful escape to Spain and consequent attempts to both learn the flamenco guitar and subsume himself within Gypsy society, he describes the experience of hearing a flamenco singer:

> I am held by the music as though any separation between myself and the rhythm has disappeared. A fat woman singing on stage, dancing in a way that seems as if she is barely moving, yet I feel she is stepping inside something and drawing me in with her. A chill, like a ripping sensation, moves up to my eyes. Tears begin to well up, while the cry from

her lungs finds an echo within me, and makes me want to shout along with her. The hairs on my skin stand on end, blood drains to my feet. I am rooted to the spot, suspended between the emotion being drawn out of me, as though bypassing my mind, and the shame of what I am feeling.

(Webster 2003: 7)

Although Webster's description of the effect of the singer and the song on him is at times hackneyed, it continues to highlight the difficulty of describing what occurs in the process of the audience experiences of duende. He finishes his description of the event succinctly and more evocatively as his host for the evening, a local man, leans over to him and asks 'did you feel it?' (2003: 7). There is *something* here to be felt and experienced, but what is 'it'?

The love song's potency to affect is categorically linked to its capacity to reflect or echo the listener's experience of love; it must make something felt. It is only successful if the listener is affected and in order to be affected, they must be moved by the rendition of the pain or joy of the writer. The love songs that travel with me are the ones that say something about *my* particular situation, *my* particular joy and/or sorrow with a particular love-object. Despite being created for a specific love-object for the writer of the song, it is only when it moves away from the original subject that the song can be ultimately successful. Duende can only be truly experienced by the listener when the song is made anew. When the listener attaches their own experience to the song, when the song takes on a love-object for the listener, in the same way it did for the writer, the song splits and becomes imbued with personal significance for the listener, that they can be truly moved by duende. I would suggest that after that happens, duende is present every time that song is heard and catapults the listener back into the ghostly arms of a lost lover or a lost time. Cave sums this capacity up when he explains that 'the Love Song holds within it an eerie intelligence all of its own – to reinvent the past to lay it at the feet of the present' (2001: 3).

Whilst Cave feels that most of his own works have been love songs, the list he produces in his essay dates from his later work with the Bad Seeds and from 1986 through to 2001 (2001: 13). Although the majority of the songs Cave cites in that list come from *The Boatman's Call*, it is his album *The Good Son*, written while Cave was living in Sao Paulo, Brazil and had fallen in love with a Brazilian woman, Viviane Carniero, that has a distinctly Spanish sound. In fact, Richard Elliott suggests that a song from the album is evidence that Nick Cave has always been a singer of Lorca's 'Deep Song', that 'Sorrow's Child' links Cave directly to the *saudade*:

[t]his is what had happened in 1994 when the controversial novo fadista Paulo Bragança recorded a version of Cave's song 'Sorrow's Child' with the guitarrista Mário Pacheco. In an interview, Bragança maintained the validity of his choice: 'throughout his life Nick Cave has been a fadista in the broadest sense of the word and the lyric of "Sorrow's Child" by itself is already a fado'.

(Elliott 2010)

Whilst *The Good Son* clearly shows the influence of living in South America in the keening sounds and mournful paeans to sorrow it contains, this influence appears intermittently throughout Cave's work. I am not suggesting that it is only the songs that sound most like flamenco in Cave's back catalogue that bring about duende. However, I do think it significant that there might be a link to an interest in the same sort of sound that inspired Lorca to write on duende in the first place. The song 'Spell' from the 2004 double album *Abattoir Blues/The Lyre of Orpheus* does not echo aspects of Spanish music, but it does contain strata of melancholy set off with Cave's restrained mournful tone. It is a pared and simple composition that, once again, evokes an ethereal quality of longing. There is an emphasis on percussion, lending the effect of gentle melancholy to the song with the underlying soft stroke of drum brushes and the rise and fall of the soft piano.

As I have already suggested, the way a love song affects an audience will depend on the environment of the heart that it is let loose upon at the time it is first heard. This is seen in Ben-Ze'ev's assertion that 'the correlation between relevance and emotional intensity is positive: greater relevance leads to greater emotional intensity' (2000: 135). In order to consider this, I will for one moment use myself as subject. I first heard Cave's 'The Ship Song', a song from the 1990 album *The Good Son*, nine years after it was released, whilst I was in the final days of a relationship. The fact that I was painfully aware of the endgame stage of my own love affair made my response to 'The Ship Song' even more painful. The lyrics suggest that this relationship is an *amour fou*, one of great passion, but ultimately doomed: '[c]ome sail your ships around me/And burn your bridges down/We make a little history, baby/Every time you come around' (2007: 175). The song, in sympathy with the lyrics, is built up of swooping piano riffs and percussion, joined together by wordless backing vocals that lend the song an ethereal quality. Cave's vocal is the only one in the song, and he sings all the accompaniment, creating an effect of longing echoes for the object that is 'a little mystery to me' (2007: 175). The lovers seem to attempt to make sense of their senseless togetherness; the inference is that they attempt to address their unsuitability to each other but their desire proves stronger: '[w]e define our moral ground/But when I crawl into your arms/Everything comes tumbling down' (2007: 175). Eventually their inevitable separation is set out: '[y]our face has fallen sad now/For you know the time is nigh/When I remove your wings/And you, you must try to fly' (2007: 175). The song, to this day, causes me to return, Proust-like, to the emotions felt during the build up to that break up and the subsequent heartache. Significantly, it is not linked to the emotions of the moment of the split, but the emotions of the time before it, a powerless sadness and resignation. My own response to this song evokes Cave's assertion that over time the love song that has duende can return the lover wholly to the relationship. Cave even suggests that beyond the love song's capacity for time travel, it is capable of existing in *place* of the relationship: 'the songs that I have written that deal with past relationships have become the relationships themselves, heroically mutating with time and mythologizing the ordinary events of my life, lifting them from the temporal plane and blasting them way into the stars' (2007: 18).

The experience of being returned to a past emotional state through the act of listening to the songs is exactly the effect that Lorca suggests the duende demands. The artist struggles with his duende, and, when he is successful in his struggle, duende comes forth. It comes through, emerging from the agony and delight experienced by the writer. When it does, the audience experiences these same emotions in the process. Nick Cave's work, dealing, as it does so often, with a dialectic of the positive and negative sides of love, enables its audience to experience duende. Cave's work sings the deep song and, in doing so, allows us to feel its keening note, its bleeding presence, and the shivering kiss of the rent heart.

References

Barton, Laura (2008), 'Duende is What I Look for in a Song', http://www.guardian.co.uk/music/2008/mar/14/popandrock4. Accessed 24 October 2010.

Ben-Ze'ev, Aaron (2000), *The Subtlety of Emotions*, Massachusetts: MIT Press.

Burnham, Douglas and Martin Jesinghausen (2010), *Nietzsche's 'The Birth of Tragedy': A Reader's Guide*, London: Continuum.

Cave, Nick (1989), *And the Ass Saw the Angel*, London: Penguin.

——— (2007), *The Complete Lyrics 1978–2007*, London: Penguin.

——— (2009), *The Death of Bunny Munro*, London: Liongate.

Chesaniuk, Marie (2006), 'Duende in the Works of Federico García Lorca', *The National Conference on Undergraduate Research (NCUR) 2006* [website], http://www.ncur20.ws/abstracts_with_media.asp. Accessed 24 October 2010.

Crawford, Anwyn (2009), 'The Monarch of Middlebrow', *Overland Literary Journal* [online], http://web.overland.org.au/previous-issues/issue-197/feature-anwyn-crawford/. Accessed 25 October 2010.

Delgado, Maria M. (2008), *Federico Garcia Lorca*, London: Routledge.

Elliott, Richard (2010), 'Duende: The Place of Longing', http://theplaceoflonging.wordpress.com/tag/duende/. Accessed 24 October 2010.

Garcia Lorca, Federico (1998), *In Search of Duende*, trans. by Christopher Maurer, New York: New Directions.

Gibson, Ian (1989), *Federico Garcia Lorca: A Life*, London: Faber.

Lindhurst, L. J. (2003), 'Book Review – And the Ass Saw the Angel', http://www.themodernword.com/reviews/cave_angel.html. Accessed 10 June 2011.

Michaels, Amanda G. (2009), 'Digital Duende: Reading the Rasp in E-Poetry Shift', http://www.shiftjournal.org/articles/2009/michaels.htm. Accessed 24 October 2010.

Nietzsche, Friedrich (1993), *The Birth of Tragedy*, trans. by Shaun Whiteside, London: Penguin.

Oxford English Dictionary 1989, 'duende', http://0-dictionary.oed.com.catalogue.ulrls.lon.ac.uk/cgi/entry/50070583?single=1&query_type=word&queryword=duende&first=1&max_to_show=10. Accessed 20 May 2010.

Reinholtz, Eric (2007), 'Morphology of the Duende', in Patricia Rae (ed.), *Modernism and Mourning*, New Jersey: Rosemont, pp. 136–53.

Webster, Jason (2003), *Duende: A Journey in Search of Flamenco*, London: Doubleday.

PART V

Sacred and Profane

Chapter 13

'There is a Kingdom': Nick Cave, Christian Artist?

John H. Baker

Soaked in blood

Nick Cave and the Bad Seeds' single 'Into My Arms' was released on 27 January 1997, and marked a departure from the style of Cave's previous album, *Murder Ballads*. *Murder Ballads* is sonically and lyrically extremely violent. The album's lyrics depict a savage world in which the various murders go unpunished and even the mass murderer of 'O'Malley's Bar' chooses surrender rather than suicide by cop. Lottie, in 'The Curse of Millhaven', slavers her way into the asylum while 'Richard Slade' leaves Mary Bellows cuffed to a bed 'with a rag in her mouth and a bullet in her head' (Cave 2007: 256–7). The serial killer in 'Song of Joy' continues to roam the land, even though 'the police are investigating at tremendous cost' (2007: 245).

The hellish atmosphere of the album is prefigured in 'There is a Light', a song that features on the bestselling 1995 soundtrack to *Batman Forever*. It seems likely that more people heard 'There is a Light' than any Cave song released before that date, considering the soundtrack's success. New listeners would have found Cave's track uncompromising: the narrator, 'Daddy-O', asks a variety of unwholesome-sounding characters about their plans for the evening, and receives a variety of unrighteous replies. 'Mr Hophead' is in search of 'some bad ju-ju', and 'Mr Gigolo' is in search of fleshly pleasures (2007: 268). 'Mr High-Roller' wants to make 'real dough' and 'Mr Killer-Man' is on his way downtown with his chum 'Mr Death' for some murderous fun (2007: 268). All sins are catered for.

Is there no beacon of morality shining in this moral void? Well, no. The 'God-fearing citizens' are 'holed up and they ain't coming out' (2007: 268). 'Mr Politician' is 'busy sucking on the guts of this town', and 'Mr Preacher', a 'carrion crow with blood on his chin', sounds unlikely to be of much assistance to his flock (2007: 268). He takes his place in Cave's gallery of demented preachers alongside 'that mad old Buzzard, the Reverend' in 'Papa Won't Leave You, Henry' and the demented Abie Poe in *And the Ass Saw the Angel* (2007: 187). 'Sugar' tells 'Daddy-O' that she is heading downtown to 'get messed up in a God-shaped hole', and it cannot be denied that God has quit this place: '[a]nd what about God and this Armageddon?/He's all blissed-out, man, up in Heaven' (2007: 268). God has abandoned His creation to wallow in this moral sewer and retreated into His own equivalent of Mr Hophead's opiate stupor. In this context the chorus seems grimly ironic: '[t]here is a light that shines over this city tonight/There is a light that shines over this city tonight/ Let it shine' (2007: 268). The light shines on, but it appears that God has nodded out without drawing the curtains. The 'little kids' 'looking to the sky' for hope in a hopeless world are unlikely to be rescued (2007: 269).

'Into My Arms'

The savage *Murder Ballads* had been the band's biggest commercial success to date. Nevertheless, Cave remained a 'cult' artist associated with violent songs about murder and mayhem. In this context, 'Into My Arms' marked a remarkable change of direction. The sound of the song made for a striking contrast with the rumbling savagery of *Murder Ballads*; the only instruments used are a piano and acoustic bass, allowing Cave's deep, crooning vocal to take centre stage. 'Into My Arms' is very nearly a solo Cave performance; the stripped-down ambience of the song allows the listener to pay particular attention to the lyrics.

The opening line is surely one of the most unusual ever written in a 'pop' song: 'I don't believe in an interventionist God' (2007: 273). The speaker rejects the possibility that God will take any active role in human existence. The Judaeo/Christian God 'intervenes' repeatedly over the course of the Old Testament, punishing His chosen people for their apostasy with numerous afflictions. In Cave's words, referring to his religious views at an earlier stage of his life, 'I believed in God, but I also believed that God was malign and if the Old Testament was testament to anything, it was testament to that' (1998: vii). The Book of Joshua, in particular, shows God vigorously supporting genocide as the rampaging Israelites exterminate the Canaanites.

The narrator of 'Into My Arms', however, denies all belief in such a God. Whether he even believes in God at all is left open, but the song rejects both an interventionist God and, later, 'the existence of angels' (2007: 273). His unwillingness to believe in such a God is perhaps informed by his fear of the merciless God of the Old Testament, and his terrible judgements; he maintains that if he did believe in such a God he 'would kneel down and ask Him/Not to intervene when it came to you/Not to touch a hair on your head/To leave you as you are' (2007: 273). There is also a certain 'gentle, high-serious humour' (in Lyn McCredden's words) in the song, as displayed when the narrator refers to God's tendency to 'direct' His creation in an almost jocular fashion: '[a]nd if He felt He had to direct you/Then direct you into my arms' (McCredden 2009: 172; Cave 2007: 273).

The song's chorus, however, is profoundly serious: '[i]nto my arms, O Lord/Into my arms, O Lord/Into my arms, O Lord/Into my arms' (Cave 2007: 273). The narrator implores the interventionist God he says he does not believe in to guide his beloved to him. The chorus of the song contributes considerably to the song's atmosphere of hushed reverence.

There is a movement, then, between doubt and faith even in the first verse and chorus of 'Into My Arms'. The song is a 'Love Song', and, therefore, by Cave's own definition, a 'sad song'; this 'sadness' bleeds through the song's continual vacillation between rejection and invocation of an interventionist God (2007: 13). The song is a sort of hymn that addresses God and the beloved simultaneously. In the second verse, strikingly, the speaker makes clear that even if he does not believe in an interventionist God, he reveres Christ; he claims that if he believed in angels, he would ask them to 'make bright and clear your path/And to walk, like Christ, in grace and love/And guide you into my arms' (2007: 273). Again the conflict between the spiritual and secular is clear: although the speaker wishes for his beloved to 'walk like Christ', he does not want her to follow Christ's stern advice and reject all love but his – he wants her to choose his earthly love (2007: 273; Luke 14: 26).

The final verse replaces doubt with faith in love. The 'path' the speaker imagined angels lighting for his beloved is one he feels he, also, can walk, although its precise nature is unclear (2007: 273). The song ends with the speaker once again imploring God to guide his beloved into his arms.

'Into My Arms' is an important song in Cave's career, and it is not surprising that he regards it with pride. It is the contention of this chapter that, like it or not, the later Cave has consciously rejected the tortured, nihilistic world-view that dominates his early work and chosen a new aesthetic. He has not 'sold out', 'got boring' or (God forbid) become a Christian, but he sees his work as a spiritual duty and himself as an artist who is, in some curious ways, Christ-like. Cave's work can, as the critical cliché has it, be seen as moving from an 'Old Testament' to a 'New Testament' period, although not in a conventionally Christian fashion.

God hates us all

Cave seems to have been a believer (of sorts) for all of his adult life: in his words, 'I've certainly never been an atheist' (Snow 2011: 178). He had an Anglican upbringing: 'at eight years old I joined the choir in our local Anglican church [...] but the God I heard preached about there seemed remote and alien and uncertain' (Cave 1997: 137). Christ, in particular, was unappealing, a 'wet, all-loving, etiolated individual'; 'even at that age I recall thinking what a wishy-washy affair the whole thing was. The Anglican Church: it was the decaf of worship and Jesus was their Lord' (1998: viii). Nevertheless, he found himself drawn back to the Bible 'in his early twenties', following the traumatic death of his father in a car crash (1998: vii). He did not go to the Good Book in search of consolation:

[w]hen I bought my first copy of the Bible, the King James version, it was to the Old Testament that I was drawn, with its maniacal, punitive God, that dealt out to His long-suffering humanity punishments that had me drop-jawed in disbelief at the very depth of their vengefulness.

(1998: vii)

What the young Cave sought from the Old Testament was confirmation that the world was a sorry place and mankind a wretched race worthy only of punishment. He found a strange comfort in 'watching a whacked-out God tormenting a wretched humanity' (1998: vii). The grim Bible stories he dimly remembered from his childhood sprang to life, newly relevant to his nihilistic state of mind, and invaluable to his art: 'I soon found in the tough prose of the Old Testament a perfect language, at once mysterious and familiar, that not only reflected the state of mind I was in at the time but actively informed my artistic endeavours' (1997: 138). It seems valid to ascribe the appeal of the Old Testament – at least in part – to Cave's own feelings of guilt and self-loathing that followed his father's death: '[f]or every bilious notion that I harboured about myself and the world, and there were a lot of those, there in the Old Testament was its equivalent leaping off the pages with its teeth bared' (1997: 138).

The world-view the youthful Cave found reflected in the Old Testament is in some ways Gnostic. 'Gnosticism' is a term that loosely describes a wide variety of beliefs and practices in the first centuries of the Christian era, but most of the groups that are now associated with this term believed that the material world was evil and that escape from its bonds could only be achieved through esoteric knowledge ('gnosis'). The material world was the creation of a 'demiurge', a malevolent being who appeared to humanity as God and demanded worship. The 'true' God was remote and indifferent, like the 'blissed-out' God of 'There is a Light', and could only be approached by the learned, or 'gnostikos' (2007: 268). The early Church Father Iranaeus attacked Gnostic beliefs in his work *Against Heresies*, and the success of the 'orthodox' Church's attack on Gnosticism is attested by the fact that until 1945 most of our knowledge of the Gnostics came from this volume: in 1945 a large number of Gnostic treatises was discovered at Nag Hammadi in Egypt (see Pagels 2006; Meyer 2008). Cave's own interest in Gnosticism is clear in his 1996 radio address, 'The Flesh Made Word', in which he makes reference to the Gospel of Thomas, one of the Gnostic texts discovered at this time (Cave 1997: 142). By this stage, however, he had a very different view of such matters, as we shall see, and quotes this Gnostic text in support of a rather more positive world-view.

The Old Testament God certainly comes across as malevolent: in Cave's words, '[t]he God of the Old Testament seemed a cruel and rancorous God and I loved the way He would wipe out entire nations at a whim' (1997: 138). His torture of the thoroughly undeserving Job is a particularly disturbing episode; when poor Job, robbed of his wealth, family and health, has the temerity to ask God why He has treated him this way, he receives the withering reply: '[w]here wast thou when I laid the foundations of the earth? Declare, if thou hast understanding' (Job 38: 4). In the face of this bombast, the wretched Job admits his own worthlessness: 'I abhor myself, and repent in dust and ashes' (Job 42: 6).

The Birthday Party: a fucking rotten business this

The Old Testament is full of such berserk cruelty. God demands unquestioning obedience, and is intolerant of all dissent. He even exterminates the entire human race at one point, except for Noah and his family (Genesis 6–9). The sheer irrationality of this brutal patriarch seems to have appealed to the crazed, fatherless Cave of the early 1980s. He 'loved to read the Book of Job and marvelled over the vain, distrustful God who turned the life of His "perfect and upright" servant into a living hell' (Cave 1997: 138). In Cave's words, 'why wouldn't man be born into trouble, living under the tyranny of such a God?' (1997: 138). The story of Job has a weirdly masochistic appeal – there is no point questioning this God, so why bother even trying? Just let His boot stamp on your face forever and glory in your wretchedness. This self-conscious 'wretchedness' can be seen in Cave's early performances – in the 1981 promotional video for 'Nick the Stripper' an abject, loincloth-clad Cave leaps and shambles through a succession of hellish scenes, passing a crucified Christ at one point before kissing a tethered goat and messing about with a severed pig's head. For much of the video, 'PORCO DIO' (an Italian blasphemy, roughly translating as 'God is a pig') is scrawled on Cave's skinny chest. Cave saw himself as a sort of Old Testament prophet, a megaphone through which God could scream at his creation: 'all I had to do was walk on stage and open my mouth and let the curse of God roar through me [...] I was a conduit for a God that spoke in a language written in bile and puke' (1997: 138–9).

Cave's early theology involved a willing embrace of the Gnostic concept of a crippled, vicious God whose rotten creation only reflects His own wickedness. Cave's protagonists roam a world whose corruption would find its ultimate expression in *Murder Ballads*. The Birthday Party song 'Big-Jesus-Trash-Can' reduces Christ to a blasphemous combination of perverted Elvis – wearing 'a suit of Gold' – and Texan oil billionaire 'driving great holy tanks of Gold': he is 'stiff in the crypt, baby, like a rock', a remarkable image that conflates images of death (without resurrection), sexual arousal and the evil spirit of rock 'n' roll (Cave 2007: 41). Heaven is a 'Graveyard' and earth is in the thrall of gold, trash and rock; a 'fucking rotten business this' (Cave 2007: 41). No wonder that the exhausted speaker in 'Wild World' asks his beloved to 'hold [His] dish-rag body tall' (Cave 2007: 56). He is '[p]ost crucifixion baby, and all undone' (2007: 56). The demented 'Mutiny in Heaven' conflates the agonies of heroin addiction and withdrawal with a disgusted rejection of organized religion:

Ah wassa born …
And Lord shakin, even then was dumpt into some icy font like some great stinky unclean!
From slum-church to slum-church, ah spilt mah heart
To some fat cunt behind a screen

(2007: 73)

The doctrine of original sin is merged with the self-disgust of the addict: '[m]ah threadbare soul teems with vermin and louse/Thought come like a plague to the head … in God's house!' (2007: 74). Perhaps the speaker is in rehab. He also makes graphic reference to the brutal moral system that he now finds unendurable: '[a]t night my body blusht/To the whistle of the birch/With a little practice ah soon learned to use it on maself/Punishment?! Reward!! Punishment?! Reward!!' (2007: 73).

The addict of 'Mutiny in Heaven' is trapped within the deranged moral framework of the Old Testament, crushed by his own wretchedness, conscious of the way he has been taught to brutalize himself (the 'fat cunt' lurking in the confessional is another of Cave's corrupt churchmen) and irresistibly drawn to the 'UTOPIATE' that simultaneously numbs and kills him (2007: 73). This is not much of a 'mutiny'; the speaker is alone and he is desperate to escape from heaven, not seize it. Lucifer was cast out of heaven; this ragged figure is simply 'bailin out' (2007: 74). The terrible power of the song owes as much to The Birthday Party as to Cave's lyrics – 'all heavy bludgeoning rhythms and revved-up, whacked-out guitars', in Cave's own words (1997: 138). Nevertheless, Cave's lyrics are indicative of the attractions of the Old Testament for an artist who wished to convey a complex mixture of self-loathing and rebellion. The Old Testament is notoriously violent, but Cave was in search of more than violence; he 'had a burgeoning interest in violent literature coupled with an unnamed sense of the divinity in things' (1998: vii). The Old Testament allowed him access to a grim moral framework that suited his purpose: the depiction of a world of endless and almost unendurable suffering from which even death is no escape. We are reminded of Cave's later choice to cover Dylan's dispiriting 'Death is Not the End' on *Murder Ballads*, a song that reminds us that for all the misery and suffering attendant upon human existence, those of us who decline to embrace salvation have an eternity of torture to look forward to.

From Her to Eternity to *The First Born is Dead*: kings of nothing

A similar sense of abandonment, of humanity crawling across a ruined landscape under the gaze of a sadistic God, haunts much of Cave's early work with the Bad Seeds. God has abandoned the protagonist of 'Well of Misery' 'deep in the Desert of Despair' (2007: 83). In 'Wings off Flies' the drunken and misanthropic speaker sardonically offers God his 'recipe of Heaven': 'you get solitude and mix with sanctuary and silence/Then bake it' and says he would willingly be hanged (2007: 89). Even 'Just a Closer Walk with Thee', Cave's adaption of a hymn, is marked by resignation: 'if I must walk these paths alone/Then let it be, please Lord, on up to thee' (2007: 95). The tide of misery is, it must be said, relentless; 'the name of the train is/Pain and suffering' and all are aboard (2007: 108). The remarkable and complex 'Black Crow King' seems to depict the crucifixion from the perspective of the titular 'king', who may even be the crucified Christ himself, abandoned on the cross by God and man: 'and the rain it raineth daily, Lord/And wash away my clothes/I surrender up my arms to a company of crows' (the mention of arms may also be an allusion to heroin addiction) (2007: 110). Perhaps Christ's words were misinterpreted and the crucifixion entirely unplanned: 'I just made a simple gesture/They jumped up and nailed it to my shadow' (2007: 109). This king is, indeed, 'king of nothing at all' (2007: 110). It is as if Christ's last despairing cry to his father upon the cross were met by silence and a lonely death with no hope of resurrection, either for Christ himself or all mankind (Matthew 27: 46; Mark 15: 34). As Cave says of Christ, 'the sense of aloneness that surrounds Him is at times unbearably intense' (1998: x). The fundamental solitude of humankind is, in this song, shared by God's own son, left to rot upon the cross and lashed by the storm, the ultimate betrayal.

Not all Cave's abandoned souls sink into despair. The lustful protagonist of 'Hard On for Love' knows his Bible: '[w]ell, I swear I seen that girl before/Like she walked straight out of the book of Leviticus' (2007: 129). However, his focus is more fleshly than spiritual and the reference to Leviticus is evidence of Cave's often disregarded sense of humour. The speaker is aware of the moral dangers posed by his desire but is more than willing to risk them: 'they can stone me with stones I don't care/Just as long as I get to kiss/Those gypsy lips!' (2007: 129). Later he makes mocking reference to Psalm 23; his 'Lord', his lust, leads him 'like a lamb to the lips/Of the mouth of the valley of the shadow of death' and his phallus embodies 'his rod and his staff [...] his sceptre and staff' (2007: 129). Woman is the only god worth worshipping and the 'altar of love' the only altar in this Godless world (shades of *The Death of Bunny Munro*) (2007: 129). We will later see Cave return to this idea, albeit in a rather more spiritual fashion. A similar note of mockery can be found in 'God's Hotel', each verse of which outlines a supposed virtue of heaven in contrast to the petty-minded restrictions imposed down below by the pious (2007: 132–4). The problem is that heaven is unutterably boring and its numbed inhabitants blind, deaf and dumb (2007: 133–4).

Tender Prey: the living dead

Tender Prey, released in 1988, positively bulges with the living dead: the condemned murderer in 'The Mercy Seat', the born villain in 'Up Jumped the Devil', the killer couple in 'Deanna', the melancholy voyeur (and possible paedophile) in 'Alice'. 'City of Refuge' warns of hell in language reminiscent of the book of Revelation – 'the gutters will run with blood' and 'the grave will spew you out' – but there is no redemption here (2007: 150). Damnation is universal in these 'days of madness' (2007: 150). We met an abandoned Christ in 'Black Crow King'; *Tender Prey* offers us a similarly abandoned John the Baptist in 'Mercy'. Deserted by his followers, the imprisoned John is addressed through the 'speak-hole' by a 'viper' – presumably either Herodias, whose incestuous marriage to Herod he condemned, or her daughter Salomé (2007: 148; Matthew 14: 3–12; Mark 6: 17–28). In Cave's contemporaneous short play 'Salomé', Salomé's motivation for seeking John's death is her own perverted malice: '[m]y mouth asks for it. My heart weeps for it! My cunt yearns for it!! The moon, in turn, demands it. THE HEAD OF JOHN THE B.!!' (1988: 730). Like the protagonist of 'Hard On for Love', Salomé has surrendered to desire, and is perversely attractive for it in comparison to the fanatical (and misogynist) Baptist. Salomé torments the Baptist by ironically asking him to 'cleanse' her; the song gives us John's own view of her voice: '[t]hick with innuendo/ Syphilis and greed' (1988: 71; 2007: 148). The contrast between the two Johns is striking; the John of the play faces his death confident of salvation, while the John of the song is a more melancholy figure, 'touchingly vulnerable' in Lyn McCredden's words, whose death is an occasion for weariness rather than ecstasy: '[m]y death, it almost bored me/So often was it told' (McCredden 2009: 174; Cave 2007: 149). The John of 'Mercy' is an exhausted figure whose suffering has reduced him to something less than human: 'my camel skin was torture/I was in a state of nature' (2007: 148). Even the austere piety of the play's John is undermined by Salomé's necrophilic abuse of his severed head (1988: 75).

The grim *Tender Prey* concludes with the superficially hopeful 'New Morning', which equates a new dawn with rebirth:

> Thank you for giving
> This bright new morning
> So steeped seemed the evening
> In darkness and blood
> There'll be no sadness
> There'll be no sorrow
> There'll be no road too narrow
> There'll be a new day
> And it's today
> For us

(2007: 159)

In some ways the final verse of this last song on the album prefigures the more hopeful Cave of recent years. Nevertheless, the first two verses are apocalyptic. 'The sky was a Kingdom/ All covered in blood', and '[t]he moon and the stars/Were the troops that lay conquered': this bright new day has only been reached through struggle (2007: 159). We are put in mind of the rigours of detoxification. The lines are reminiscent of the Book of Revelation: '[a]nd I beheld when he had opened the sixth seal, and, lo, there was a great earthquake; and the sun became black as sackcloth of hair, and the moon became as blood; and the stars of heaven fell unto the earth' (Revelation 6: 12–13). The lines are also reminiscent of Blake's 'The Tyger', in which 'the stars threw down their spears/And watered heaven with their tears', a similar gesture of surrender before the terrifying creator (Blake 1988: 24). In the second verse of the song the speaker kneels like Christ 'in the garden' beneath the 'spears of the bright sun', hovering 'unearthly/In banners of fire' (Cave 2007: 159). He cowers like Job and covers his eyes. This rebirth seems a bloody and painful process: if this is redemption, it is only achieved through surrender to a violent God. The God of love we encounter through Jesus is a long way away.

The Good Son: universal misery

We seem to meet Him on the opening track of the Bad Seeds' next album, *The Good Son* (1990). The chorus of what Robert Eaglestone calls a 'half-lullaby', 'Foi Na Cruz', is taken from a Protestant Portuguese hymn Cave heard in Brazil: it translates as 'it was on the cross, on the cross, that one day, my sins were punished in Jesus. It was on the cross, that one day, it was on the cross' (Eaglestone 2009: 147). The song's hushed ambience is also somewhat hymnal. However, the verses are as bleak as ever: '[d]ream on 'til you can dream no more/For all our grand plans, babe/Will be dreams for ever more' (Cave 2007: 168). The soothing quality of the music is undercut by the verses, which promise only 'trickery and deceit' (2007: 167). Perhaps the song implies that mankind should turn to Christ's sacrifice for consolation; this is by no means clear, however.

We encounter another of Cave's 'Biblical' characters in the album's title track, and his virtue has led only to misery. 'The Good Son' is the dutiful elder brother of the prodigal, who has demanded his share of his father's inheritance and left for 'a far country', where he wastes it in 'riotous living' (Luke 15: 13). The elder son plays a supporting role in Christ's parable; his role is to complain to his father that his loyalty has won no reward while the prodigal's return has been greeted with rejoicing: '[l]o, these many years do I serve thee, neither transgressed I at any time thy commandment: and yet thou never gavest me a kid, that I might make merry with my friends: But as soon as this thy son was come, which hath devoured thy living with harlots, thou hast killed for him the fatted calf' (Luke 15: 29–30). There is a real sense of resentment (and, perhaps, frustration) in the reference to the 'harlots'. This complaint allows the father to stress the subversive point of the parable – that God rejoices more in the return of a sinner than in the loyalty of the pious (Luke 15: 10).

Once again Cave presents a Biblical story from a perspective that takes human frailty, suffering and resentment into account. The song implies that the elder brother's resentment pre-dated his brother's return: '[a]nd he calls to his mother/And he calls to his father/But they are deaf in the shadows of his brother's truancy' (Cave 2007: 169). The elder brother labours loyally in the fields – '[h]e is a tiller, he has a tiller's hands' – but his heart is full of violence: 'down in his heart now/He lays queer plans' (2007: 169). It is no coincidence that Cain was also 'a tiller of the ground' and killed his brother out of jealousy and a desire for paternal affection: 'his father, he says, is an unfair man' (Genesis 4:2, 8; Cave 2007: 169). The elder son has, like the crazed Euchrid Eucrow in *And the Ass Saw the Angel*, been born beneath a 'malign star' and hears voices from the night 'of good and evil' (2007: 169). Ultimately, he 'curses his virtue like an unclean thing' (2007: 169). We are still in a world dominated by dark passions, and the Good Son is every bit as abandoned as the Black Crow King and the Baptist. Cave continues to undermine Biblical narratives of faith by plunging them into a world of resentment and suffering in which misery is universal, as in 'Sorrow's Child' and 'The Weeping Song' on the same album. 'The Hammer Song', which may depict the prodigal's suffering after he has frittered away his inheritance, shows us yet another despairing figure battered by a malign fate, wandering through a frozen landscape and met with hostility by those he encounters. Human love provides no comfort on this album: the protagonists of 'Lucy' and 'Lament' have been abandoned by their lovers, as has the protagonist of 'The Train Song', a contemporaneous composition, who obsessively demands the details of his lost love's departure. Even though the music on *The Good Son* is Cave's softest yet, the brutal world-view is much the same.

Henry's Dream and *Let Love In*: hell on earth

By *Henry's Dream* (1992) and *Let Love In* (1994) the pattern is clear – Cave's protagonists are mainly wanderers, reminiscent of Cain or the Wandering Jew, deprived of either spiritual or human comfort and denied even the blessing of death's release. We are close to the hellish universe of *Murder Ballads*. Long-term drug addiction may have coloured these desolate narratives, but they are also marked by a profound sense of spiritual yearning. Henry's father 'bellow[s] at the firmament' in rage at his friend's murder; he traverses a post-apocalyptic landscape inspired by Cave's time in Brazil: '[e]ntire towns being washed away/Favelas exploding on chemical spillways/Lynch-mobs, death squads, babies being born without brains/The mad heat and the relentless rain' (Cave 2007: 187, 190). In 'I Had a Dream, Joe', Jesus is 'shadowy', flitting 'from tree to tree'; he offers no salvation (2007: 192). The landscape of 'Straight to You' is, like that of 'Papa Won't Leave You, Henry', apocalyptic, although there seems no chance of redemption in this chaos: drunken saints howl at the moon and angelic chariots collide (2007: 192, 195). The penniless drunkard of 'Brother, My Cup is Empty' and the paranoid wanderer of 'When I First Came to Town' are locked into relentless patterns of self-destruction, as is the abused protagonist of 'Jack the Ripper'. The sombre 'Christina the Astonishing' even depicts the pious heroine crawling into an oven 'to escape the stench of human corruption' (2007: 199). Cave's account of Christina, a medieval holy woman noted for the extreme privations she voluntarily underwent (including, indeed, roasting herself in furnaces), does not mention the vision of purgatory that inspired her to mortify her own flesh during her lifetime to alleviate the sufferings of those imprisoned there (see Thomas of Cantimpre 2008). Without this explanation Cave's Christina seems motivated solely by misanthropic disgust, which fits in with the nightmarish ambience of the album as a whole. John Finn's murderer wins the affections of his beloved only by planting his bolo knife in her husband's neck; although the narrator of the ominous 'Loom of the Land' seems affectionate towards Sally, we are uncomfortably aware of the knife in his jeans and his repeated entreaties to her to fall asleep (as well as their isolation). He has no motive for murder, but who needs a motive in such a world? The couple have, after all, already passed 'Reprobate Fields', and a 'reprobate' is already damned (2007: 205).

Let Love In (1994) is similarly bleak. 'Do You Love Me' depicts another doomed relationship: 'I knew before I met her that I would lose her' (2007: 216). 'Part Two' of the song, which concludes the album, tells a heart-rending story of child abuse. The bereft lover of 'Nobody's Baby Now' has 'searched the holy books/Tried to unravel the mystery of Jesus Christ the Saviour' in vain for an explanation of his desertion (2007: 217). Cave's wretched protagonists seek salvation in the arms of women but simply find more pain. In 'Ain't Gonna Rain Anymore', the abandoned narrator is 'left to drift on a dead calm sea', his loneliness numbing him like some narcotic (2007: 228). By contrast, the devilish 'Loverman', like the narrator of 'Hard On for Love', has surrendered to the fires of lust. He is no hedonist, however; his desire is a torment: '[a]nd he's old and he's stupid and he's hungry and he's sore/And he's blind and he's lame and he's dirty and he's poor' (2007: 219). Like an addict, he 'got no choice at all' (2007: 219). In 'Let Love In' the narrator bewails the 'Despair and Deception' he invited into his life when he fell in love (2007: 225). Desire is not the only addiction afflicting these unfortunates: poor Jangling Jack is gunned down in a bar by a 'grinning man' for no apparent reason while in 'Thirsty Dog' the habitual toper's only explanation for his appalling conduct is a sort of metaphysical starvation: 'my heart and soul are kind of famished' (2007: 221, 227).

By the time he released *Murder Ballads*, Cave had reached an artistic impasse. The album's world of carnage is so extreme as to be almost parodic, something Cave seems to acknowledge with the frequent moments of black comedy that pepper the record. Over almost 15 years Cave's art had come to depict a grim landscape of guilt, loss and desertion, traversed by lonely (almost always male) figures who fail to find salvation through their various addictions – drugs, alcohol, sex, murder. Euchrid's 'faith' in *And the Ass Saw the Angel* is simply a manifestation of his madness and organized religion is reduced to deranged fanaticism. This is a world of spiritual starvation, of desperate and doomed attempts to fill the 'God-shaped hole' of 'There is a Light' (2007: 268).

There is a definite shift in mood between *Murder Ballads* and *The Boatman's Call*, however, and not merely a musical one. This shift is signalled by the spoken-word piece 'Time Jesum Transenteum Et Non Revertentum', which first appeared as a hidden track on the *X-Files* soundtrack, *Songs in the Key of X*, released in March 1996. Over a melancholy instrumental backing, Cave recites a strange tale in which the narrator, 'searching for the secrets of the universe', forces demons to reveal the 'message': '[d]read the passage of Jesus for He will not return' (2007: 270). The narrator and his companion(s) fail to heed this advice and instead indulge in consumerism, listening to the imprisoned song of caged birds; the latter implies that the worse sin is not greed but the imprisonment of inspiration. The song concludes with apocalyptic imagery – '[n]ow the stars they are all angled wrong/And the sun and the moon refuse to burn' – but the song's conclusion makes it clear that salvation *was* on offer and the narrator scorned it (2007: 270). For all its melancholy, the piece is indicative of an entirely new – and more positive – attitude that marks Cave's work from *The Boatman's Call* onwards.

Jesus Christ, artist

This new attitude is outlined in a number of prose works written by Cave in the late 1990s: 'The Flesh Made Word', a lecture delivered on BBC Radio 3 in March 1996, a short introduction to the Gospel of Mark published in 1998 and a lecture entitled 'The Secret Life of the Love Song' delivered in Vienna in 1998 and in expanded form in London in 1999. The appearance of these works marks what Robert Eaglestone calls 'a key intellectual-aesthetic moment in [Cave's] career' (2009: 142). The prospect of the raging Cave of the early 1980s writing or delivering such material would have been inconceivable, and Cave acknowledges this when he speaks of the 'abject *horror*' that fills him at the prospect of '*teaching, lecturing*', like his father (2007: 5).

In 'The Flesh Made Word' Cave claims that he simply grew tired of the nihilistic rage that marked his early work: '[a]ll that sustained hatred was a painful and tiring business' (1997: 139). In his introduction to Mark, however, he ascribes this shift to more than simple weariness:

> you grow up [...] Buds of compassion push through the cracks in the black and bitter soil. Your rage ceases to need a name. You no longer find comfort watching a whacked-out God tormenting a wretched humanity as you learn to forgive yourself and the world. That God of Old begins to transmute in your heart, base metals become silver and gold, and you warm to the world.
>
> (1998: vii)

What Cave is describing here is in part a process of maturation, but it is also a spiritual and artistic process. Cave's 'Old Testament' period was marked by his consciousness that in some curious and violent way his writing and performance were conduits 'for a God that spoke in a language written in bile and puke' (1997: 139). Over time, that voice began to 'transmute' into a voice that was 'softer, sadder, more introspective' (1997: 139). This process of transmutation was achieved through a growing focus on Christ himself.

Cave's new fascination with Christ was not conventionally Christian. There is little focus on the crucifixion or redemption from sin. Cave sees Christ as the ultimate artist. He claims that the 'shameful fantasies' that tormented him as a child 'were coming from God' and that his father's curious habit of reciting 'great bloody slabs' of literature to his baffled son 'elevated him, tore him from normality, lifted him out of the mediocre and brought him closer to the divine essence of things' (1997: 137). As he grew older, Cave claims, his own creative urge manifested itself in an entirely appropriate way – his rage was reflected in the deranged God of the Old Testament who presides over his early work. Cave claims, in retrospect, that a great deal of the nihilistic rage that dominates his early work stemmed from an unresolved grieving process – an attempt to fill 'the great gaping hole' of his father's death with art, to come to terms with his despair through an engagement with the imagination (2007: 6). The youthful Cave who ranted and screamed was allowing God to speak through him in the way of all genuine artists: 'wherever two or more are gathered there is a communion, there is language, there is imagination. There is God. God is a product of the creative imagination and God is that imagination taken flight' (1997: 137).

In the light of this almost romantic theology, it is not surprising that the narrator of 'Into My Arms' does not believe in an 'interventionist' God (2007: 273). The God of Cave's later work is already *within* us, a product of our human imagination, liberated through artistic expression. In Cave's words, 'I found that through the use of language I was writing God into existence. Language became the blanket that I threw over the invisible man, which gave him shape and form' (2007: 6). In this light, 'O'Malley's Bar' is every bit as 'godly' as

'Into My Arms'. The imagination that allowed Cave access to the mind of the former song's mass murderer is expressed with equal validity in the sadder, more questioning voice we hear in the latter. Nevertheless, in 'The Secret Life of the Love Song', Cave maintains that his most profound works are 'Love Songs', 'the cry of one chained to the earth and craving flight, a flight into inspiration and imagination and divinity' (2007: 7). It is striking that in this lecture, delivered in 1999, Cave lists ten songs that he regards with particular pride, only two of which – 'Deanna' and 'From Her to Eternity' – are marked by the musical and lyrical violence of the earlier work (2007: 13). The rest of the songs are 'softer, sadder, more introspective' (1997: 139).

Nick Cave, Christian artist?

Is the post-1997 Cave a 'Christian artist'? Not in any straightforward way. He cannot be compared to Bob Dylan, whose full-on embrace of Evangelical Christianity in the late 1970s shocked his fans; he has not used his fame as a pulpit, or written songs of praise. He explicitly denied he was a Christian to Robert Sandall in 2003 and again to John Payne in 2010 (Snow 2011: 127; Payne 2010). The post-9/11 Cave is particularly concerned about the way religion has become identified with terrorism and violence: as he told Debbie Kruger in 2004, 'the words of Christ have been so violated and hijacked and used for deeply unrighteous political purposes', and in the same year he told Phil Sutcliffe that he was troubled by 'the more fanatical notions of what God is and where that can lead' (Snow 2011: 136, 172). Similarly, he told Thomas Bartlett that 'the name of God has been hijacked by a gang of psychopaths and bullies and homophobes', by American extremists (Bartlett 2004). He is at pains to point out that he belongs to no 'church or organised religion' and that his faith is 'open, doubtful, sceptical' (Snow 2011: 172). Nevertheless at some point his Bible reading became more about 'spiritual enlightenment' than simply confirming his nihilistic world-view (2011: 136). In recent years he has been keen to relegate his love of the Old Testament firmly to the past: 'I've always been more interested in the New Testament. Apart from very early on' (2011: 136). One wonders how, exactly, Cave defines 'very early on'. He has also agreed that the division of his work into 'Old Testament' and 'New Testament' periods is 'tosh' and that his interest in the Old Testament was mainly motivated by his research for his first novel (2011: 215). This seems a trifle disingenuous in the light of the way his work up to *Murder Ballads* positively drips with Old Testament themes and language (as well as the fact that he himself has agreed with – or even suggested – such a division of his work several times) (2011: 127, 191). Cave seems keen to distance himself from this period.

All the same, it is impossible to ignore the passionate focus on Christ that we find in 'The Flesh Made Word', in particular, and the way Cave uses Christ to symbolize the artist. Cave displays no interest in the crucifixion. It is the humanity of Christ that attracts him; the only one of his miracles he dwells upon is his healing of a sick woman who touches the hem of his garment, since, in his words, 'to be made whole is to be made human; that was the human nature of him' (2011: 171). Cave makes Christ the artist *par excellence*: 'a man of flesh and blood, so in touch with the creative forces inside himself, so open to His brilliant, flame-like imagination, that He became the physical embodiment of that force, God' (Cave 1997: 139). Cave's Christ is a rebel whose contempt for the forces of order is reminiscent of the fury that flowed through the young Cave: 'Christ was forgiving, merciful and loving but He was after all the Son of the Old Testament God and His Father's blood still boiled in His veins' (1997: 140). He rebels even against his father, and comes 'to right [His] wrongs' (1997: 140). Cave is claiming that his own role as an artist is a spiritual one: '[d]ivinity must be given its freedom to flow, through us, through language, through communication, through imagination. I believe this is our spiritual duty made clear to us through the example of Christ' (1997: 142). Euchrid Euchrow is a blocked artist whose 'internalised imagination' turns to 'madness' (1997: 142). Cave goes so far as to compare himself as a successful creator of art (unlike his own father, whose own creative endeavours came to nothing) to Christ: '[l]ike Christ, I too come in the name of my father, to keep God alive' (1997: 142).

Cave has resisted the temptation to compare himself to Christ in subsequent years (and has even generously claimed that 'you can get that same link sawing a piece of wood or looking after your children or being an accountant'), but it is plain that he believes his art allows him to rise above the 'ordinariness' and 'mediocrity' of mundane human existence (Snow 2011: 137; Cave 1998: xii). It is in this way that we can understand Cave's working life, in which he 'goes to the office' six days a week, clad in a suit, to write; to Cave, this is anything but mundane. This is his own way of allowing divinity to flow through him into the mundane world, although it is 'most of the time numbingly hard work' (Snow 2011: 137).

It would be too much to claim that Cave 'found Christ' (or that Christ found him) at this time, but a profound change is evident. The old nihilism is absent, and Cave's world-view, while still hardly rosy, is somewhat warmer. Cave seems to have reconciled himself to God through his vision of Christ as the exemplar of the artist, and this has profoundly changed his art. Since 1996 his songs have been much less bloody. Women are still present, but rather less frequently as the victims of murder or violence; the 'softer, sadder' voice of Cave's later work tends to dwell upon the more melancholy aspects of love. As previously mentioned, Cave declared himself proudest of ten 'Love Songs' in 1998, and only one – 'Deanna' – deals with the familiar theme of murder (Cave 2007: 13). Whisper it softly, but Cave's later work can be seen as 'mature' in its focus on the realities of love and desire rather than the Gothic horrors of his earlier work. This 'maturity' has led to a certain degree of criticism from those, like Emma McEvoy, who feel Cave's work now lacks the deranged Gothic intensity that once marked it, but it is hard to see how Cave could have gone on making albums like *Murder Ballads* without slipping into simple self-parody (McEvoy 2007). Perhaps Cave himself was aware of these criticisms – his most recent Bad Seeds albums, *Abattoir Blues/The Lyre of Orpheus* and *Dig, Lazarus, Dig!!!*, as well as the two albums he has made with Grinderman, certainly 'rock' in a way that most of, say, *Nocturama* simply does not. However, it would be a mistake to see Cave as somehow creating a pastiche of his earlier work in these latter albums. Lyrically, they are very different, particularly in the way they deal with religious themes and with love. As Will Self points out, it would be a serious error to pigeonhole Cave merely as a lyricist of violence and fury (2007: xii).

Idiot prayers

It is, perhaps, a relief to note the lack of explicitly Christian songs in Cave's recent catalogue – the piano-led 'Bless His Ever-loving Heart' is about as close as Cave has come to writing a hymn (Cave 2007: 345). Cave's contempt for conventional Christianity is clear in what Robert Eaglestone calls 'an overtly political song' – one of very few by Cave – 'God is in the House', whose protagonists seem happy in their infinitely dull (and creepily fascistic) pseudo-paradise (shades of 'God's Hotel') (Eaglestone 2009: 141; Cave 2007: 324–5). This 'God' is thoroughly tamed, the antithesis of both the Christ Cave admires for his 'ringing intensity' and of all creativity (Cave 1998: xi). The protagonist of 'Little Empty Boat' amusingly rejects evangelical Christianity in favour of casual sex: '[g]ive to God what belongs to God/And give the rest to me' (2007: 291). The road offered by conventional Christianity is closed for good; 'Swing Low' makes this clear: '[p]ray like Peter, preach like Paul/Jesus died to save us all/I climbed through the window, I crawled on the floor/ I ripped apart the furniture/But I still couldn't find what I was looking for' (2007: 377). Characteristic of this later period is the 'open, doubtful, sceptical' spirit Cave described to Phil Sutcliffe in 2004, and a tendency to seek spiritual meaning in earthly love (Snow 2011: 172). Perhaps God 'lives only in our dreams', as 'There is a Town' has it, but we should remember the way Cave has linked God and the creative impulse – dreams can in this way be seen as messages from God, the only way He can speak through (and to) us (2007: 360). In Cave's words, 'the emphasis is placed clearly on man […] without him as a channel God has no place to go' (1997: 142). These songs are honest in their appraisal of both the pains and pleasures of love: 'those songs that speak of love, without having within their lines an ache or a sigh, are not Love Songs at all' (2007: 8). This honesty allows these songs to 'fill, with language, the silence between ourselves and God, to decrease the distance between the temporal and the divine' (2007: 11). The abiding theme of Cave's post-1996 work is love, not God. God is not absent for Cave; the very act of writing these love songs is his way of 'actualizing' Him (2007: 6).

'Wife', for example, tells us that 'God is gone. We got to get a new one/Not Lock Him down in cathedrals and cages' and seeks salvation in 'the eternal woman' (2007: 298). The chorus of 'There is a Kingdom' – '[t]here is a Kingdom/There is a king/And He lives without/And He lives within' sounds thoroughly Christian, as does the reference to Kant's 'starry heavens above' and 'moral law within', but the speaker's 'faith' is in a woman, not God, and 'this day so sweet' 'will never come again' (2007: 279). 'Sheep May Safely Graze' may sound like a lullaby but on a closer reading the world outside the window becomes a bleak and terrifying place: '[a]ll you can hear outside is the roar of a city being razed/That's just the powers that be making it safe to graze' (2007: 308). The song ends with a reference to Christ's own admission of a sense of homelessness (and, perhaps, persecution) in Luke's Gospel: '[t]he fox has its home, the bird has its nest/But the son of man has no place to lay his head and rest' (2007: 309; Luke 9: 58). The protagonist of 'Brompton Oratory' finds himself wryly unable to forget the absence of his beloved even while receiving a Pentecostal mass: 'I look at the stone apostles/Think that it's all right for some' (2007: 278). His mind is on a rather different body than that of Christ: '[t]he smell of you still on my hands/As I bring the cup up to my lips' (2007: 278). As Lyn McCredden argues, '[s]exual and religious submission conjoin here' (2009: 170). In 'Idiot Prayer' the speaker seems to be facing execution, but his thoughts are with his victim rather than the torments that await him. His 'prayer' is to her and his muttered 'Glory Hallelujah' ironic (Cave 2007: 285). Later, in 'Gates to the Garden', the speaker rejects 'angels', 'saints' and 'the dead' he finds in a churchyard – a world that is, in Lyn McCredden's words, 'haunted, ancient and dying' – in favour of his beloved: 'God is in this hand that I hold' (McCredden 2009: 181; Cave 2007: 334). A bleaker experience is found in 'Darker with the Day', in which the speaker seeks 'the presence of a God' in a church but finds only images of a weak and helpless Christ: 'I found a woolly lamb dosing in an issue of blood/And a gilled Jesus shivering on a fisherman's hook' (Cave 2007: 336). Outside, an apocalyptic scene is ignored by 'cunts' jabbering on their mobiles and the 'earth yawns/Bored and disgusted' at their banality (2007: 337). Again, the focus is on the speaker's separation from his beloved and the inability of religion to help. Similarly, in 'Grief Came Riding' the unhappy protagonist has a grim vision of a drowned Christ who has 'found his final resting place' '[w]ith the fishes and the frogs' (2007: 342). The later 'Get Ready for Love', for all its Gospel stylings, makes it clear that the only way of reaching God is through love on earth: 'I was just hanging around, doing nothing and looked up to see/His face burned in the retina of your eyes' (2007: 384).

Salvation, then, cannot be found in dedication to this flickering and helpless God; nor, however, can it be permanently found in love, which for Cave is always marked by 'the whispers of sorrow and the echoes of grief' (2007: 8). Nevertheless, we are no longer marooned in the world of pain we find in the 'Gothic' Cave, compelled to obliterate our suffering through alcohol, drugs, abusive relationships and murder while we await damnation. Cave has not 'found God' and he is no Christian artist, although Christ and art are inextricably linked in his later work. The salvation mankind seems doomed to seek can be found through creative inspiration, in Cave's case the art of songwriting, which can at its finest transform the misery of an unhappy relationship into a love song that 'beats its wings heavenward' (2007: 18). This act of creation allows Cave to, in his own words, 'keep God alive' (1997: 142). His later work is, itself, a form of (idiot) prayer: '[t]he Love Song is the light of God, deep down, blasting up through our wounds' (2007: 7).

References

Bartlett, Thomas (2004), 'The Resurrection of Nick Cave', http://dir.salon.com/story/ent/feature/2004/11/18/cave/index2.html. Accessed 29 August 2011.

Blake, William (1988), *The Complete Poetry and Prose of William Blake*, ed. by David V. Erdman, New York: Anchor.

Cave, Nick (1989), *And the Ass Saw the Angel*, London: Penguin.

—— (1997), *King Ink* II, London: Black Spring.

—— (1998), 'Introduction' to *The Gospel According to Mark*, Edinburgh: Canongate.

—— (2007), *The Complete Lyrics 1978–2007*, London: Penguin.

Eaglestone, Robert (2009), 'From Mutiny to Calling upon the Author: Cave's Religion', in Karen Welberry and Tanya Dalziell (eds), *Cultural Seeds: Essays on the Work of Nick Cave*, Farnham: Ashgate, pp. 139–252 [kindle edition].

McCredden, Lyn (2009), 'Fleshed Sacred: The Carnal Theologies of Nick Cave', in Karen Welberry and Tanya Dalziell (eds), *Cultural Seeds: Essays on the Work of Nick Cave*, Farnham: Ashgate, pp. 167–85 [kindle edition].

Meyer, Marvin (ed.) (2008), *The Nag Hammadi Scriptures: The Revised and Updated Translation of Sacred Gnostic Texts Complete in One Volume*, London: HarperOne.

Pagels, Elaine (2006), *The Gnostic Gospels*, London: Phoenix.

Payne, John (2010), 'Nick Cave's Masterplan', http://articles.latimes.com/2010/nov/29/entertainment/la-et-nick-cave-20101129. Accessed 28 August 2011.

Snow, Mat (ed.) (2011), *Nick Cave Sinner Saint: The True Confessions*, London: Plexus.

Thomas of Cantimpre (2008), *The Collected Saints' Lives: Abbot John of Cantimpre, Christina the Astonishing, Margaret of Ypres, and Lutgard of Aywieres*, ed. by Barbara Newman, trans. by Barbara Newman and Margot H. King, Turnhout: Brepols.

Welberry, Karen and Tanya Dalziell (eds) (2009), *Cultural Seeds: Essays on the Work of Nick Cave*, Farnham: Ashgate.

Chapter 14

'The Time of Our Great Undoing': Love, Madness, Catastrophe and the Secret Afterlife of Romanticism in Nick Cave's Love Songs

Steven Barfield

T his chapter will examine Cave's work as song lyricist in two principal contexts: his inheritance of a 'Romantic tradition' (I explain my use of quotation marks below) and interpreting his relationship to the place of an excessive love and desire within our contemporary social world. My chapter takes seriously the claims that Cave advances for the love song in 'The Secret Life of the Love Song' (hereafter in text 'Secret') and attempts to situate these claims in a broader cultural context (Cave 2007: 1–19). I use the version of 'Secret' printed in *Complete Lyrics 1987–2007* rather than the original spoken word version. However, the fact that this was given in Vienna in 1998 for the Poetry Festival, and that Vienna is the home of Freudian psychoanalysis, suggests that it is perhaps not a coincidence that it was there that Cave made this statement about desire and its secrets.

Insofar as the chapter concerns Cave's love songs, the choice of the romantic tradition as a context may not seem surprising, whatever might be missed in such easy formulations as the 'Romantic tradition'. (This problem has been frequently noted. It was A. O. Lovejoy who first worried at the value of the term 'Romanticism' and such critical anxiety is now something of a cliché (Lovejoy 1924: 229–53)). However, romantic in my use of the term is intended to convey something significantly wider than the purely British romantic tradition, which usually includes Blake, Wordsworth, Keats, Shelley and Byron, sometimes adding Mary Shelley and John Clare. The romantic tradition with respect to Britain is often considered dead and gone as a movement by the 1830s, to be replaced by the new spirit of Victorianism. In contrast, what I mean by romanticism, at least for the sake of my argument here, includes all of that disparate and fragmented continental European work of romanticism and post-romanticism (including Ireland), often barely separated from the Gothic, and which, as if only half-glimpsed from the corner of the eye, weaves its way through the subterranean quarters of the great expanse of nineteenth-century realism and naturalism. Sometimes such work may be classed as late romanticism, transitional to modernism (such as that of Rainer Maria Rilke or W. B. Yeats), as symbolism (such as that of Charles Baudelaire) or as the proliferation of the European avant-garde, including the strange and extreme scene of surrealism, which in turn, I would argue, threads itself into the contemporary period and Cave's own work.

Surrealism (for instance as practised by André Breton, Paul Éluard or Joyce Mansour), while immensely varied and disparate in its very nature, possessed an energetic wish to disrupt socially acceptable bourgeois norms through its transgressive re-situation of the fundamentals of desire, based on a sometimes eccentric reading of the work of Freudian psychoanalysis. In addition, it has an addiction to what it sees as the secrets and mysteries that lie behind the surface of everyday life, often revelling in the pathological and intoxicating, and therefore has a habit of finding the marvellous secreted amongst the mundane in the ephemera of theatre posters, street advertising and commonplace objects and situations such as the trysts of lovers.

The secondary literature on surrealism is vast and growing. Mary Ann Caws' (1996) astute introduction, 'The Poetics of Surrealist Love', in her edition of *Surrealist Love Poems* is a useful place to start in terms of this chapter, as it focuses on the genre of surrealist poetry rather than the better-known visual material. Jennifer Mundy's *Surrealism: Desire Unbound* (2001) is the catalogue to the exhibition of the same title at Tate Modern (2001–02) and provides a range of incisive essays that focus critically on surrealist ideas of desire in all of the arts. David Lomas (2000) explores the surrealists' complex relationship with psychoanalysis, as does David Bate (2003); while Katharine Conley (1996) discusses surrealism and the idea of women as muse, as do the contributors to Natayla Lusty's (2007) collection of essays.

Louis Aragon's *Le Paysan de Paris/Paris Peasant* (1926), the first surrealist novel, showed the secret life of vanishing nineteenth-century Paris as a city of reveries and dreamers, of unknown desires, in which at any moment the decaying streets and half-hidden passages could lead on to ecstatic territory.

Breton's own semi-autobiographical *Nadja* (1928) recounts his obsessive affair in Paris with a young woman, Nadja, who suffers from visual and auditory hallucinations. In Breton's dreamlike prose the hysterical beloved's absence is often more affecting to the protagonist than her presence. *Nadja* concludes in Breton's memorable phrase: '[b]eauty will be CONVULSIVE or will not be at all' (1999: 160). As Breton's muse and lover, the young woman's illness has formed the definition of surrealist beauty by means of her 'hysterical' psychopathology. The surreal Paris of Aragon and Breton is itself the strange fruit of Baudelaire's earlier depictions of Paris and its efflorescent, lowlife characters (such objects of desire as prostitutes, 'a consumptive negress' or 'a red-haired beggar-girl') in *Les Fleurs du Mal* (1857), although that collection of poems also contains many about Baudelaire's lovers/muses. According to Linda and Michael Hutcheon the title of *Les Fleurs du Mal* (where 'mal' can mean 'sick', 'evil' or 'pain' in English) links together images of flowers and syphilitic sickness typical of the nineteenth century via the unspoken connection of the figure of the prostitute and is echoed in the quotation often attributed to Baudelaire: 'to make love is to do evil' ('*faire l'amour, c'est faire le mal*') (Hutcheon 1999: 77). While Cave's songs do not spend much time in the grit of the city, nonetheless his cast of characters and the situations in his poetic world are similar to those seemingly mundane, but in reality marvellous, creations we find in surrealist writing. For example, a song such as '(Are You) The One That I've Been Waiting For?' tells of a narrator's anticipation of a woman who exists only in the possible future: 'I've felt you coming, girl, as you drew near/I knew you'd find me, 'cause I longed you here' (Cave 2007: 137–40). The narrator's obsessive desire can almost create his fantasy as something probable and palpable, because of his need for her. As the song's narrator claims: '[o]ut of great longing great wonders have been willed' (2007: 280).

'The Mercy Seat', with its wonderfully relentless rhythm and Old Testament echoes, concerns a prisoner's final confession as he is executed in the electric chair and weaves in at all levels the convulsive beauty of the sublime that Breton recommended: '[a]nd the mercy seat is waiting/And I think my head is burning' (2007: 137). Bearing in mind the often grisly endings of many characters in Cave's songs, he might appreciate that surrealism shares a keen interest in the importance of death for the living, and in turn what it can tell us about the hidden reality of our life. As Breton half-offered, half-joked, in his 1924 *First Manifesto of Surrealism*: 'surrealism will usher you into death, which is a secret society. It will glove your hand, burying therein the profound M with which the word Memory begins' (2005: 733). Breton suggests that surrealism's interest in death promises a hermetic society in which participation can alchemically reinvigorate those lives lived half-asleep and half-forgotten and thus repressed in the *ennui* of bourgeois society. Breton, like many young Europeans, had been deeply affected by World War I; he had witnessed many horrific injuries while working in a neurological ward of a hospital and came to believe French society could not simply forget the war and continue afterwards with business as usual.

Surrealism, therefore, has a particular role to play within such an expanded and less exclusively British history of romanticism. Love poetry as a genre is of particular value to poets from the surrealist tradition, as Mary Anne Caws has shown in *Surrealist Love Poems* (1996), which collects many fine examples of such work. For an example of a surrealist love poem, consider Breton's extended anthem to the glory of his then lover and muse, Jacqueline Lamba, in *L'Amour Fou/Mad Love* (1937), which, as Caws suggests in her introduction to her translation, 'stresses the overwhelming power of surrealist love as it participates in the arational marvellous' (1988: xiv). Breton in effect strives to deconstruct the oppositions between rationality and irrationality in order to create a new sense of possibility and transformation through writing about his beloved and desired muse. Love, for surrealism, is both commonplace and extraordinary; apparently unique, while simultaneously available to all; antagonistic to the logic of the machine age of materialism, while secular enough to avoid a relapse into religious values: all factors which, for surrealism as much as romanticism, are of signal importance. As Cave himself suggests in 'Secret', 'through the writing of the Love Song one sits and dines with loss and longing, madness and melancholy, ecstasy, magic and joy' (2007: 20). Such thoughts sound not dissimilar from the surrealist or romantic impulse in the love poem.

My aim is not to give a history of this larger romantic tradition, even a sketch of such a history, but rather to argue that one of the contexts required to understand Cave's love songs is a far wider conceptualization of romanticism than the Anglo-American version alone. This is in order to understand the continuities to the history of the love poem that his work assumes. In particular, my argument contends it is this continental tradition(s) of romanticism in writing and other arts that has in turn marked the work of continental European thinking in psychoanalysis, literary theory and philosophy that will be used within the chapter. These thinkers are engaged in an imaginative dialogue with this expanded and continuing sense of the romantic tradition of the avant-garde and surrealism. I will use such contexts to try to illuminate Cave's lyrics and songs in the series of close readings that follow.

'The Secret Life of the Love Song': scattered moments of the marvellous and the ecstatic

Why is it that love songs should have a 'secret life': that is to say, one hidden away from the surface? The phrase 'secret life' is like Freud's theoretical formulation of the unconscious as the secret unknown thoughts and fantasies we all hold within us, and suggests the way a surrealist or romantic should read the potential of the love song, as a thing which conceals more than it divulges at first and plain sight. Freud used the phrase 'secret life' [*geheimes Leben*] in his essay 'A Seventeenth-Century Demonological Neurosis' (1923): '[w]e also know from the secret life of the individual which analysis uncovers, that his relation to his father was perhaps ambivalent from the outset, or, at any rate, soon became so' (1965: 85). The case study concerns Christopher Haizman, a seventeenth-century painter who believed that he had made a Faustian pact with the devil. The Freud-inspired surrealist artist Salvador Dalí also used or perhaps re-used the phrase. His relationship to his father and to masculinity was exposed as extremely ambivalent in his 1942 autobiography, *The Secret Life of Salvador Dalí*. Common usage of the phrase probably stems from Dalí. It is interesting that Cave is discussing his complex reactions to his own father's death in his essay.

Cave's answer to this question in his account is multiple and complex, and within the space available can only be dealt with in part. His writing, he tells us, was a response to the traumatic loss of his father, which Cave describes as causing a 'palpable sense of loss', 'a vacuum' and 'a great gaping hole' (2007: 6). Writing, therefore, became for Cave the means of at least temporarily suturing that hole ('a poultice to the wounds incurred by the death of my father') and 'writing God into existence' (2007: 6). However, 'God' here is not necessarily a personified presence, as in orthodox Christianity, as much as the possibility of something spiritual beyond the self; since, as Cave suggests, 'it is the haunted premise of longing that the true Love Song inhabits. It is a howl in the void for love and comfort, and it lives on the lips of the child crying for its mother' (2007: 7). This is, for Cave, what causes the sadness behind the love song, which he calls a song of sorrow itself ('what the Portuguese call "saudade"'), and represents a longing to be transformed: 'a flight into inspiration and imagination and divinity' (2007: 7). The song needs to be sad, Cave tells us, drawing on Lorca's arguments in 'The Theory and Function of *Duende*', because such sadness is also ecstatic in the sense that it decreases the distance between human beings and the divine, which is to say that the love song is intrinsically spiritual (if not necessarily religious) even when it appears most profane and based within the material world (Lorca 1998: 48–63). Cave goes on to describe the location to which the love song can transport singer and audience in terms that could almost be Breton's in describing the desire of *L'Amour Fou*: '[t]he Love Song must be borne into the realm of the *irrational*, the absurd, the distracted, the melancholic, the obsessive and the insane, for the Love Song is the clamour of love itself, and love is, of course, a form of *madness*' (Cave 2007: 11, emphasis mine).

Cave's song 'Where the Wild Roses Grow', sung as a duet with Kylie Minogue, is most commonly regarded as one of his more famous murder ballads as well as being his biggest hit single to date, but for my purpose here it can be regarded as if it were a contemporary rewriting of the idea and symbols of William Blake's 'The Sick Rose' (one of Blake's *Songs of Experience*) (Cave 2007: 250–1):

O Rose, thou art sick!
The invisible worm,
That flies in the night,
In the howling storm,

Has found out thy bed
Of crimson joy;
And his dark secret love
Does thy life destroy

(2000b: 196)

While much more can be said about Cave's song than I have space for here, it is worth saying that while Cave's ballad, a dialogue (duet) between murderer and victim, narrates an actual set of events (similar to those recorded in the nineteenth-century murder ballad 'Down in the Willow Garden', of which Cave and the Bad Seeds have recorded a version), and thus seems generically different from Blake's poem, at its dark heart is the same idea shown in Blake's poem. This same idea is that of an obscure and frighteningly intense love that destroys the very thing it desires most – in the shape of the rose or Elisa Day – and both function as exemplars of an absolute beauty. Compare Cave's last lines to those of Blake, above: '[a]s I kissed her goodbye, I said, "All beauty must die"/And leant down and planted a rose between her teeth' (2007: 251).

Leaving aside the use of characters and consequent psychologization of themes in Cave's ballad, at the level of motif there is perhaps surprising similarity. In both cases beauty (symbolized by using the rose, which is a traditional emblem of female beauty in the West) must be destroyed by the very subject by which it is desired. Such destructive desire is paradoxical in several ways, if we consider desire as normally a productive or procreative phenomenon. Destructive desire brings death to the beloved, beautiful object rather than enhancing the other's life. It departs from the pleasurable admiration of straightforward beauty and ushers in the terror and awe of the sublime for the desiring subject. Therefore, Cave's song and Blake's poem (or song) both end up producing a sense of the sublime from what would be more commonly seen as the realm of the beautiful (the more straightforward desire for the rose). The feeling of the sublime, unlike the beautiful, is associated with a sense of awe, fear and the infinite, which radically reduces the importance of the desiring subject, while giving, in turn, a sense of the absolute. (The 'indescribable' sublime is another complex topic; however, Philip Shaw's *Sublime* (2005) is a pithy and useful introduction to this very influential idea).

In Blake's case this is marked both by turbulent nature and the severe obscurity of the action (how can we possibly picture an invisible worm, flying in the night through a howling storm?). Why would the worm, which supposedly loves the rose – for whatever mysterious reasons – then wish to destroy it? In Cave's case we ask what kind of man can kill the woman he desires most of all (as this is clearly an obsessive love) with a rock found by the side of a river, leaving her dead in the water with a wild rose between her teeth (the latter detail emphasizing the physicality of the desire as well as the image of the rose)? How, indeed, can he go on living, burdened simultaneously by the sense that he has perpetually deprived himself of the thing he apparently desires most and the accompanying guilt towards the murdered object of his desire?

One uncomfortable answer is the fact that it is the punishment of guilt itself that is the sublime agony. The guilt and consequent agony are both penalty and prize for the narrator: the knowledge, as in Blake, that human desire can be destructive. Moreover, the fact that we can begin to theorize such destructiveness demonstrates our consciousness of the strange vicissitudes of human desire. As Jonathan Culler suggests in his introduction to *Les Fleurs Du Mal*, one ambition of Baudelaire's extraordinary range of love poems in that volume is to demonstrate that because love is a 'Satanic religion', it can help us understand and become 'educated' about the 'Satanic' within the everyday (2008: xxxv, xxxvii). Culler defines Baudelaire's idea of the 'Satanic' as 'an articulation of the uncanny forces (forces of evil) that structure our lives and imaginings' (2008: xxxvii). To learn of such (apparently) irrational knowledge is to face up to the world of desire, ourselves and our fantasies. This shift in love poetry, from the aesthetics of the beautiful to those of the sublime, is a characteristic development that began with the romantics and remains a constant in much surrealist poetry. Mario Praz, in his encyclopaedic thematic study *The Romantic Agony* (first published in 1933 and thus contemporary with the work of the surrealists) had already argued that nineteenth-century romanticism was obsessed by eroticism and death and he traced a line from Blake and Lord Byron to the Marquis de Sade and then to Baudelaire (1978). As Benjamin Péret, a leading surrealist poet, stated in regard to the sublime as a mode of desire: 'I don't think the temptation of sublime love can be erased for a man once he has been able to surrender totally to it' (cited in Balakian 1987: 241).

Another trait typical of many romantic surrealist poems is a candid representation of embodied sexuality between lovers, an eroticism that may often seem to border on the obscene as it was determinedly transgressive towards bourgeois propriety. It was an erotic desire that remade the profanity of the physical and material body, by a process of resacralization, into a receptacle of marvellous energy. Joyce Mansour was one of the more candid surrealist exponents of such eroticism (though it is a common feature of surrealist poems), as when she writes in the now quite well-known 'Je veux dormir avec toi/I want to sleep with you' (1955) in Mary Ann Caws' translation:

> I want to sleep with you side by side
> Our hair intertwined
> Our sexes joined
> With your mouth for a pillow.
> I want to sleep with you back to back
> With no breath to part us
> No words to distract us
> No eyes to lie to us
> With no clothes on.
> To sleep with you breast to breast
> Tense and sweating
> Shining with a thousand quivers
> Consumed by ecstatic mad inertia
> Stretched out on your shadow
> Hammered by your tongue
> To die in a rabbit's rotting teeth
> Happy

(Caws 2004: 348)

We can find some examples of this erotic intensity in Cave's work, although – perhaps indicating the difference between popular music and modern poetry – there is less physicality concerning the erotic in his songs than there is concerning dismemberment and violence towards the body. 'Brompton Oratory' is an unusual example, set amidst a Roman Catholic church service (Cave 2007: 278). The song makes a series of sharp connections between profane and sacred love, which are, to some extent, leveraged from the real name of the church (the two and often symbolically opposed Marys of the New Testament, the Virgin Mary and Mary Magdalene) and the problematic depiction of women in the Bible. The song mentions that the reading the narrator hears is from Luke 24, and while it is not directly noted in the song, this Biblical passage emphasizes the key role of women in witnessing Jesus' resurrection: Mary Magdalene, Joanna and Mary the mother of James are those present on the first visit to the empty tomb and it is they who will inform the male disciples. 'It was Mary Magdalene, and Joanna, and Mary the mother of James, and other women that were with them, which told these things unto the apostles' (Luke 24: 10; 1998: 112).

However, while there is space for some kind of reading of Cave's unexpectedly female-centered appreciation of Christianity in this song, it is not that I wish to focus upon here, but rather the way in which he intertwines sacred and profane love as motifs. The sublime and unendurable beauty of which the song speaks is one to which the narrator kneels, as if in prayer: '[a] beauty impossible to define/A beauty impossible to believe' (Cave 2007: 278). Despite the setting this is not a submission or supplication to God, but rather to his lover: '[n]o God up in the sky/No Devil beneath the sea/Could do the job that you did/Of bringing me to my knees' (2007: 278). Throughout the song it is the physicality of the woman – and of the narrator's experience of love – that is at stake, rather than the ostensible rituals of Christianity, and, like Breton in *Nadja*, he finds his beloved's absence is more powerfully cathartic and provocative than her presence ('forlorn and exhausted, baby/By the absence of you') (2007: 278). Daringly, and in the manner of the surrealists, he conflates the profane love of his beloved's body with that of the sacrament (which in Roman Catholic tradition, through transubstantiation, makes the spiritual physical, the bread and wine becoming the body and blood of Christ). The body of his muse therefore becomes the locus of the secret of the spiritual and sexual acts become haunted, as it were, by the possibility of the sublime and the absolute: '[t]he blood imparted in little sips/The smell of you still on my hands/As I bring the cup up to my lips' (2007: 278).

'Where Do We Go Now But Nowhere?': singing love's disaster as madness

'Straight to You' (hereafter 'Straight') and 'Where Do We Go Now But Nowhere?' (hereafter 'Nowhere') seem, as love songs, more puzzling than most in Cave's *oeuvre*, even though Cave seldom writes straightforward love songs (2007: 194–5, 281–2). In the next two sections I will argue that these songs explore love's intersection with themes of madness (in 'Nowhere') and disaster (in 'Straight'), and that madness is a kind of disaster. While madness and disaster are by no means rare themes in Cave's work, their relationship to the theme of love within these songs is what makes them so interesting. I will make these arguments via some intersections with the French writer, philosopher and critic Maurice Blanchot (1907–2003) and his unusual account of disaster in *L'Ecriture du Desastre/The Writing of the Disaster* (1995).

'Nowhere' adopts the retrospective narrative strategy of telling a story and it affirms that intention in its first line: 'I remember a girl so very well' (Cave 2007: 281). Either we as listeners, some unknown interlocutor, or the narrator themselves appear to be the audience for most of the song, but the simple chorus seems, in contrast, to directly address the woman in the song as apostrophe: '[o] wake up, my love, my lover, wake up/O wake up, my love, my lover, wake up' (2007: 281–2). The narrator is at present (or at least thinks they are) in some kind of institution, perhaps a mental hospital or hospital, as indicated by the lines: '[i]f they'd give me my clothes back then I could go home/From this fresh, this clean, antiseptic air' (2007: 282). Hospitals keep a patient's own clothes and have such air and the gates to their grounds are usually 'locked' (as we are told they are later), especially if they are of the psychiatric variety. However, as we shall see, the song avoids a coherent or logical linear narrative of that past situation leaving us uncertain to a high degree about these events, narrated as fragments, many of which prove to be obscure: to make some sense of the story therefore requires a very strong interpretation in the form of reconstruction, somewhat like reading a dream, as I demonstrate here.

The events seem based in Latin America (there are 'a missionary bell' and a 'colonial hotel' as well as a stereotypical image in which an 'old donkey moans' in the grounds of wherever the narrator actually is) (2007: 281–2). It is perhaps Mexico, as the first verse mentions a carnival and seems to allude to the festival of the Day of the Dead, which is best known in its Mexican version (*Día de los Muertos*, usually held late October till early November): '[g]rim reapers and skeletons and a missionary bell' (2007: 281). The use of the setting of the *Día de los Muertos* to symbolize mental collapse and catastrophe for Europeans and Americans is not a new idea. Malcolm Lowry's *Under the Volcano* (1947) with its alcoholic protagonist, Geoffrey Firmin, the former British consul, is a famous example of such a *katabatic* narrative (a descent into the underworld) set in Mexico, in which the exotic setting presents the opposite of rational, bourgeois European/North American values (2000). Firmin, in his mescal-soaked and hallucination-haunted purgatory, becomes jealous after the arrival of his estranged wife, Yvonne (sometimes depicted from his point of view as a phantasmal figure), who will try unsuccessfully to save him. (For a survey of the use of Mexican settings in twentieth-century Anglo-American fiction, see Elisabeth Mermann-Jozwiak (2009). For *katabatic* narratives more generally, see Rachel Falconer (2005)). However, another intertext, which uses images of church bells, may be alluded to here, perhaps unconsciously, a song of lost love and the impossibility of its mourning by Warren Zevon, 'Empty Handed Heart' (1980).

The following lines (below) are sung as a sudden, unexpected descant by Linda Ronstadt (note the use of *we* in the verse), and thus with a female voice, while Zevon sings the repeated refrain at the same time: '[t]hen I've thrown down diamonds in the sand' (1980). Zevon alone sings the rest of the song. Therefore, it is sung by the speaker in the present with what is presumably the ghostly memory/fantasy of the lost woman to whom the song's lyrics are addressed and which is symbolized by Ronstadt's vocals: the descant structure reinforcing the idea she is both present and absent. She erupts into being present through the subject's fantasy. As Freud suggests in his essay 'Mourning and Melancholia', the disturbance of melancholia demonstrates that an object, who has not been fully mourned by the subject and thus successfully internalized as a memory, must of necessity be an object to whom that subject is still painfully attached (1957b). This lost object is therefore neither simply present nor absent for the grieving subject. The lost woman from the narrator's past returns in Zevon's song, as revenant, through her voice, in this case bringing happiness mixed with pain: '(Remember when we used to watch the sun set in the sea/You said you'd always be in love with me/All through the night we danced and sang/Made love in the mornings while the church bells rang)' (parentheses in original lyrics perhaps indicate the difficulty of deciding on the temporal status of the woman's voice) (Zevon 1980). Warren Zevon (1947–2003), as a Californian singer-songwriter, made continued use of such Mexican settings in his songs; while such images of Mexico are sometimes restorative and sometimes examples of *katabasis*, they are frequently associated with various forms of destructive addiction to drugs and alcohol that mirror Zevon's notorious real-life addictions. Like Cave, Zevon was a formidable and celebrated writer of contemporary ballads and love songs and he seldom wrote the latter without a sense of accompanying doom and loss, although his love songs lack any manifest hostility towards the lost loved object by the melancholic subject, such as we frequently see in Cave's work. See Crystal Zevon's biography (2007) for further discussion.

The story of 'Nowhere' is shot through with a memorable image of visceral passion: in this case, of sex (as we have already seen, this visceral quality, of the marvellousness of the body of lovers, is important for Cave): '[i]n a colonial hotel we fucked up the sun/Then we fucked it down again' (Cave 2007: 281). These lines suggest common ideas in the *carpe diem* ('seize the day') tradition in poetry, where passion is proposed as an alternative to the inevitability of decline and death and the sun is often figured as a marker of the passage of time and of human mortality. Cave seems, indeed, to be alluding directly in these lines to the last lines of Andrew Marvell's 'To His Coy Mistress', one of the best-known examples of the *carpe diem* tradition: '[t]hus, though we cannot make our sun/Stand still, yet we will make him run' (2005: 55). In these lines Marvell also makes a pun on a future pregnancy ('son' for 'sun') in the idea that what will outlive them in this race against time is their future child.

However, 'Nowhere' is also clearly a song about broken lives. There is the haunting, traumatic, but ultimately obscure image of a dead child: '[w]hile the bones of our child crumble like chalk', and the flicker of a suggestion that the child perhaps fell from a balcony due to the noise of a drum from the carnival band (2007: 282). However, there is no mention of an actual fall and it seems rather strange to take any child on a holiday to Mexico of the kind described here, while the evocative image of bones that 'crumble like chalk' does not suggest a fall in any logical way: '[t]he crack of a drum a little child did scare/I can still feel his tiny fingers pressed in my hand' (2007: 282). The vivid and poignant image of the narrator with a child, perhaps his son, hand in hand, also makes little sense within my reconstructed narrative, as it is an image of fatherly plenitude and protection. The song also contains a memorable image of the revenge-filled former lover, presumably the girl once remembered, as the narrator says: '[y]ou come for me now with a cake that you've made/Ravaged avenger with a clip in your hair/Full of glass and bleach and my old razor blades' (2007: 281). Why she would want to take revenge, though (the line probably alludes to the female Erinyes – or Furies – of classical mythology who had serpents instead of hair, hence the 'clip'); or why she is ravaged (though this again may simply suggest the Erinyes, who are always depicted as monstrous); or why she wishes to obtain revenge through bringing the narrator a cake filled with poisons and the traces of their life together (in the form of 'his old razor blades') remains unexplained. There is no suggestion of anything more than the child's accidental death, if that, in the song, but the Erinyes often punished those who committed murder within the family, most notoriously in Aeschylus' *Oresteia*, in which they pursue Orestes for the revenge-motivated murder of his mother, Clytemnestra. However, as I will argue later, it is by no means clear whether the child cited in 'Nowhere' actually ever existed, let alone whether s/he died through an accident or through something more suspicious, or indeed whether the narrator's projection of guilt makes the death seem more causal than it actually was. There is some possible guilt evoked in the mention of Reinhold Niebuhr's Serenity

Prayer in the song, as the prayer asks: 'God, give us grace to accept with serenity the things that cannot be changed,/Courage to change the things which should be changed, and the wisdom to distinguish the one from the other' (www.aahistory.com 1992). While the prayer exists in many versions of differing lengths and wordings, these are the essential sentiments. The prayer is most familiar because of its long established use by Alcoholics Anonymous, which began in a New York office in 1942 (www.aahistory.com 1992). When this detail is combined with the Mexican setting in the song and the intertext of Lowry's *Under the Volcano* (which focuses on an alcoholic's disintegrating life), it may hint at some influence of alcohol upon the traumatic events that are being narrated.

The point here is that while we can make sense of a partial story of sorts, it requires a very determined reading through gnomic fragments created by a deeply unreliable narrator, and this uncertainty and incoherence is the dominant frame within the song. But why would Cave have rejected a more traditional and linear version of the narrative that I have laboured to reconstruct with only partial success? This is not a typical choice in Cave's work, where often his grim stories work as traditional ballads with linear stories; consider, for example, 'Henry Lee' or 'O'Malley's Bar' (2007: 246–7, 260–5). The second issue is that, rather like interpreting a dream, I have linked images and signs together in the song to create coherence in order to recover meaning much as Freud suggests as a method in *The Interpretation of Dreams*: even so, much in the lines remains obscure and problematic and therefore any attempted interpretation on the listener's part seems problematically overdetermined (Freud 1953). For instance, is it just the narrator or also the woman he loved/loves who is in hospital: 'I remember a girl so bold and so bright/Loose-limbed and brazen and bare/Sits gnawing her knuckles in the chemical light' (2007: 281)? If she is visiting him in hospital (though that in itself seems odd, in terms of how he reads her current attitude towards him) then why is she 'gnawing her knuckles', which makes it sound like he is visiting her in hospital where she is the patient (2007: 281)? Does he simply want her to be there with him in his fantasy and has he thus willed his fantasy into being? In fact, the continued use of phrases such as 'chemical light', 'clinical benches' and 'antiseptic air', which suggest the hospital context of the song, make it unclear if the woman is actually in hospital with him or not, and instead raise the real possibility that the woman is the narrator's hallucination, a memory returning as a ghost, as we saw happening more clearly and unequivocally in Zevon's song of his lost love (above).

In the last verse of the lyric there is an odd and terse construction that is easy to miss, where the narrator in referring to that fateful day on the balcony calls his beloved his 'future wife' (2007: 282). At first sight this might simply suggest that they were engaged in the past at the time of the mysterious incident, but why wait until the last verse to tell us this? 'Future wife', from an emotional point of view, is at once a stronger construction than fiancée, but perhaps also more ambiguous as, unlike fiancée, it does not suggest public formalization and could be merely a projected fantasy of the narrator. As the events of the song on the balcony are set in the past, perhaps he had projected her in that past as his future wife and therefore his own life's future. 'If I could relive one day of my life' is also a problematic line, as while it is easy for the listener to jump in and say the narrator wants to change something, we do not actually know that, and perhaps he simply wants to relive that one day of his life (the word 'relive' is used twice) rather than wishing to change the past. He wishes simply then to return to the past moment like a regretful ghost from the future as that was where his/their future effectively ended with the death of their love and their (perhaps merely hoped for) child.

This process of interpretation is further complicated by the song's emotionally powerful refrain, repeated thrice, which seems to make no sense within my reconstructed reading of the fragmented narrative of the lyric: '[o] wake up, my love, my lover, wake up/O wake up, my love, my lover, wake up' (2007: 281–2). This sounds more like it belongs to the romance of a fairy tale, 'Sleeping Beauty' perhaps, or the narrator trying to rescue his beloved from death, a coma or some such scene of stasis. What, in any case, should she wake up to? In fact, she always seems awake when we see her in the present of the song: '[a]round the duck pond we grimly mope/Gloomily and mournfully we go round again' (2007: 282). The refrain speaks to the narrator's continued love for the woman he refers to as his 'future wife' and, in fact, this is one of the abiding themes of the lyric. This is probably the main reason for this tender and romantic refrain, which otherwise seems deliberately out of place. It returns thrice within the song's verses, because it helps to underpin its framework as a love song.

The title of the song itself, 'Where Do We Go Now But Nowhere?', insists on failure, and, importantly, is repeated in various ways throughout the lyric, but it speaks to the idea of a failed relationship or a relationship that has reached a dead end (like the image of the narrator and his 'future wife' endlessly tracing a futile figure round the perimeter of the duck pond, which seems the most literal embodiment of the title in terms of the song's own imagery). If this seems curiously at odds with the reconstructed narrative I have suggested, then it may be because the dead end of this moment of 'nowhere' is the place from which the narrator cannot tell the story, and we as an audience cannot understand what is being told. This is not, then, a resolvable issue, but rather an effect of the narrative; too much of the lyric is fragmentary and elliptical and at one level the lyric is not only without a coherent narrative, but is so much a product of the unreliability of madness that we cannot as listeners create a coherent narrative without the kind of overdetermined and thus problematic reading that I have demonstrated. While the song forces us to repeat the narrator's unsuccessful efforts in struggling to create a logical narrative of his past, our attempts as listeners to create meaning seem to fail and break down in a very similar way to his own. We are obliged to repeat, as it were, in our attempts at interpretation, the narrator's failure to narrate lucidly the crucial events of his life.

Instead we come to an *aporia*, a narrative impasse that is one way to read the title of the song itself. The last verse offers a strange line that dramatizes this *aporia* of being stuck at a dead end, a nowhere from where escape or going forward or backwards is impossible: '[o] who could have known, but no one?' (2007: 282). This line cleverly picks up the repeated line 'where do we go now, but nowhere?', a sign of the figure and theme of *aporia*. But this is an odd line, as to say 'who could have known', or no one could have known, would make obvious sense, but instead the line literally suggests that only (I am substituting only for 'but') 'no one' could have known. But who, indeed, is 'no one'? The unnamed narrator himself is a kind of 'no one', so is he saying he now knows he knew in the past what would happen, even if we, the listeners, do not know what it is he knows? What is it that he could have known?

Rather than following the narrator in struggling to reconstruct a cogent narrative – which, I have shown, is undermined by so much within the song and therefore cannot seem more than elusive – I would argue that we would do better to turn instead to the idea that the incoherence and fragmentation of narrative, as a form of retrospective madness, has created the cracks and fissures in the substance of the lyric. It is a consequence of an extreme form of something that Cave himself notes: '[t]he Love Song holds within it an eerie intelligence all of its own – to reinvent the past and lay it at the feet of the present' (2007: 3). The love song, then, at some level can be (perhaps always is) a potential fantasy, which breaches the barrier between past and present as a perpetual recreation of the past it attests to; like Marcel Proust's *petite madeleine,* it becomes an exercise in the melancholia that Freud discussed and which I considered earlier (Freud 1957b). The love song repeats the past not simply and originally as it was – that is to say, as a fixed memory – but rather as a differential repetition within the present, because the past is changed by this activity of repetition as it is brought into the subject's present.

Love's relationship to madness is not a novel theme, of course, as Shakespeare playfully suggested by means of Theseus, in *A Midsummer Night's Dream* (Act V, i): '[t]he lunatic, the lover and the poet/Are of imagination all compact' (2005: 419). In the song, through the melancholia of a failed relationship, a failure that in the end may itself be imagined, what has been created is a madness affecting the lyric at the level of form wherein there is no way out, only a perpetual recirculation within 'nowhere'. I am reading the image of the son as a fantasized hope for the future that literally crumbled into dust – which is what happens to chalk, something we can use to draw our imaginings with. We might notice again the importance of the allusion to Marvell here, as in those lines a son, via a pun on 'make our sun', is a future possibility weighed against the effects of time in the race that the speaker imagines himself and his beloved conducting. I would suggest that Cave's song is reutilizing this ghosted possibility in terms of the idea of the loss of the possibility of a future child to concretize the failure of the dreams of the narrator and his beloved's relationship.

Madness, then, in this song, is an everyday consequence of love and reminds us of the way in which, at its strongest, love is marked by a kind of disaster that uncannily shadows it – the disaster here epitomized by the child who may or may not have existed and the woman who may not or not be real in the present. They are impossible objects of continuing desire, but still felt as irrevocably lost and thus they bear the traces of guilt and failure. As Shoshana Felman remarks (of Gustav Flaubert's *Mémoires d'un Fou/Memoirs of a Madman*): '[m]adness is the illusion of being able to salvage something from time, the belief in the possibility of eternity, of the absolute; in love, or in God. [...] Madness is not simply love, but *the belief in love*' (Felman 2003: 84, italics in original). This conflict is at the heart of the song, as even when he recalls Marvell's magisterially optimistic lines the narrator cancels the sentiment almost immediately, recalling his present situation: '[w]ell, the sun comes up, and the sun goes down/Going round and around to nowhere' (Cave 2007: 281). In effect, it is the continuing belief in love in its possibility to transcend the everyday contingencies of the progress of time, to turn chance into the cannily serendipitous, as opposed to a reality that sees the idea of love as absurd and ridiculous because of contingency, which has driven narrator and narrative to fragmentation and madness. Love's fondly imagined *nowhere* is a place beyond reality, a fantasy of transcendence beyond the world such as it is, while the other *nowhere* of love is also an impasse beyond which there is nothing, which cannot be passed over and which itself is the reminder of the contingency of the fragile world in which we live, in which love is an impossibility. Such then is the madness that love risks knowingly (*l'amour* is always *l'amour fou*, as Breton might say), and such is the fate that love entails and which the song dramatizes; 'no one' knows, indeed, what happened, happens or will happen. To love truly is perhaps always madly, to take the risk of becoming 'no one', a 'no one' who can only narrate their life as a ruin of fragments, dislocated memories and uncertain images.

'Straight to You': singing love's disaster as the end of the world

Disaster as the uncanny and necessary relation to love, the shadow from which it cannot and will not escape, is strongly marked, not only as mental disaster as in 'Nowhere', but as apocalypse in the lyrics to what is in all other ways a singularly affecting love song: 'Straight to You' (2007: 194–5). Leaving aside the title and the key theme (that of the relationship between the speaker of the lyric and the beloved) for the moment, it is worth noticing how everything about the lyric is apocalyptic and magnified in truly mythic dimensions, which often recalls the Biblical account of the end of days, but intertwines these with a variety of more intimate images of disaster.

It begins with the crumbling of 'the towers of ivory', and Cave might be referring to the end of knowledge here, 'ivory tower' standing as an allusion to the university's disinterested pursuit of knowledge for its own sake, rather than in service to the needs of commerce (2007: 194). The fact that the 'swallows have sharpened their beaks' is deliberately peculiar and makes the birds appear to be preparing for war, while it also draws our attention to global change (they leave when winter appears) (2007: 194). This apocalyptic tone is affirmed in the third line: '[t]his is the time of our great undoing' (2007: 194). But, we may ask, who is the 'we' – is the entire world suffering this 'undoing', or is it just the speaker of the lyric and the woman who is the object of the address? What, exactly, is being 'undone'?

Throughout the song we find similar images of catastrophe, and sometimes these images are domestically intimate; for instance, the candles 'guttering' (2007: 194), which recall W. B. Yeats' similarly catastrophic opening lines from 'Moods', from *The Wind Among The Reeds* (1899): '[t]ime drops in decay,/Like a candle burnt out,/And the mountains and woods/Have their day, have their day' (2000: 44). The world affects the private realm, for the 'light in our window is fading' (presumably the day outside the home is being extinguished as part of the apocalyptic undoing) and in the greater world we see: '[g]one are the days of rainbows/Gone are the nights of swinging from the stars/For the sea will swallow up the mountains/And the sky will throw thunder-bolts and sparks' (Cave 2007: 194). The days of rainbows have gone, presumably, because the rainbow signifies God's promise in the Bible to not send another deluge, but this compact made with humanity now appears to be void (Genesis 9: 8–17; 1998: 9–10). The third line of the verse recalls Psalms 46: 2, as the King James version puts it: '[t]herefore will not we fear, though the earth be removed, and though the mountains be carried into the midst of the sea'. However, in the case of 'Straight' there is no implication that anyone should trust God anymore or not be afraid under the circumstances.

Yet, even here this is balanced with more romantic and personal images such as that of 'swinging from the stars', which in fact probably alludes to the 1944 song 'Swinging on a Star': '[w]ould you like to swing on a star?' (Van Heusen 1944). Although in its new context it seems almost unrecognizable (and the song is associated with adults speaking to children, which I will return to later on), it is an image Cave reuses in 'Brother, My Cup is Empty' (2007: 197). The Chilean poet Pablo Neruda, who had links to surrealism, was fond of star imagery, as is Cave (see also Cave's 'Your Funeral, My Trial', 'Lucy', 'Faraway, So Close!', 'There is a Kingdom', and '(Are You) the One That I've Been Waiting for?', among others) (Cave 2007: 126, 183, 208, 279, 280). Such domestic blissful images, set against more world-devouring ones, help the song to keep in play the question I asked at the beginning: who is this 'we'?

The final verse of 'Straight' works more closely to tie together the personal and more global sense of catastrophe, principally through the fact that heaven itself 'has denied' the protagonists 'its Kingdom', while saints and angels – who are presumably reliable servants of God – seem also to be undone by the forces at hand: it is the end of everything, perhaps even God (2007: 195). To be denied a heaven might seem a problem, but in its profane and earthly vision the line draws our attention to two things. First, the narrator and his beloved exist most purely and surely in this moment of return from the narrator to the beloved, rather than any transcendence beyond the body into another immortal world. Second, like Madeline and Porphyro in John Keats' 'The Eve of St. Agnes' or Shakespeare's *Romeo and Juliet*, it is the desperate lovers isolated against the rest of the world that Cave wishes to emphasize.

At the same time as this elaboration of the end of the world, the interwoven theme within the lyric is at first sight simple and uses modified variations of a single image that is reused four times in the lyric: 'I'll come running/Straight to you/For I am captured/Straight to you/For I am captured/One more time' (2007: 194–5). Here the key ideas are the directness of return to the beloved and the idea of capture, both in the past and as continuation in the present. The male captured by love, like a hart by the mythological huntress and Goddess Diana, is a traditional trope of love poems, of course; it works to render the male narrator powerless and, to some extent, reverses the normal male to female oppositional dynamics of activity and passivity ('I am captured' is therefore in the passive voice). This idea is reminiscent of William Blake's surreal lines (though *avant la lettre* of surrealism) in 'The Crystal Cabinet': '[t]he Maiden caught me in the wild,/Where I was dancing merrily;/She put me into her Cabinet,/And lock'd me up with a golden key' (Blake 2000a: 117–18). As

Elizabeth Butler Cullingford has argued, the medieval courtly love tradition (which featured such tropes of male lovers being captured and made powerless by their beloved) became popular in the late nineteenth and early twentieth century due to its prominence in the love poems of W. B. Yeats (Butler Cullingford 1993). Surrealists too, such as Breton, were much enamoured of the idea of courtly love with its paradoxical formulations and cult of suffering, as has been discussed by Caws in her introduction to *Surrealist Love Poems* and analysed by Bate using a Lacanian methodology in the context of surrealist photography (Caws 1996; Bate 2003: 145–72).

The idea of running to return to the beloved is mainly made strange in the song by two features. First, there is its continuous repetition within the structure, rather than being, as we might expect, a singular event at the end of the narrative, an Odysseus-like return to home and Penelope, keeping the promise he made before and which he has kept throughout his exile. It is a movement that keeps returning and repeating itself in Cave's song as a literal recapture, at the secondary level, of the song's structure. Why, indeed, does she need to continually capture the narrator 'one more time' or desire him to be so caught by her, again and again? One caught once should surely remain caught forever? The lines suggest, instead, that capture is a present action, always as if for the first time, maintaining what Dorothy Tennov described in a neologism as the state of 'limerence', of being in love (1998). Second, there is the odd hesitation created by the word 'more', which suggests it is a singular event in a series, haunted by the facts of finitude and mortality, rather than one that can go on forever (there is no heaven for them after the catastrophe, we notice; each moment of return as recapture is, therefore, one snatched madly across the Nietzschean abyss created by the death of God and meaning).

In fact, this repetitious movement is a version of a kind of loss and return familiar from the *fort/da* (gone away/there) game in Freud's *Beyond the Pleasure Principle*, in which the small child, his grandson, uses a cotton-reel to represent or play (*spiel*) with his mother's loss and return and, to some extent, is thus able to master this loss of the mother through such actions (1957a: 14–18). However, in the case of 'Straight', it is not mastery of loss that seems to be the object of the exercise (as it was with the game Freud observed his grandson playing), but rather the pleasure taken in the return and reunion with the beloved, though it is a pleasure that is starkly finite. 'One more time' suggests that there may be a time when such a reunion can no longer be true, because return will be impossible (and, after all, the world is coming to an end).

In Blanchot's *L'écriture du desastre/Writing of the Disaster*, his rich text of limpid fragments responding to the many disasters that haunt the contemporary period, he explores a scenario that is relevant to 'Straight to You' because of the song's sense of catastrophe. This catastrophe is not imminent in the future, but imagined as if it is happening already, and has been set into motion for reasons unknown (the song is not of the straightforward 'I'll love you until the world ends' type). For Blanchot this catastrophe is 'the experience that none experiences, the experience of death', but it is recast by Cave in less personal and more universal terms (Blanchot 1995: 66–7).

Blanchot goes on to imagine a child seven or eight years old, who looks up to the sky and sees:

the sky, the same sky, suddenly open, absolutely black and absolutely empty, revealing (as though the pane had broken) such an absence that all has since always and forever been lost therein – so lost that therein is affirmed the vertiginous knowledge that nothing is what there is, and first of all nothing beyond.

(1995: 72)

In a sense, the apocalyptic catastrophe that has happened (and which, for the child in Blanchot's account, is a source of a silent and incommunicable joy) is the fact that the human world has ended; the sky is a void, the universe is bereft (from our human point of view), there is no meaning and of course, no God. It is, perhaps, like the 'hole' in reality Cave describes resulting from his father's untimely death in 'Secret', but with rather different consequences (Cave 2007: 6).

This continual process of the subject being recaptured by an origin, and therefore of having been away or lost in order to make this return to the beloved, which seems the most noticeable feature of Cave's lyric, is the process that fills this hole or void that Blanchot describes in his account. This return to fill the void of the world's ending is not a process that can happen forever, and therefore it occurs with a sense of finitude (eventually the return must fail) and precariousness (will it be this time that the return to the beloved fails?). The song is aware that the world is already lost, so the value of the possible reunion lies in the fact that human beings are both mortal and impermanent. For 'one more time' in the lyric, we should therefore read the possibility of *one last time*.

Thus, to answer the question at the beginning of this analysis, the end of the world is both their, and the world's, 'great undoing'. If this seems to indicate that I am suggesting that Cave is (unconsciously) casting the beloved of the song as the figure of the mother (psychoanalytically speaking) and the narrator as a child, then this is no more than to claim a kind of fundamental otherness for the relations between subject and object, wherein the first move of loss (and return) always lies in the relationship of the child to the body of the mother and becomes the model for subsequent others, as in Freud's observation of the *fort/da* game. Cave suggests significantly, in 'Secret', that '[the love song] lives on the lips of the child crying for its mother' (2007: 7). Not for nothing, then, does Cave seem to allude to 'Swinging on a Star', in which an adult sings to a child about the future. To be together 'one more time' (or one last time) before the end is the implicit promise made by lovers to one another, as well as that of parents to their children (although that order is perhaps reversed as children become adults and parents become elderly).

Love is, therefore, a form of anguished happiness amidst catastrophe in 'Straight to You'. It is a catastrophe, not in Blanchot's sense of being something incommunicable and silently held within the subject as a knowledge only s/he can know, but one constituted through the relationship of the subject and the other in Cave's song as it is created via language and music. Our primal scene of catastrophe, Cave suggests, is made up of signs made towards the other and however atavistic that scene might be (for instance in the cited example of the child crying for its mother), it is still a catastrophe that is addressed to the other and therefore represents shared and communicable knowledge between human beings. Such language in the lyric traces the possibility of recapture as capture, as if always for the first time, as if always between a simple present tense and a simple past tense, and thus marks that precariousness, because of the feared and inevitable termination of this struggled-for ecstasy of returning to the other. Indeed, while we might have expected sadness at the end of the world, the song is marked by a surprised sense of moments of joy and rapture amidst these final things; the guitars ring like bells, for a joy that can only be found because it is perpetually haunted by the final disaster that has already happened, is always happening.

Love.

References

The Bible: Authorized King James Version (1998), ed. by Robert Carroll and Stephen Prickett, Oxford: Oxford Paperbacks.

Aeschylus (1984), *Oresteia*, ed. by W. B. Stanford, trans. by Robert Fagles, Harmondsworth: Penguin.

Aragon, Louis (1999), *Le Paysan de Paris/Paris Peasant*, trans. by Simon Watson-Taylor, Boston: Exact Change.

Balakian, Anna (1987), *Surrealism: The Road to the Absolute*, Chicago, IL: University of Chicago Press.

Bate, David (2003), *Photography and Surrealism: Sexuality, Colonialism and Social Dissent*, London: I.B. Tauris.

Baudelaire, Charles (2008), *Les Fleurs du Mal*, trans. by James McGowran, Oxford: Oxford University Press.

Blake, William (2000a), 'The Crystal Cabinet', in Duncan Wu (ed.), *Romanticism: An Anthology*, Oxford: Blackwell, pp. 117–18.

——— (2000b), 'The Sick Rose', in Duncan Wu (ed.), *Romanticism: An Anthology*, Oxford: Blackwell, p.196.

Blanchot, Maurice (1995), *L'écriture du desastre/The Writing of the Disaster*, trans. by Ann Smock, Lincoln, NE: University of Nebraska Press.

Breton, André (1988), *L'Amour Fou/Mad Love*, trans. by Mary Ann Caws, Lincoln, NE: University of Nebraska Press.

——— (1999), *Nadja*, trans. by Richard Howard, Harmondsworth: Penguin.

——— (2005), *First Manifesto of Surrealism*, in Lawrence Rainey (ed.), *Modernism: An Anthology*, Oxford: Blackwell, pp. 718–41.

Butler Cullingford, Elizabeth (1993), *Gender and History in Yeats's Love Poetry*, Cambridge: Cambridge University Press.

Cave, Nick (2007), *The Complete Lyrics 1978–2007*, Harmondsworth: Penguin.

Caws, Mary Ann (1988), 'Translator's Introduction', in André Breton (1988), *L'Amour Fou/Mad Love*, trans. by Mary Ann Caws, Lincoln, NE: University of Nebraska Press, pp. i–xvi.

—— (ed.) (1994), *The Yale Anthology of Twentieth-Century French Poetry*, New Haven, CT and London: Yale University Press.

—— (ed.) (1996), *Surrealist Love Poems*, London: Tate Publishing/Chicago, IL: University of Chicago Press.

Conley, Katherine (1996), *Automatic Woman: The Representation of Women in Surrealism*, Lincoln: University of Nebraska Press.

Culler, Jonathan (2008), 'Introduction' in Charles Baudelaire (2008), *Les Fleurs du Mal*, trans. by James McGowran, Oxford: Oxford University Press, pp. xiii–xxxviii.

Dalí, Salvador (2009), *The Secret Life of Salvador Dalí*, Mineola, New York: Dover.

Falconer, Rachel (2005), *Hell in Contemporary Literature: Western Descent Narratives since 1945*, Edinburgh: Edinburgh University Press.

Felman, Shoshana (2003), *Writing and Madness: Literature/Philosophy/Psychoanalysis*, trans. by Martha Evans, Palo Alto, CA: Stanford University Press.

Flaubert, Gustav (2003), *Mémoires d'un Fou/Memoirs of a Madman*, trans. by Andrew Brown, London: Hesperus.

Freud, Sigmund (1953), *The Interpretation of Dreams. Standard Edition* (vol. 4), trans. and ed. by James Strachey, London: Hogarth.

—— (1957a), 'Beyond the Pleasure Principle', *Standard Edition* (vol. 18), trans. and ed. by James Strachey, London: Hogarth.

—— (1957b), 'Mourning and Melancholia', *Standard Edition* (vol. 14), trans. and ed. by James Strachey, London: Hogarth.

—— (1961), 'A Seventeenth-Century Demonological Neurosis', *Standard Edition* (vol. 19), trans. and ed. by James Strachey, London: Hogarth.

Homer (2008), *The Odyssey*, trans. by Walter Shewring, Oxford: Oxford World's Classics.

Hutcheon, Linda and Michael Hutcheon (1999), *Opera: Desire, Disease and Death*, Lincoln, NE: University of Nebraska Press.

Keats, John (2000), 'The Eve of St. Agnes', in Duncan Wu (ed.), *Romanticism: An Anthology*, Oxford: Blackwell, pp. 1043–52.

Lomas, David (2000), *The Haunted Self: Surrealism, Psychoanalysis, Subjectivity*, New Haven, CT and London: Yale University Press.

Lorca, Federico Garcia (1998), 'Play and the Theory of Duende', in Christopher Maurer (ed.), *In Search of Duende*, San Francisco: New Directions, pp. 48–63.

Lovejoy, Arthur O. (1924), 'On the Discrimination of Romanticisms', *PMLA*, 39: 2, pp. 229–53.

Lowry, Malcolm (2000), *Under the Volcano*, Harmondsworth: Penguin.

Lusty, Natayla (ed.) (2007), *Surrealism, Feminism, Psychoanalysis*, London: Ashgate.

Marvell, Andrew (2005), 'To His Coy Mistress', in Jonathan Bate (ed.), *The Complete Poems*, Harmondsworth: Penguin, pp. 50–5.

Mermann-Jozwiak, Elisabeth (2009), 'Writing Mexico: Travel and Intercultural Encounter in Contemporary American Literature', *Symplokē*, 17: 1–2, pp. 95–114.

Mundy, Jennifer (ed.) (2001), *Surrealism: Desire Unbound*, London: Tate Publishing.

Praz, Mario (1978), *The Romantic Agony*, trans. by Angus Davidson, Oxford: Oxford University Press.

Shakespeare, William (2005a), *Romeo and Juliet,* in Stanley Wells, Gary Taylor, John Jowett, William Montgomery (eds), *The Complete Works*, Oxford: Oxford University Press.

—— (2005b), *A Midsummer Night's Dream,* in Stanley Wells, Gary Taylor, John Jowett, William Montgomery (eds), *The Complete Works*, Oxford: Oxford University Press.

Shaw, Philip (2005), *Sublime,* London: Routledge.

Tennov, Dorothy (1998), *Love and Limerence: the Experience of Being in Love,* Chelsea, MI: Scarborough House.

Van Heusen, Jimmy (1944), 'Swinging on a Star', composer Jimmy Van Heusen, lyrics Johnny Burke, New York: Chappel/Elite.

www.aahistory.com (1992), 'Serenity prayer', http://www.aahistory.com/prayer.html. Accessed 15 January 2011.

Yeats, W. B. (2000), *The Collected Poems of W. B. Yeats,* London: Wordsworth.

Zevon, Warren (1980), 'Empty Handed Heart', *Bad Luck Streak in Dancing School*, Elektra Records.

Zevon, Crystal (2007), *I'll Sleep When I'm Dead: The Dirty Life and Times of Warren Zevon,* New York: Ecco.

Chapter 15

From 'Cute Cunts' to 'No Pussy': Sexuality, Sovereignty and the Sacred

Fred Botting

Rag and ruin

During a night of drunken wandering, the first-person narrator of Georges Bataille's story, 'Mme Edwarda', enters a teeming brothel. He kisses the eponymous heroine of the tale; he comes. Then she raises her leg: 'her "old rag and ruin" loured at me, hairy and pink, just as full of life as some loathsome squid'. 'I'm GOD', she says. He falls to his knees, pressing his lips 'to that running, teeming wound' (1997: 229–30).

Cloven gender

'Cute Cunts' is the title of two simple collages copyrighted by Nick Cave in 1985: two pale-skinned baby-fleshed angelic female infants in white gowns and white wings, with big bright eyes, round rosy cheeks, gleaming smiles and light glossy hair (Dax 1999: 18). Standing in idyllic meadow scenes surrounded by flowers, one plays a flute and the other feeds a flock of bright yellow ducklings. In both cases Nick Cave's artistic intervention takes the same form: a large patch of black bristle is glued – out of scale – to their respective midriffs. Below the hair, large crudely splashed patches of pink and a black-ringed deep red occupy the centre of the picture, spreading a dark and obscene stain across the pastel surfaces of obscene innocence. Childhood and maturity, angels and whores, sexual innocence and experience are crudely and irrevocably stuck together. Gender is multiply cloven: an image of the female sexual organ itself, the cleavage refers to the polarised and heavily policed cultural constructions of femininity and the hoofs that signal animality and mark the Beast. Cloven genders extend across the text of Cave. Birthday Party songs depict female genitalia lasciviously 'grinning at me from hip to hip' or declare the need 'to feel your lips around me', an ambivalently oral and vaginal embrace (Cave 2007: 44, 43). One-act plays abound with cunts and cars, and with Salome calling for the head of the Baptist: 'my cunt yearns for it!!' (1988: 131). Euchrid Euchrow, the mute swamp-dwelling outcast-voyeur and narrator of *And the Ass Saw the Angel*, cut from the womb with a broken bottle, describes his violent, alcoholic mother with as much loathing as he can muster: a 'great whopping whale of a hog's cunt with a dry black maggot for a brain' (1990: 75). The inner sleeve of *Your Funeral, My Trial* has a pen drawing in the style of illustrations from mid twentieth-century woman's magazines. A woman in a polka-dotted headscarf and loose blouse seated on a sofa gazes into a mirror. The reflection she admires is, albeit unconventionally, her own: naked from the waist down but for stockings and high heels, her raised left leg unashamedly reveals her sex. Less an appreciation of the 'Origin of the World', the satisfied and self-contained gaze has more in common with the resistant confidence of Manet's Olympia, though more narcissistic in its absorption. 'Little Empty Boat' tells of a drunken encounter with a female evangelical Christian, involving thoughts of 'that grave you've dug between your legs' (2007: 290). 'No Pussy Blues', sung in the persona of an old rock star, details an inability to possess the object of desire no matter what romantic cliché (poetry, flowers, walks in woods) or banal trials (washing-up, mending gates, stroking Chihuahuas) he endures (2007: 435). While the song's object of desire is no embodiment of 'madhouse longing' able to rub 'a lamp between her legs' and release a singing genie, the singer may end up like Henry, losing his way 'deep in the forests of Le Vulva' and putting a gun to his head ('Hold On to Yourself' and 'Albert Goes West' from *Dig, Lazarus, Dig!!!*) (2008).

In Cave's words, '[t]here are things that preoccupy me now that feel weirdly adolescent … Like sex' (Quawson 2008: 43). Bunny Munro also thinks about sex a lot, pussy in particular. From the early pages until the end, vaginas dominate. There is Libby's 'joyful pussy', young life's potential as opening up 'like, um, a vagina or something' and summertime as 'beached pussy prostrate beneath the erotically shaped cumulus' (2009: 7, 15–17). His refrigerator magnets read 'FUCK YR PUSSY' and a social worker's moisturised legs suggest 'a waxed pussy' (2009: 54). We are also told of Cynthia's 'oscillating playground pussy', Charlotte's 'sparky vagina', Penny's 'sculpted domino of black fuzz balanced on top of her gash like a pirate flag on a Jolly Roger or something' (2009: 96, 131, 139). Celebrity vaginas abound: Madonna's 'waxed pussy (probably)', Pamela Anderson's '(almost) shaved pussy', and a 'blizzard of imagined pussy' – Kate Moss', Naomi Campbell's, Kylie Minogue's, Beyoncé's (2009: 55, 112, 188–9). And Bunny repeatedly fantasises about Avril Lavigne's vagina, 'the fucking Valhalla of all vaginas' (2009: 97, 139, 160, 189, 154). Bunny's devotion is played out with one of his clients: does he like pussy? 'I love it', he replies, 'beyond all things', 'more than life itself', 'beyond measure', 'till the cows come home' (2009: 140). Vaginas, historically figured as the absence confounding and constituting male sexuality, become, in Bunny's imaginings, the excess before which man bends and bows, an overabundance that escapes and overwhelms him, and before which his illusions of mastery and sovereignty slip away.

She's coming

In the first half of the twentieth century, conceptions and depictions of female sexuality – theoretically, artistically and socially – developed out of images of the New Woman and Suffragettes. Popular accounts registered concerns about telling the difference between respectable womanhood and prostitution (Dean 1992: 70). For Elisabeth Roudinesco, the 'new representation of woman' in the inter-war years was evident in surrealism's constructions of female animality, in psychoanalysis' engagement with female psychosis (the Papin Sisters) and the 'female ecstatic' as presented in Bernini's statue of St Theresa (1990: 18–20). 'She's coming', observed Lacan, as he outlined an idea of jouissance, inaccessible to men (except in fantasy) (1998: 76). Female sexuality situated woman as 'radically Other', 'on a path of existence', a trajectory towards 'one face of the Other, the God-face' (1998: 77, 83). Freud's 'specimen dream' involved female resistance, silence and excess. For Lacan, it signals an 'abyssal relation' to the unknown and the real, Irma's dream mouth associated with the female sexual organ and 'the essential object that isn't an object any longer, but this something faced with which words cease and all categories fail, the object of anxiety *par excellence*' (1988: 176, 154, 164). Site of horror and joy, anxiety and desire, the central locus and void of female excess becomes the core of psychoanalysis, its question, its mystery, its object. Bataille's writings, his cultural theory as much as his fiction, stand out in this process of reimagining sexuality, his Mme Edwarda preeminent in her very modern enactment of sex and the sacred: 'a triumphant madwoman, capable of inscribing the name of God on the "raps" hanging from her scarlet sex' (Roudinesco 1990: 19). In his theoretical writings, sexual forces are articulated with modes of expenditure and excess, profane things and sacred values, work and festivals, waste and consumption, sovereignty and sacrifice, positioned on an axis of taboo and transgression, prohibition and limit, site of the organization of life death, and a more vital, exuberant overflow of energies. In *Eroticism*, Bataille explores the role and effects of sexuality and death in respect of culture, religion and subjectivity, plotting lines of ambivalence and excess in the manner in which sacrificial rituals and festivals expend and delimit exuberant forces, breaking and reaffirming the sacred prohibitions sustaining the banal, organized, homogeneous world of work. Women are still passive, degraded, animal, pathways, it seems, to a sphere from which they are excluded: symbolizing 'the negation of the object, she herself is still an object', 'the nakedness of a limited being' (Bataille 1987: 131). The assumption of women's 'passive attitude' leads to the claim that 'prostitution is the logical consequence of the feminine attitude' and the assertion of feminine ambivalence: 'the beauty of the desirable woman suggests the private parts, the hairy ones, to be precise, the animal ones' (1987: 17, 143). Eroticism, furthermore, takes the form of a sacrificial violence in which woman is stripped of her identity, 'despoiled of her being' and subjected to 'impersonal violence that overwhelms her from without' (1987: 90). As 'mirror' to man in the erotic conflagration, her sacrifice allows him to become sovereign (1997: 267). But eroticism is 'that within man which calls his being into question' and 'entails a breaking down of established patterns [...] of the regulated social order basic to our discontinuous mode of existence defined as separate individuals' (1987: 29, 18).

Long-lost dress

'Cute cunts' appears to follow an all too familiar pattern of the objectification, idealization and commodification of women, playing out oppositions and taboos sanctioned, for centuries, in patriarchal culture: angels, virgins, whores, demons, unashamed sexuality, figures of mystery, desire, adoration, objects of possession, violence and murder. Cave's songs sing of and from the position of Marys, virginal innocents and naive but faithful lovers, all tragically alone in their desperate suffering (Cave 2007: 123, 147, 256). Abandoned, they endure extremes of loss and pain. Others are objects of all-too accessible desire and ready brutality, of sticking a six-inch gold blade in the head of a kewpie doll zoo-music girl Crow Jane; or relishing the murder of female victims ('woman-pie', Mary Bellows, Elisa Day, Joy) (2007: 44, 45, 23, 258). Otherwise women are implicated as the cause of male sin and violence (Lucy in 'Swampland'; Nancy in 'Knockin' on Joe'), complicit in crimes (Deanna, John Finn's wife) or downright diabolical in their own terms (the delightfully unrepentant Loretta in 'The Curse of Millhaven') (Cave 2007: 75–6, 112–3, 144–6, 202–4, 252–5). Obscenely combining angel and whore, beauty and 'hairy parts', surface and void, feminine excess confronts male desire with its own ambivalence. The image of prostitution – in the gate-fold sleeve of *Your Funeral, My Trial* – literally closes upon a drawing of Mary holding a shroud depicting the face of Jesus. Mary is both Mother and Magdalene at the same time, cause of adoration, desire, hatred and self-disgust: 'a thousand Marys lured me', the singer in 'Your Funeral, My Trial' wails, before venting his rage against this singular multiplicity, demanding that 'all the bells in whoredom ring/All the crooked bitches that she was' (2007: 126). Norms, limits, oppositions and divisions are strained to breaking point. In exposing the conjunctions of fear and desire, disgust and joy, the complicity between desecrations and idealizations of femininity, an obscene excess appears in masculine positions: in 'From Her to Eternity' the fantasies surrounding the unseen and unknown woman in room 29 are wound up to a febrile state in which desire and possession are wrenched apart (2007: 84).

Dresses repeatedly signify the surface that is femininity, a surface often discarded to leave nothing but a memory of loss. 'Mr Clarinet', medium and go-between, is called by the song's voice to help him woo his beloved: she is composed purely of clothing (2007: 34). Kewpie Doll wears a 'cheap red dress' while 'Nobody's Baby' leaves behind a dress covered in 'blue quilted violets' (2007: 45, 217). Nancy is, like her prisoner-lover, a simulacrum of death, wearing not only 'a dress of red and gold' but 'her body like a coffin', as stiff in her box as he is in his cell (2007: 112–13). More powerfully, the slow-moaning lament 'Well of Misery' conjoins dress, body, loss and anguish: '[d]own that well lies the long-lost dress/Of my little floating girl' (2007: 83). She is gone and he wanders the deserted landscape in misery. Like the 'legs of lace' (rather than legs in lace), damp dress and drowned body are almost identical. Desire withers and crumples in rags and anguish, the stripping away of surfaces disclosing death's deep hole. The dress, well and dead girl have appeared earlier: 'her dress floats down the well and assumes the shape of the body of a little girl' (2007: 58). The image has a double function: as surface, veil over nothing, masquerade; and killing off that image as ragged image. The surface then is discarded, cast away like the dress/girl down the well, the covering emptied out as a construction of femininity, as image and artifice. Made visible as construction, it is stripped away to show that it is only empty-dress-body, a surface whose consistency cannot be sustained or lived.

The mirror of eroticism is not the object-dress-body of the beloved, but loss itself. Nothing is left but the well, a deep, dark hole of misery, a greater void embracing and consuming the dejected (male) singer (and murderer). His object – her (now dead-gone) dress-body – is evacuated just as he is in the process, as hollow and dark as the well into which he gazes. Holes open within men, voids tearing being apart. In the funereal, post-coital 'Wild World', the singer has a 'dish-rag body', a cloth-form like so many dead girls' dresses cast down wells (2007: 56). Sexually exhausted 'post-crucifixion' bodies are, in a world without God, 'all undone': abandonment is rendered continuous, a repeated, slave-driven marking of nothing and time, a dirge moving backwards and forwards, forever and unresolved, to the panting, gasping, grunting voice that declares '[i]t's a wild world' (2007: 56).

Dissolution

'Theoretically', Bataille notes, 'a man may be just as much the object of a woman's desire as a woman is of a man's desire' (1987: 130). Objects of desire dissolve in eroticism, males 'generally' being active and females passive, becoming 'dissolved as a separate entity'. For the male, dissolution paves 'the way for a fusion where both are mingled' since eroticism aims 'to destroy the self-contained character of participators as they are in their separate lives' (1987: 17). Dissolution, beyond sexual expenditure, is linked to inner experiences like laughter, communication, horror: it engenders mystical, ecstatic rendings of discontinuous existence. It implies other senses of 'dissolute': sexual immorality, drunken intoxication, madness, corporeal paroxysm, mass hysteria, violent explosiveness, idleness, wild exuberance and wasteful behaviour like gambling, a consumption and expenditure of energies sweeping away meaning, purpose, use. Upsetting mirrored roles of master and slave, eroticism situates women between a double movement, a double negation of both nature and culture (Guerlac 1990: 98). Object of exchange, woman is also image signifying loss, a figure of absence on the basis of which erotic ecstasy and joyful dissolution in sacred continuity – for men – can be posited. As image, woman discloses a residual difference not overcome in eroticism. If feminine dissolution is prior, his self-loss comes later as an effect of (the image of) hers: remaining at a distance, still discontinuous, the active/male position initially experiences fusion by means of an image of feminine excess (Surkis 1996: 20–1). Asymmetry between sexes remains, perhaps even enabling eroticism's intensity in sustaining the desire's tension. 'Love is a kind of immolation', substituting 'persistent discontinuity' with 'miraculous continuity' (Bataille 1997: 269; 1987: 19). It 'obliterates the antithesis of good and evil', carries lovers 'beyond the source of moral values, beyond pleasure and pain, beyond the realm of distinction – into a realm where opposites cancel out' (de Rougemont 1993: 39). Abandonment is a sacrificial loss and expenditure comparable to the abandon of erotic activity: 'by dissolving the separate beings that participate in it, [abandonment] reveals their fundamental continuity, like the waves of a stormy sea. In sacrifice, the victim is divested not only of clothes but of life (or is destroyed in some way if it is an inanimate object)' (1987: 22). Sacrifice consumes materiality in order to restore being's excess; it destroys things to return them to values (1997: 210; 1987: 157). Its aim 'is always the totality of being':

> the object of desire is the *universe,* in the form of she who in the embrace is its mirror, where we ourselves are reflected. At the most intense moment of fusion, the pure blaze of light, like a sudden flash, illuminates the immense field of possibility, on which these lovers are subtilized, annihilated, submissive in their excitement to a rarefaction which they desired.
>
> (1997: 267)

The mirror, then, is not the other person, remaining unchanged, if sanctified, by the reciprocal gaze of adoration: what is reflected is an impossible totality. Generally the position of the object is taken by a woman: her loss precedes and paves the way for his; her body occupies a place of 'duplicity' ('asexual maternal and sexual feminine') marking the 'contradictory coexistence of transgression and prohibition, purity and defilement' essential to eroticism's inner experience and to its textual performance (Surkis 1996: 20; Suleiman 1986: 131). Woman, object of desire, more than desire, embodies, suffers and performs the 'double movement' of prohibition and limit, locus of exchange, objectification and luxurious generosity. Her loss-plenitude defines the human as 'erotic animal' (both sacred and thing), figuring 'man's larval state': the chrysalis, *'nymphe'* (in French the 'small lips of the vulva'), signifies 'woman's sex, and clothes or figures it, if you will, with the image, the form of nakedness' (Guerlac 1990: 98–104).

And the same God that abandoned me

The last thing Elisa Day sees is the stone with which her lover kills her. His part of the duet transmutes the rock into a rose planted between her teeth. Love's fleeting temporality and materiality is transformed to a permanent symbol – the ever-present rose – transcending time and body. Elisa becomes myth, the 'wild rose' replacing her given name. In Cave's lecture, amorous relations are 'by nature abusive': Kylie Minogue's 'Better the Devil You Know' declares her willingness to remain with a bastard no matter what he does (Cave 2007: 12). She presents herself as passively tied to love and suffering: a 'sacrificial lamb, bleating an earnest invitation to the drooling, ravenous wolf, to devour her time and time again, all to a groovy techno beat' (2007: 12). The love song must engage with sadness and sorrow: without a deep sense of loss, neither wonder, nor magic, nor joy can be fully appreciated; without encountering evil, one cannot grasp goodness. The movement between poles links Kylie and Psalms and defines love's meaning and intensity through an association of God and loss. Cave's songs reiterate losses of the beloved, either in death or in break-up (2007: 106, 228, 179). In 'The Train Song', the lover sings of missing her departure, torturing himself by asking a series of questions that replay the moment (2007: 184). Loss and departure are drawn out doubly in the painful and plaintive reconstruction.

If love means abandonment, it also leads to abandon: a total, amorous immersion in which nothing exists except love and the rest of the world falls away or apart. Loss, here, appears on a grander scale, a mirror of totality in which the beloved is the hole and whole into which everything is absorbed: natural landscapes and phenomena present love's sublimity, wild, desolate, populated only by a solitary wanderer, lost in 'deserts of despair' (2007: 83). Love is both impermanent and solid, fixed and always in motion, a matter of rock, sea, wind and waves (2007: 361). Love and beloved enjoy kisses raining 'down in storms', are 'a force of nature' or 'a storm in the form of a girl' (2007: 319, 390, 228). Love is the All sweeping all else away: 'when I crawl into your arms/Everything comes tumbling down' (2007: 175). Like the sun, it is as big as the diurnal rhythms of nature: 'in a colonial hotel we fucked up the sun/And then we fucked it down again' (2007: 281). Passion runs from before dawn and until after dusk, its rise and fall moving the sun, rewriting the course of nature and universe. 'Straight to You' announces amorous apocalypse, jettisoning institutions and knowledge ('towers of ivory are crumbling') and clichéd happiness ('days of rainbows', 'nights of swinging from the stars') for chaotic cosmic reverberations: saints 'drunk and howling at the moon'; angels 'colliding' in their chariots, the sacred overwhelmed and reversed in a divine car-crash (2007: 195).

The God that reappears in many songs is not so much the divinity that presides over religious and social institutions or moral judgements, not the house-proud, curtain-twitching, racist, homophobic small-town God of prurience, self-satisfaction and barely suppressed hostility ('God is in the House'); nor is He the figure locked 'down in cathedrals and cages': that 'God is gone. We got to get a new one'. And She is 'Eternal woman' (2007: 298, 324). God and woman, figures of absence and suffering, mirror of global pain and image of the despair that touches on the sacred, elevating – and abasing – humanity. Sex opens up in the absence of the sacred: in the quiet tragedy of post-coital separation, a lover enters a church and takes communion: 'the blood imparted in little sips/The smell of you still on my hands/As I bring the cup up to my lips' (2007: 278). Sacrifice, sex, transubstantiation: blood and bodily fluids conjoin. But religion does not give sexuality its sense of sacredness: neither god nor devil had the power to do what she did, the power 'of bringing me to my knees' (2007: 278). In prayer, he acknowledges a higher power; the physical position suggests the payment of a different oral homage as he kneels before her sex.

Ain't there nothing sacred anymore?

Love songs address the absence of the sacred, divine absence, crying out 'into the yawning void, in anguish and self-loathing for deliverance' (2007: 12). Poetry, in cherishing great depths of loss, allows sorrow to become a 'creative act': it distinguishes true – sad – love songs from other popularly mediated forms of music, their 'hysterical technocracy' 'littering' broadcasting to 'deny us our human-ness' (2007: 8). Identifying God as a 'product of the creative imagination', of 'imagination taken flight', links poetry and divinity as heterogeneous forms in opposition to the homogeneous, soulless and narrow spaces of modernity (1997: 137). In the Gospel of Mark Christ represents 'divine inspiration' opposed to 'dull rationalism', raging 'at the mundane' and becoming a 'victim of humanity's lack of imagination' pinned to the cross with 'nails of creative vapidity' (1998: x, xi). The void opening up in the love song is thus associated with poetic heterogeneity: it stands apart from profane homogeneity, above and below a world of haste and hysteria. Writing fills and addresses, and takes its energy from, loss; it involves risk, openness, absence: 'one can write only to fill a void or at the very least to situate, in relation to the most lucid part of ourselves, the place where this incommensurable abyss yawns' (Leiris 1968: 144). The abyss of loss underlies the way that expenditure, sovereignty and divinity contribute to creativity, art, poetry. Working according to a 'principle of loss' and as 'creation by means of loss', poetry 'is the power of words to evoke effusion, through the excessive expenditure of its own forces' (Bataille 1997: 169, 2004: 95). It partakes of a sacred, marvellous, imaginative and sovereign impulse 'to create a sensible reality whereby the ordinary world is modified in response to the desire for the extraordinary, for the marvellous' (1955: 34, 15).

Sovereignty: a refusal to be subordinated to rules, conventions, limitations of time or knowledge, to work, rationality, utility or, even, death itself, 'the movement of free and internally wrenching violence that animates the whole, dissolves into tears, into ecstasy and bursts of laughter' (1997: 277–8). Sovereignty uses up resources, expends violently and unproductively, has no purpose or aim other than the moment. At odds with profane existence, sovereignty produces mythical figures as 'concrete symbols of the kind of grandeur and perdition reserved for those who violate taboos', the 'damned ones' coloured with the 'glory of not having accepted any divine or human limitation when it was a question of satisfying one of the unquenchable appetites of feeling, knowing, and dominating' (Caillois 2001: 136). Nor do sovereign figures accept the limitation of time or death. To live in a sovereign manner is to live as though 'the representation of death is impossible, for the present is not subject to the demands of the future' (Bataille 1997: 317). For Caillois, as for Bataille, the sacred and sovereignty disappear in a modern, bourgeois world of work and Christian conservative morality (Caillois 2001: 126–9). Transgression, the latter suggests, cedes to profanation and degradation associated with abjection and identified with the 'thieving rabble', with those who 'lie down and scoff' (Bataille 1987: 135–9).

Fifty good pussies

'Stagger Lee' reworks blues mythology in sovereign fashion. A gambler, killer and self-proclaimed 'bad motherfucker' finds a bar, shoots the barman, spurns the town's most popular whore and waits for her pimp (White 1996). His readiness to deliver death is calibrated to his willingness to stare it in the face. Vocal self-assertions are violently punctuated by shots from his pistol and, performatively, in the drumbeat-shot repetition cutting across rolling drum-bass rhythms (like the 'pow pow pows' of 'Hamlet (Pow, Pow, Pow)' (Botting and Wilson 2001a)). Death, rather than sex, is on the top of his agenda, so he waits for Billy Dilly: having his dick sucked is no more than the whore d'oeuvres to ejaculating bullets into the pimp's head. To state that 'I'll crawl over fifty good pussies just to get to one fat boy's asshole' is not so much a declaration of sexual preference but a sovereign assertion of death's intensity (White 1996). Sovereignty evinces a caprice, indifference and an utterly insubordinate curiosity that allows a man to shoot someone 'just to watch him die'. In contrast, the killings of 'O'Malley's Bar' are accompanied by pseudo-philosophical musings and narcissistic reflections (Cave 2007: 260–5). This is not sovereignty, despite the setting and the explosive violence, only small-town murders by a small-town man. As the police arrive and he is left with his last bullet, he gives up (2007: 260).

For other sovereign characters, living beyond the fear of death underwrites the intensity of their lives, evinced by captives whose loss of freedom and suffering enables them to attain a different state of consciousness. 'Knockin' on Joe', according to the sleeve notes of 'The Firstborn is Dead', describes the activity of causing oneself injuries serious enough to avoid enforced hard labour: 'crushing fingers, hands, legs' (1985). Sung from the position of a cell-bound inmate, it announces a prisoner's freedom from repressive – chains or bars – and ideological institutions: the warden's fists can no longer hurt him; the preacher's words no longer terrify. Afraid no more, the prisoner repeats his suffering in a general offer to assume any emotional burden as well as his own (2007: 112). More dramatically, in 'The Mercy Seat', the prisoner chants an account of moving from incarcerated abjection (and religious delusion) to a sovereign embrace of death. Its driven rhythm and dissonant swirl of instruments accompanies an Old Testament invocation while the over-running conjunctions (serial killing?) and repetitions-with-difference suggest non-equivalence rather than a simple balancing of the scales: eye for eye, tooth for tooth, truth for truth, lie for lie, life for life, do not add up in the changing rhymes of the chorus. It introduces an element of uncertainty into justice, suggesting one life is not equivalent to another. Even the key repetition (the sovereignty of 'I'm not afraid to die') varies: 'I'm not afraid to tell a lie', declaring sovereign indifference to systems of truth and justice, becomes 'but I'm afraid I told a lie' (2007: 137). Fear, after insisting throughout he was beyond it? And what lie: undermining a presumption of innocence and lessening the pain of his death sentence, disturbing the thrust of the song towards sovereignty? The lie forms the death drive of the song, a wish to hasten the flicking of the switch, the lie that he is not afraid to die.

Figure of fun

Sovereignty comes closer to abjection with other mythical figures in Cave's writing, death subordinated to disgust and degradation. Their song-worlds, spaces of idleness, violence, consumption, are appropriate: bars, dance-halls, brothels, jailhouses, ports, fleabag hotels, run-down shacks, dusty small-towns and swamplands envelop the songs in violence and despair. The drunks, whores, preachers, convicts, outcasts, killers, gamblers, writers and singers are all part of the landscape, figures of a negative community, rabbles wasting time, money, lives. 'Gun wears his alcoholism well': booze swills from the page and stage (2007: 57). As his name suggests, this dance-hall gigolo is unafraid when it comes to shooting off. 'Black Paul', writer and murderer, is utterly abandoned, the song a dirge calling for someone to care enough even to box and bury him (2007: 91–3). 'Guitar thugs' and singers roll into town, able to fight and kill as much as play and sing, bards, lonely wanderer-adventurers, misunderstood prophet-outcasts like Johnny Cash's 'The Singer' (2007: 96). Generally loathsome creatures, they are disgusting, repulsive, abject, cartoon, comic-book and literary grotesques, the hideousness of Ed Roth's glossy gargoyles (the cover for *Junkyard*) meeting the freaks and fairground monsters of Southern Gothic fiction: Nick the Stripper is 'hideous to the eye', a 'fat little insect', 'a fucked little insect'; stinky, sandy, sooty King Ink sniffs like a dog and feels like a bug; 'Junkyard King' yack yack yacks his way through the garbage (2007: 26, 28, 47). Sleeve illustrations present similar figures of degraded manhood: scrawny, unshaven pen-and-ink doodles of naked male bodies, abject forms, ugly, repulsive, stringy-dicked. Fucked little insects, half-beasts, tramp-devils: the cultural icon of these used-up vestiges of humanity, exploited, commodified, fucked over detritus of life's wasting process and their own loathsome selves, is an image (copyrighted 1985) ink-drawn on cheap hotel notepaper of a figure in flares and bare torso, seen from behind, sitting on a stool hunched over a guitar, a dark-quiffed face and curled lip turned towards the viewer. He has hair growing over his shoulders and a long gash extending the length of his naked back: 'cuntback Elvis' (Dax 1999: 89). 'Loverman', too, is abject, miserable, exhausted: 'howling with pain', 'weak with evil', 'crawling up the walls', 'broken by the world', 'old', 'stupid', 'hungry', 'sore', 'blind', 'lame' and 'dirty' (Cave 2007: 218). Too repulsive to be loved, the inverted image of a blues and rock 'n' roll tradition of potency, a self deflated by its own desire. 'Thirsty Dog' is a long, slavish and urgently repetitive apology for numerous marital and social inadequacies, for which the bottle is the only and permanent compensation. Put more directly in 'Abattoir Blues', 'I wanted to be your Superman but I turned out such a jerk' (2007: 397). Jerks, cuntbacks, fuck-ups: male inadequacy, abjection and self-loathing is paraded to an almost mythical level. Declarations of potency – from 'I Put a Spell on You' to the self-mocking 'No Pussy Blues' and the comic dark masculinity of 'Mr Sandman the inseminator' ('Today's Lesson') – manifest ironic and parodic inversion, ridicule rather than sublimity, servility rather than mastery, abjection rather than selfhood (2008).

'The inaccessible nature of the totality of the instant motivates less remorse than humour (simultaneously angelic and black)' (Bataille 2004: 108). Cave's text is rife with comic modes, cartoonish, ridiculing, ironic, self-mocking, defensive and dark. Cave has described himself as 'a *funny* misanthropic miserabilist' (Keenan 1999: 32). Biba Kopf sees him as a writer of 'grotesque comedies' (Gray 1997: 26). Will Self notices Cave's ability to pile irony upon irony (Cave 2007: xii). Irony, multiple identification, is part of a process of self-reflection and self-consciousness that allows the combined use of cliché, diverse literary, musical and cultural traditions, all involving a doubleness evident in the use of different personae held up for recognition, examination, sympathy, identification and/or mockery. When it comes to considering sex there is a greater irony. Bunny Munro originates in Valerie Solanas' *S.C.U.M. Manifesto* and its 'wonderful description' of 'the male type': 'half-dead blobs somewhere between a human and an ape, incapable of relating to anything but its own sensations and incapable of mental passion or sensitivity or any of those sorts of things' (Medd 2009: 23). Ironies multiply in the reference to a text subtitled 'Society for Cutting-Up Men': a 're-ironisation' of *Loaded*, irony deflecting sexism into self-conscious, and therefore harmless, quotation marks; a shielding under the name of extreme feminism; a spurious diversion or spicing-up of tiresome interview questions? Or a more pervasive hyper self-consciousness, perhaps of the kind a former collaborator, Lydia Lunch, finds in the work of this 'shy' but 'hyper-conscious and sensitive' poet (Quawson 2008: 41)? Or, irony of ironies, the claim might simply be true! (Cave had already written a song called 'Scum' (Cave 2007: 119–20)). The *S.C.U.M. Manifesto* presents males as biological 'accidents' (Solanas 1968). Guilt-ridden, insecure and shameful, 'he'll swim through a river of snot, wade nostril-deep through a mile of vomit, if he thinks there'll be a friendly pussy awaiting him' (1968). Solanas identifies a reversal of conventionally gendered characteristics. 'Pussy', for her, represents the desire to overcome his anxiety and emptiness, as 'men are more and more becoming fags or are obliterating themselves through drugs' (1968). According to Avital Ronell, 'fagginess' dismantles 'essential and defining characteristics by means of an unavoidable "feminization"' (2004: 19). The identification of a process of 'feminization' resonates with other readings of the effects of postmodern economic practices on gender distinctions. Jean-Joseph Goux wonders 'what has become of proletarians, women, and artists', noting how western market ideology suppresses ideals of corrective or distributive justice and threatens social ties and subjective bonds. In modernity they were sustained in respect of the exceptions defining moral authority and as guarantees of social feeling and attachment: proletarians (the value of solidarity), women (humanity) and artists (the aesthetic bridge between conception and realization) are invoked in the defence of society against capitalism (Goux 1998: 42). Workers once channelled their alienation from the means of production and from the benefits of their labour, women opposed the delimiting social and subjective effects of paternal law and artists opened up the horizons of human reality, form and meaning. When exchanges move to a more abstracted and alienating level governed by 'autonomisation of the general equivalent' things change decisively: 'we are all', so the system declares, 'structurally and ontologically, proletarians, women and artists' (Goux 1998: 45, 49). The economy thus disregards gender conventions and feminizes all consumers in a process of lack-desire, evacuating and refilling the void of human wanting, commanding more and more luxurious expenditure. Consumption is abject rather than sovereign, driven not by ultimately sacrificial expenditure or the possibility of sacred heterogeneity, but by the imperative for more and by a tacit anxiety-induction of never having enough, with the safety net of credit holding off fatally damaging expenditures. Loss is no longer final, no longer devastating. We are all like Solanas' men;

or are all women now, consuming voids of evacuation and expenditure (Lieberman 1993: 246–7). And if the 'logical consequence' of the 'feminine attitude' is prostitution, then The Pop Group was right: 'we are all prostitutes'.

Cuntsumption

Desire pulses over a void constantly occluded by the flickering of commodities. Everything returns to a feminized, evacuated consumer fucked over (and over again) in a process far from sovereign in its expenditure. With Bunny Munro's pussy-obsessed and pusillanimous misogyny, the sexual commodification of femininity appears paramount. Pussy becomes the figure of consumption's intense, dis-satisfying and endlessly repeated process of expenditure, holes in search of wholes. Capitalism turns impossible, sacred joy and luxuriousness into the ultimate imperative to consume:

> [p]ussy, pussy, pussy! [...] We got white pussy, black pussy, Spanish pussy, yellow pussy, hot pussy, cold pussy, wet pussy, tight pussy, big pussy, bloody pussy, fat pussy, hairy pussy, smelly pussy, velvet pussy, silk pussy, Naugahyde pussy, snappin' pussy, horse pussy, dog pussy, mule pussy, fake pussy! If we don't have it, you don't want it!
>
> (Tarantino 1996: 61)

The sales pitch for the delicatessen of dark and dirty delights is, in *From Dusk Till Dawn*, a lure: the 'Titty Twister' is a vampire bar and any punters who enter to enjoy the exotic entertainments soon find that they are on the menu (Botting and Wilson 2001b). The generalization, abjection and pervasiveness of sexual commodification – cuntsumption – are played out in Bunny's incessant musings on pussy. Sitting in McDonald's, he reflects: 'with its flaccid bun, its spongy meat, the cheese, the slimy little pickle and, of course, the briny special sauce, biting into a Big Mac was as close to eating pussy as, well, eating pussy' (Cave 2009: 146–7). Cuntsumption's obscenity renders everything the same, pussy representing both the metaphysical uncertainty, the void, at the centre of human desiring and the general equivalent, which guarantees and enables all exchanges, an abstraction and reduction rendering all commerce possible.

Bunny's pursuit of pussy is haunted by an expenditure that is beyond him, an inedible emptiness: the void-continuity of death, a loss without return or reserve. Masturbating in response to his wife's suicide, he fails to excise 'the day's horror' (2009: 40). Intimations of his mortality recur. As if that final expenditure gives meaning – even in denial – to his countless little expenditures. Throughout the novel death shadows pussy: one night on the road as he falls asleep in front of the television, a 'wall of darkness' approaches (2009: 160). He thinks, 'with a sudden, terrible, bottomless dread, of Avril Lavigne's vagina', the 'Valhalla' of vaginas (2009: 160). One of his last sexual encounters brings the relationship of sex and death vividly into view. Visiting an almost comatose female junkie, Bunny is compulsively drawn to 'her blueing lips and trickle of bright blood in the crook of her arm, the mortal weaponry of hypodermic syringe and blackened spoon in front of her': he had 'walked through the looking glass, into death itself, hers and perhaps his own' (2009: 227). 'Oh, my dear Avril', he says as he positions her: 'it is exactly as he imagined – the hair, the lips, the hole – and he slips his hands under her wasted buttocks and enters her like a fucking pile driver' (2009: 227). From sexual fantasy to fatal expenditure, Valhalla mirrors his desire, terminus of his pursuit of pussy. Grotesque, obscene, pathetic, the act signals Bunny's exhaustion and inability to assume a dignified or sovereign relationship to himself, others or death. He remains the same smarmy, sexist salesman of beauty products, as much in thrall to the cosmetic industry's promises of desire, image and aspiration as his female customers. His assumed sovereignty as 'cocksman' becomes steadily and visibly more abject: sex involved nothing erotic or sacred; entailed no sovereign expenditure, no real loss, costs, nor stakes. That other expenditure that haunts him, an absence more total and consuming than all the holes that stand in its place, indicates a curiously fetishistic disavowal of death's finality by means of the conventional, psychoanalytic, site of fetishism.

Bunny's double emphasizes the disgusting and serious comedy of manhood. News reports punctuate the narrative: a man dressed in a red devil suit terrorises Northern women with his 'trident' (a garden fork). Nicknamed the 'horned killer', this cartoon figure of evil (another 'loverman') is stupid, amusing, contemptible and frightening all at once: though a caricature, he is, despite suit and media construction, a sexual predator and a killer, ridiculous and terrifying, comical yet obscene. His movements and crimes chart a southerly trajectory towards Brighton, Bunny's home town. These caricatures of pussy-obsessed, abject masculinity seem to be very much a redundant, if not dying (in the case of Bunny and his father), breed. The story repeatedly mentions a building firm: 'Dudman'. A Dudman concrete mixer is the cause of the crash that kills Bunny. Dudman: dead man and fake man, useless, an explosive device without the spark to explode, a blank, it sums up Bunny Munro in life as it ends it. No glorious death, no sovereign expenditure; no forgiveness or redemption sought before death, only a last desperate, pathetic attempt to find pussy: soaked to the skin in a rainstorm he clutches at the knees of a woman crying 'will somebody please fuck me?!' (2009: 251).

References

Bataille, Georges (1955), *Lascaux*, trans by A. Wainhouse, Geneva: Skira.

———— (1987), *Eroticism*, trans. by Mary Dalwood, London and New York: Marion Boyars.

———— (1997), *The Bataille Reader*, ed. by Fred Botting and Steven Wilson, Oxford: Blackwell.

———— (2004), *Unfinished System of Non-Knowledge*, ed. by Stuart Kendall and Michelle Kendall, Minneapolis, MA: University of Minnesota Press.

Botting, Fred and Scott Wilson (2001a), *Bataille*, London and Basingstoke: Palgrave Macmillan.

———— (2001b), *The Tarantinian Ethics*, London: Sage.

Caillois, Roger (2001), *Man and the Sacred*, trans. by Meyer Barash, Urbana and Chicago: University of Illinois Press.

Cave, Nick (1988), *King Ink*, London: Black Spring.

—— (1990), *And the Ass Saw the Angel*, London: Penguin.

—— (1997), *King Ink II*, London: Black Spring.

—— (1998), 'An Introduction to the Gospel According to Mark', *The Gospel According to Mark*, Edinburgh: Canongate.

—— (2007), *The Complete Lyrics 1978–2007*, London: Penguin.

—— (2009), *The Death of Bunny Munro*, Edinburgh: Canongate.

Cave, Nick and the Bad Seeds (1985), *The Firstborn is Dead*. CD. Mute.

—— (2008), *Dig, Lazarus, Dig!!!*. CD. Mute.

Dax, Max (1999), *The Life and Mind of Nick Cave*, trans. by I. Minock, Berlin: Die Gestalten Verlag.

De Rougemont, Denis (1993), *Love in the Western World*, trans. by Montgomery Belgion, Princeton: Princeton University Press.

Dean, Carolyn J. (1992), *The Self and Its Pleasures*, Ithaca and London: Cornell University Press.

Goux, Jean-Joseph (1998), 'Subversion and Consensus: Proletarians, Women, Artists', in Jean-Joseph Goux and Philip R. Wood (eds), *Terror and Consensus*, Stanford: Stanford University Press, pp. 37–51.

Gray, L. (1997), 'Old Nick', *The Guardian Weekend Magazine*, 18 January, pp. 24–30.

Guerlac, Suzanne (1990), '"Recognition" by a Woman!: A Reading of Bataille's L'Erotisme', *Yale French Studies*, 78, pp. 90–105.

Hattenstone, Simon (2008), 'Old Nick', *The Guardian Weekend*, 23 February, pp. 37–43.

Keenan, David (1999), 'Under a Black Sun', *The Wire*, 81, pp. 32–8.

Lacan, Jacques (1988), *The Seminar of Jacques Lacan Book II*, trans. by S. Tomaselli, Cambridge: Cambridge University Press.

—— (1998), *The Seminar of Jacques Lacan Book* XX, trans. by B. Fink, New York and London: Norton.

Leiris, Michel (1968), *Manhood*, trans. by Richard Howard, London: Cape.

Lieberman, Rhonda (1993), 'Shopping Disorders', in Brian Massumi (ed.), *The Politics of Everyday Fear*, Minneapolis: University of Minnesota Press, pp. 245–65.

Medd, J. (2009), 'Original Sin', *The Word Magazine*, October, pp. 23–4.

Ronell, Avital (2004), 'The Deviant Payback', Introduction, in Valerie Solanas, *S.C.U.M. Manifesto*, London and New York: Verso, pp. 7–21.

Roudinesco, Elisabeth (1990), *Jacques Lacan & Co.*, trans. by Jeffrey Mehlman, London: Free Association.

Solanas, Valerie (1968), *S.C.U.M. Manifesto*, http://www.churchofeuthanasia.org/e-sermons/scum.html. Accessed 29 August 2011.

Suleiman, Susan Rubin (1986), 'Pornography, Transgression, and the Avant-Garde', in Nancy K. Miller (ed.), *The Poetics of Gender*, New York, Columbia University Press: pp. 117–36.

Surkis, Judith (1996), 'No Fun and Games Until Someone Loses an Eye: Transgression and Masculinity in Bataille and Foucault', *Diacritics*, 26.2, pp. 18–30.

Tarantino, Quentin (1996), *From Dusk Till Dawn*, London: Faber.

White, Nick (1996), 'Stagger Lee: NC Interview and List', http://www.bad-seed.org/~cave/info/songs/mb_staggerlee.html. Accessed 7 July 2011.

Notes on Contributors

John H. Baker is Senior Lecturer in English Literature at the University of Westminster. His book *Browning and Wordsworth* was published by the AUP in 2004 and his current research interests include Philip Pullman, David Peace, Howard Barker and Anne Rice, as well as literature and the Bible more generally. His chapter on Morrissey and skinhead culture, 'In the Spirit of '69? Morrissey and the Skinhead Cult', was published in *Morrissey: Fandom, Representations and Identities*, ed. by Eoin Devereux, Aileen Dillane and Martin J. Power (Bristol: Intellect, 2011).

Steven Barfield is currently a freelance theatre critic (*The Lady*, *Plays to See*, *The Public Reviews*, *One Stop Arts*, *Exeunt*) and book reviewer for *The Lady* , as well as an educational consultant. He was Senior Lecturer in English Literature at the University of Westminster until 2012 and has published widely in such areas as the work of Samuel Beckett, contemporary British theatre, children's fantasy literature, the literature of London and post-colonial literature. He is Deputy Director of the UK Network for Modern Fiction Studies and was co-editor and founding editor of the UKNMFS journal *Critical Engagements: A Journal of Criticism and Theory* from 2005 to 2011 (6 book-length issues). His edited volumes include Steven Barfield, Paula Hixenbaugh, Liz Thomas, (eds) *Critical Reflections and Positive Interventions: An Electronic Casebook on Good Practice in Personal Tutoring* (Higher Education Academy UK, 2006) available online; Steven Barfield, Philip Tew, Anja Muller-Wood, Leigh Wilson, (eds) *Teaching Contemporary British Fiction*, Series: *Anglistik und Englischunterricht* (University of Heidelberg Press, 2006); Steven Barfield, Matthew Feldman, Philip Tew, (eds) *Beckett and Death* (Continuum, 2009); Steven Barfield and Katharine Cox (eds), *Critical Perspectives on Philip Pullman's His Dark Materials: Essays on the Novels, the Film and the Stage Productions* (McFarland USA, 2011). He was managing series co-editor of two book series for Continuum, the *Continuum Handbooks to Literature* and Culture (10 volumes, series 1) and the *Continuum Guides to Modern Theatre* (9 volumes), and has also edited or co-edited several special issues of various journals. In addition, he was managing co-editor of *Critical Engagements – A Journal of Criticism and Theory*, editorial Board Member of *Literary London Interdisciplinary Studies in the Representation of London* and *Odisea: Revista de Studio Inglesas*, and is also associate editor of *Symbiosis: A Journal of Anglo American Literary Relations*. He is a Fellow of the Royal Society of Arts and the Royal Asiatic Society.

Peter Billingham is Head of the Department of Performing Arts at the University of Winchester. He is an experienced teacher and researcher, an award-winning playwright and the author of numerous books on contemporary British theatre and television drama. His most recent monograph was *At the Sharp End* (Methuen 2008). He is a specialist on the plays of Edward Bond and his forthcoming monograph will be *Edward Bond: A Critical Study* (Palgrave Macmillan, 2012).

Fred Botting is Professor of English Literature and an executive member of the London Graduate School at Kingston University. His most recently published books are *Limits of Horror* (MUP, 2008) and *Gothic Romanced* (Routledge, 2008). And, with Scott Wilson, *Bataille* (Palgrave Macmillan 2001) and *Tarantinian Ethics* (Sage, 2001).

Karoline Gritzner is Lecturer in Drama and Theatre Studies at Aberystwyth University. She has co-edited *Theatre of Catastrophe: New Essays on Howard Barker* (2006) and is the editor of *Eroticism and Death in Theatre and Performance* (2010). Her research focuses on British and European drama and performance, and on the connections between Theodor W. Adorno's critical theory and theatre.

Nick Groom is Professor in English at the University of Exeter's Cornwall Campus. His first book was a study of eighteenth-century English ballads (*The Making of Percy's Reliques*), which was followed by studies of literature and forgery (*The Forger's Shadow*), Shakespeare (*Introducing Shakespeare*, republished as *Shakespeare: A Graphic Guide*), and national identity (*The Union Jack*), as well as several editions and articles. He has recently completed an introduction to the Gothic for Oxford University Press.

Rebecca Johinke is a member of the Department of English at the University of Sydney, Australia, where she teaches a range of courses on literary cities, street cultures, writing and rhetoric. Her research interests are varied and include Australian genre film and representations of street cultures (including car cultures, *flânerie* and psychogeography). In addition to her recent work on Nick Cave, she is currently working on a number of projects, including essays on Edgar Allan Poe and Charles Dickens.

Carl Lavery is Senior Lecturer in Performance and Theatre at Aberystwyth University. His most recent books are *The Politics of Jean Genet's Late Theatre: Spaces of Revolution* (2010), *Contemporary French Theatre and Performance* (2011), *'Good Luck Everybody': Lone Twin: Performances, Conversations and Journey* (2011) and *'On Foot': Performance Research* (2012). He is planning a new book on Van Morrison and *Astral Weeks*, but it might take a while.

Paul Lumsden teaches contemporary literatures at Grant MacEwan University in Edmonton, Alberta, Canada. As well as an interest in the relationship between music and literature, he has published on the television series *The Sopranos* –'Tony's Menagerie: Animals in the Sopranos' – and the applicability of narrative theories in a work by Louise Erdrich, "And Here Is Where Events Loop Around and Tangle": Tribal Perspectives in *Love Medicine*'. His latest projects involve music, narrative and rhetoric.

David Pattie is Professor of Drama at the University of Chester. He has published extensively in a wide number of areas: Scottish literature and drama, Samuel Beckett, contemporary theatre, theatre history, popular music and popular culture.

Dan Rose is a Clinical Psychologist who is active in training and supervising pre-doctoral and post-doctoral psychology candidates. He is affiliated with Columbus State University and also has a private practice. His areas of interest and study include but are not limited to aesthetic experience, the psychological utility of art and the application of contemporary psychoanalytic theory to clinical practice and cultural objects.

Isabella van Elferen is assistant professor of Music and New Media at the Department of Media and Culture Studies of Utrecht University. She has published widely on German Baroque music, film and TV music, videogame music, mobile phone ringtones and Gothic theory and subcultures. She is the author of *Mystical Love in the German Baroque: Theology – Poetry – Music*, and the editor of *Nostalgia or Perversion? Gothic Rewriting from the Eighteenth Century until the Present Day*. Her new book, *Gothic Music: The Sounds of the Uncanny*, appeared with University of Wales Press in 2012.

William Verrone teaches film and literature at the University of North Alabama, where he founded and chairs the film studies minor. He is the author of *Adaptation and the Avant-Garde: Alternative Perspectives on Adaptation Theory and Practice* (Continuum 2011) and *The Avant-Garde Feature Film: A Critical History* (McFarland 2012). He has published widely on many different historical and theoretical issues in film, including essays on Ken Russell, Mike Leigh, Neil Jordan and Werner Herzog.

Nathan Wiseman-Trowse is Senior Lecturer in Popular Culture at the University of Northampton. He has taught at the university for 12 years over a range of media related courses and is currently Course Leader for the University's BA Popular Music degree. Nathan's research has covered the multiple *Blade Runner* narratives, discourses of identity in British indie music, the guitar solo and symbolic disruption and shamanism in the music of Julian Cope. His doctoral thesis, *Performing Class in British Popular Music*, was published by Palgrave Macmillan in 2008. He has subsequently published 'Oedipus Wrecks: Nick Cave and the Presley Myth' in *Cultural Seeds* (Ashgate, 2009) and 'Marvel or Miracle: (Re)placing the Original in Alan Moore's Marvelman' in the journal *Critical Engagements* (2010). Nathan has also organized the *Magus: Transdisciplinary Approaches to the Work of Alan Moore* conference at the University of Northampton (May 2010). He is currently writing a monograph for Reaktion books, *Nick Drake: Dreaming England* (2012). Nathan is a member of the International Association for the Study of Popular Music.

Sarah Wishart is a writer and artist, currently living in Leeds, working on her Ph.D. on political live art and the audience at Leeds University. She is particularly interested in theatre writing and performance, photography, walking practice, storytelling and the city and performance wrestling.